To Val,

To celebrate y

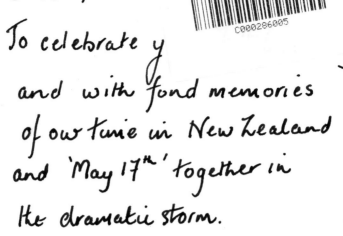

J

and with fond memories
of our time in New Zealand
and 'May 17ᵗʰ' together in
the dramatic storm.

May 17ᵗʰ 2007.

With my love and continuing
prayers.

Anne.

Sᵀ A of D.
xxx

Once a Doctor

Ron Mulroy

ISBN No. 1-905546-10-6
978-1-905546-11-4

Published by Write Books, Ferrybridge, WF11 8PL
Tel: 01977 678371
Website: www.writebooks.org.uk

Photograph on back cover:
David Ward LMPA

Ron Mulroy was born in Stoke-on-Trent and educated at St Thomas' RC Junior School and St Joseph's College, Trent Vale. He studied Medicine at the University of Edinburgh and graduated M.B., Ch.B. in 1959. After junior hospital posts in Scotland, Chester and Stoke, he worked as a locum in Cheshire and Bedfordshire before joining the practice at Chapelthorpe, Wakefield where he remained until his retirement. He also worked part-time in the Wakefield hospitals.

He passed the membership examination of the Royal College of General Practitioners in 1973 and was elected to Fellowship in 1978. He received the Yorkshire Award in 1996. After retirement he studied History at the University of Leeds and graduated B.A. (Class 1) in 2002.

He still lives at the Old Vicarage, Chapelthorpe with his wife Julie. Most of their children are married and have produced fifteen grandchildren (at the time of writing).

Foreword

It seemed to me a good idea to write down something of my professional life so that my family might at some time know what I had been doing while they were growing up. For fathers in my day were not like those of today. I was of the school that expected the wife to feed and clothe us all and to bring up the children. I am not particularly proud of my attitude; I accept that that was how I was and I look back with some regret. Perhaps I can offer this account as an apologia.

I have been helped in recalling patients and events by the habit I developed during my medical career of doodling. Occasionally, the doodling grew into writing and sometimes I fiddled with it and shaped it. I found I enjoyed it. There were many benefits from writing about one's work. As you write, you think and as you think you learn. I found it was possible to modify exasperation and frustration by writing it down. And important emotions could be better preserved in the written word. Moreover, analysis of error and the subsequent learning were better accomplished by a planned, written account.

The essays and anecdotes I have included stem from some of those jottings accumulated over the years and supplemented by more recent memories and some meditations on life in retirement. Some of the pieces have been published, perhaps in an edited or abbreviated form. I am grateful to the publishers and editors noted below for permission to use them here.

Are they all true? Yes. Well sort of. Names of patients and places have been changed where necessary. And it is important to remember that the accounts I give are my own. A patient's view of an incident will be quite different to mine. Myself and the patient will necessarily have different agenda. And in writing of an incident, it is self evident that the account is retrospective. Inevitably too, there is some literary embellishment, if only to emphasise a point. I think it unlikely that any patient will be recognisable from these pages.

I have to admit that what follows is largely about me. But it is also about patients and I hope that none feel slighted. I was privileged to meet so many who taught me so much. They transformed a medical graduate into a 'proper doctor'. But they also taught me a lot about patience, fortitude, endurance and a courage that verged on the heroic. Above all, they taught me much about good humour, even in the worst situations. And they have shaped this book as they shaped my life over the last forty or fifty years. I am grateful to them all.

Ron Mulroy Summer 2006

I am grateful to the following for allowing me to incorporate, whole or in part, some of my previous writing:

The Times (NI Syndication Ltd)
Radcliffe Publishing Ltd (*Alimentary My Dear Doctor* 1988 and *Myocardial Medley* 1990)
The Bryansground Press (*Hortus*)
The Society of Medical Writers (*The Writer*)
Leeds University Dept of Postgraduate Medical and Dental Education (*Yorkshire Medicine*)
British Medical Journal Publishing Group
Triangle Magazine (Parish of Ss Peter and Paul, Sandal)
Medicom (UK) Ltd. *(Medical Monitor)*
GP Magazine.
Pulse Magazine.
World Medicine
The Physician

This book is dedicated to my wife Julie,
who lived through the reality.

Origins

I was born in the 'New Block' at the City General Hospital, Stoke-on-Trent in the days before the war when nurses dressed like angels. We lived in the end house of what was then Queen Street, one of the many streets of terraced houses that fed into Liverpool Road, Stoke, not far from the centre of the town. The street was a cul de sac, closed at one end by the embankment of the canal, protected by a high wall. The house has long gone, replaced by a corner shop, and the street is renamed. I suppose Queen Street was rather a grand name.

Stoke-on Trent at that time was both ugly and unhealthy. Few buildings were memorable. Only the Co-Op Emporium, just down the road, stood out in my childhood memories. It was, curiously, a white building in the style of an Indian temple. You could buy clothes there, but I don't remember going in much. Everywhere else was grey black and grimy. The pottery factories, the 'potbanks', had grown up among the houses within the town itself and the great bottle kilns dominated. They were coal fired and, during smoking time, would belch great clouds of black sooty smoke into the streets. I recall one occasion when, on my way home from school, I was caught out by smoking time. Driven by a breeze, the smoke billowed down the street. I ducked into a doorway to avoid the worst, but was still marked by the soot. Things didn't change a lot until some years after the Second World War when the tunnel kilns were invented and powered by gas or electricity.

At the time, all this was accepted as the norm, the grey faces of the potters, the 'No Spitting' signs in the streets and on buses. It was a few years after the war that that the ugliness of Stoke struck me. The Michelin Tyre Company on the outskirts of the city held a large open Sports Day. They invited some of their French workers over to compete. They were elegant and bronzed and stood a head taller than the locals. They wore proper tracksuits and running shoes. Some were black. We had never seen anyone black before. The contrast between the French group and the local competitors was striking.

There were five children in our family, though my younger brother and I never knew Vera, our eldest sister. She died before we were born and a large photograph of her hung on the wall. It was originally black and white, but it had been tinted. You could have photos tinted in those days before colour photography. We gathered that she had just started to go to school by herself and was killed crossing the road outside our house. I do not remember my mother or father talking much about Vera, apart from an odd reference, nor do I remember asking

Mum and dad both worked at the potbanks in those days. Dad worked on the kilns. I suppose the firing of the kilns was quite an art, controlling the temperature simply with the rate of firing alternating with 'banking down'. The temperatures achieved were very high and the firing had to be maintained without a break for three or four days and nights. Then the kilns needed emptying. Officially, there was a cooling period, but this was often perceived as lost time and the unloading of the kiln began in intense heat. The men were issued with salted beer. Mother worked in the transferring department, where the ware was decorated with transfers and hand painting. If she couldn't collect us from school, we would walk the short distance to the factory and wait there.

Our home life was frequently affected by flare ups of chronic disease. Our elder sister, Eileen, suffered from severe asthma and dad already had silicosis, though I think it had not yet been defined. It was because of these health problems that we moved to a council house in a small village on a hill outside Stoke. I am not sure how it came about, but certainly mother always felt that our GP, Dr Gamble, had a lot to do with it.

Life changed. We had a garden – which we never fathomed. I fear my father never understood gardening and I do not recall anything thriving there, though he seemed to dig it up a lot. We had a small lawn. For some reason, whenever he cleared the ashes from the fire, he would scatter them on the lawn. Why he did it I have no idea, but the results were pretty disastrous. There was never any grass to speak of and sitting on it was an uncomfortable experience. Mother, though, liked the idea of gardening and we did grow some potatoes once I think. She always had a dream of living in the country and running a smallholding. Once she won a prize on the football pools and the dream grew. The week before the prize was several hundred pounds and the week after, over a thousand. It was a heady weekend. Alas, on the Tuesday, she received a cheque for £4.11s, not a sum that dreams are made on.

Around us were fields and trees. Sometimes the smoke from the town would reach us, but not often. There was an air raid shelter in the garden. We used it for its intended purpose only two or three times. It was quite exciting. But Hitler obviously didn't feel that breaking Britain's cups and saucers would necessarily win the war. As a result, Stoke was comparatively unscathed, apart from bombs that strayed from attacks on Shelton Bar, the nearby iron foundry and steelworks. When a bomb did drop locally, the news sent all the kids off in search of shrapnel – a highly valued collectable in the school playground. Eventually, the superfluous Anderson shelter was used to house first rabbits, then chickens. The great slaughter every December was not one of my happiest memories, though we enjoyed delivering the meat to various friends and relatives. We usually got a penny or two for our trouble.

Most memories of my youth were inextricably bound up with school and with the Church. People sometimes ask "Were you happy at school?" The short answer is that I don't know. It never occurred to me to consider it. You just went to school and did as you were told. It seemed to work out all right. I never objected to going. After the second day, that is, when the inevitability of my fate first hit me. St Thomas's was an infant and junior school of its time. I was fascinated by the floor boards. They were badly worn except where they were nailed and, as a result they were very uneven. When I think of the school, I can smell that special smell of boiled cabbage and humanity. The routines of school life would now be considered criminal. Both Miss Wallace and Miss Barnes (lady teachers were expected to remain unmarried in those days) were not above wielding the cane or the ruler. Miss Wallace's cane was bound with sticking plaster. I can only remember being caned once. I can't remember why, but once was plenty. Yet both those teachers were respected, even loved. When Miss Wallace told us we had "...*to work like billyoh..*", we did.

I think I was a sore disappointment to Miss Barnes who produced plays and concerts. I played *Grumpy* in *Snow White and the Seven Dwarfs*, but refused to go on when the time came. I was persuaded by a piece of chocolate, but wolfed it so fast that I was sick on stage and ruined my crepe paper costume. A further disaster ensued when I was obliged to stand in for Jean Shaw in the title role of *The Pied Piper of Hamelin*. I reckon I was miscast. I couldn't play the recorder and her costume was a tad too big for me. And then my voice shrank to a squeak on the night. Sometimes I find myself singing the songs again and even wishing I could have another go at it. Most of the time, though, the memories are the stuff of nightmares. And the nightmares of those two nights are always compounded by the vision of Canon Twiney. He was a large bulk of a man with a loud deep voice. As children we were terrified of him and he exploited our fear. Kindliness and gentleness were foreign to him and psychology was a far distant land. The morning after my theatrical debut, he marched into the classroom and asked me to stand up. In a loud voice, he berated me for my puny performance of the night before. "You were just like a girl" was the insult that hurt most. He died a few years ago. People said nice things about him and talked of 'a Pillar of the Church' and 'a beacon of Christianity', but to a ten year old boy he was a bully.

I passed a scholarship and went to St Joseph's College, which was not that far from home. My sojourn there was almost entirely happy. Of course, physical punishments were employed, but that was the norm throughout society. You knew where you were. I thought that overall the Brothers were fair. I was surprised recently when my brother and others who attended the school considered their time there as deeply unhappy. Yet they had all achieved a lot – at school and beyond. I suppose I did have my traumas. I was cast out of the choir as a 'drone' and clipped with a cane as I left; I was thrown out of the cast of the Gilbert and Sullivan opera when I was accused of damaging the scenery. I never did, honest. I was dismissed from the violin class as a tuneless incompetent. I was struck on my backside one cold November afternoon during games practice, because I failed to scrum down properly. Yet somehow I accepted all this as being how life was.

I did enjoy the sport at school and while I can't say I excelled, I kept my head above water and Wednesday and Saturday afternoon were always anticipated with pleasure. Rugby was a religion second only to Catholicism. In my final year, I did flit in and out of the first XV, though I was only ever the last resort and never distinguished myself. It's amazing what you learn from competitive sport. There was, for a while, an interform rugby league. On one occasion I captained our team when we were playing a team from the form below. We were a much better team than them and averaged a year older. We overan them, scoring tries at will. We used the conversions as kicking practice for the whole team. I felt quite pleased with myself as we walked off until the referee, Brother Lovelady, called me over. "Never, ever do that again", he said, angrily. "Never patronise or show contempt for an opponent, no matter how superior you are. Always play your best, it's the greatest compliment you can pay. And you always leave them with some dignity". I often thought about that when I took on the children and still do with the grandchildren.

The inter-form competition had an interesting side effect. There was a weight limit to iron out some of the disparity between the forms. I was half a stone over, one year and took up running to lose the weight. Soon I was enjoying the running for its own sake and eventually won both the senior cross-country and the open Mile. The cups were still there when I last looked. If you turn them round you see my name.

Cricket, though was a different kettle of fish. For the Irish Christian Brothers it was a foreign game. I still feel that whatever talent I had was eliminated at school. I was never able to regain my hook shot after that. Many years later I tried to re-ignite my skills playing for the scratch parish team. I played six times.

My batting was at least consistent (average 0.5 runs/innings). My bowling was less impressive for the fast medium swingers of my youth had become cunning spinners – but not cunning enough. I did take a catch once though,

The teaching at St Joe's was a bit thin in parts, I suppose, but much of it I still remember. Now, when I try to learn another language, I still revert to 'O' level French and the lesson on the accession of Elizabeth I remains indelibly in my mind. I will never forget that when she came to the throne, '..*the treasury was empty..*'. I used the phrase half a century later when I studied history. But, one way and another I did manage to acquire enough knowledge to get to University.

'Church' was simply part of the normal run of life. Together with the wireless, school, books, the cinema and playing in the street, it completed a rounded sort of childhood. Sunday morning was a day for best clothes and Mass and bacon and egg and oatcakes. It was a special day too because the pot ovens did not smoke on a Sunday and the air was clean and fresh. Perhaps that's why I always remembered Sundays as sunny days. When we came out of Mass, mother would talk to other mothers and we would wait. I used to watch the men talking. They wore trilbies and overcoats and had clean shoes. As they puffed their pipes and fags, they talked seriously. Quite often, the priest was with them. I was always amazed that people could stand about and talk to a priest, just like a normal person. One of the men was tall and thin and always looked serious. He took the collection. I asked my mother who he was. She told me, then added, "He's a Big Catholic". From that time, I decided that when I grew up, I wanted to be a 'Big Catholic'. I have tried, but I still don't think of myself as one, not a really Big Catholic. Perhaps it's the changing perspective of age, but somehow, I've never developed the style.

That my parents influenced me is self-evident. I hear people boast that they do not indoctrinate their children and that they want them '..to make up their own minds..' Silly beggars. Whoever we are we are of our parents and the environment they create. Yet, having said that, it is often difficult to define just how you were influenced. Mother, for instance, was not so much a person as a presence. She was just there. She was always just there. She fed and clothed us and at Christmas, provided presents (I later discovered). I remember little of her story. Sometimes she would reminisce about her time as a girl in service with a Jewish family. We heard snippets about her time working in 'Munitions'. Accidents were common and often serious. One phrase she used comes back to me, "…if you worked there for long, your skin went yellow…" It conjured a frightening picture. I'm ashamed to say that Peter and I did not have a lot of interest in these topics at the time and used to take it turns to listen, especially when Saturday Night Theatre was on the wireless and Eileen and Bernard, our much older sister and brother, were out.

Nowadays, when chaps of my generation meet over a pint or more, the conversation is more likely to drift towards the subject not of mothers, but of fathers.[1] It is common for most of us to express the wish that our fathers were still alive, but they rarely are. We would like to talk to them - and to listen. We would like to tell them how we are and show them our achievements, perhaps seek their approbation. For fathers were different in our day than they are now. They didn't often tell you how good you were and not many of us recall overt affection.

Few of us remember conversations with our fathers. They worked, came home, read the paper, listened to the wireless and

[1] A version of *Aphorisms of a Father* originally appeared in *The Writer* (The Journal of the Society of Medical Writers). Vol 2 No 4. 2004.

sometimes went out for a pint. "Don't bother your father", mother would say. We sometimes went to the park on a Sunday, but I don't remember much, apart from the band. My father would occasionally take me and my brother to the pictures. He would not, however, watch 'Cowboys', 'Love Stories' or any film with aeroplanes in it. This limited our cinematic experience somewhat. But I do remember Paul Robeson in *'Sanders of the River'*. I can still sing *'Ay-ee-ok-o'* if pressed.

Curiously, despite this lack of remembered intimacy with our fathers, many of us had inherited aphorisms, most of which had a touch of the proverbial about them. (Mothers tended to have 'sayings' or 'expressions'). It is odd how these became imprinted on our minds. I was quite surprised to hear my youngest son use such an aphorism recently. I suppose it's what you call the oral tradition. *'Hunger is the best sauce'* was said at the beginning of a meal more often than Grace. I think about that when I see people walking the streets, eating. I reckon, by a very approximate count, that nearly 50% of people in Wakefield in an afternoon are eating or drinking. I worry that they will not enjoy their tea when they get home.

I often used to puzzle over the meaning of *'Little fish are sweet'*. I had always thought of it as a consoling sort of expression, an aid to coping with disappointment or noting even the most minor achievement. Now I find in it all sorts of meanings; an encouragement to assiduous application in work; a guide to happiness and contentment; a sensitivity to the delights of our world and the people in it. But I still tend to use it most often in my original understanding – as a consolation when I score poorly at dominoes or cards.

Like most working men, my father had a best suit. On Friday and Saturday nights, after a 'good wash' in the kitchen, he would put on his suit and a collar and tie and go for the 'last hour'. He would often remark that '*A clean neck, a white collar and clean shoes and a man can go anywhere*'. In retrospect, dress was very important to him. When I first played cricket, he was insistent that I had proper flannels and that they were washed and pressed before each game. '*If you can't play like a cricketer, at least look like one*'. So important was this, that he once soaped the creases in my flannels so that they would last. They did, until it rained. I was the only fielder foaming at the trouser.

Sunday was always a day for 'Best', especially for Mass. '*Remember where you're going*' he would say, though he rarely came with us. I still feel the need to wear a collar and tie at the weekend Mass. The Holy Father did not mention this in his recent address on our respect for the Eucharist, but I'm sure he would have done had he thought on. After all, in our other lives, do we not dress for the occasion? Do we not speak through what we wear?

My father's parents, whom I never knew, were both Irish and he inherited the Celtic tendency to see dark clouds even on the brightest day. How often would we hear him say, as me and my brother noisily enjoyed some game after tea, '*There'll be tears before bedtime*'. There often were, of course, but I always thought there was no need for him to say so. His only advice to me when I left for university was '*You'll spend the first six weeks making friends and the next six years avoiding them*'. A funny thing to say and I wonder about it to this day. I'm sure there's a grain of truth in it, but I find it difficult to define.

He was critical of people who stayed up late and never could believe that anything worthwhile could be achieved after ten o'clock. A good night's sleep was important, '*an hour before midnight is worth two after it*'. Until I left home at eighteen, I was expected back from any outing before half past ten. If I was not, I could expect that infuriating question *'What time d'you call this?'* Even though I knew that the question was rhetorical, as I got older I was tempted to give a literal answer, but for the sake of peace, I would usually mutter merely an apology or excuse.

Sometimes my father showed remarkable psychological insight. If we were dilatory in performing some task, or starting our homework, he would state *'Hard work never killed anyone, but the thought of it killed thousands'*. It is a saying that occurs to me on many an occasion as I anticipate a thankless or unwelcome task. And I take a certain pride in knowing that my father's wisdom runs parallel to the Chinese philosophers - *In the journey of a thousand miles, the most difficult step is the first'*, There was another call to action he used and for some reason, it used to drive me mad. Usually said when we were at ease, but with some action planned, he would stand and declare *"This and better might do; this and worse will never do"*. I don't know why it irritated me so, perhaps the subtlety escaped me.

I don't think he – or anyone else of his generation – would have understood the modern fashion for 'working out' or 'getting fit'. *"Fit for what?"* would be his immediate response. And I know he would have resented lining the pockets of the Gymnasium entrepreneurs. As for 'personal trainers'. *"I'll give you personal trainers the other side of your face"* I can hear him say. It doesn't make much literal sense, but you get the gist. No. At that time, many of the men of that generation were old at forty, broken by disease and industrial working conditions. Not surprisingly, his attitude to physical activity was the reverse of that of the present day. I think it was after a prolonged spell in a sanatorium for his silicosis and TB that he evolved his dictum *"Never walk when you can stand; never stand when you can sit down; never sit down when you can lie down; and never stay awake when you can go to sleep".* I have to admit, the dictum has always appealed to me and has sustained me thus far. I know that I am drifting towards portliness, but at least it gives me an air of affluence.

When I reached an age when I could go out with him for a drink, I was admitted to a previously unknown world with its own behaviour and etiquette. On those occasions, I would sit with him and his friends, most of whom were what was then called 'working class'. I would be acknowledged, but not encouraged to contribute. It was unspoken that if you couldn't buy a round, you had few rights. I do not remember any dirty stories, nor even a hint of bad language. We were, after all, in a public space. To put your glass on a table, not using a beer mat, was frowned upon. You always returned your empty glasses to the bar as you left. *'Always do your own fielding. Nobody else will, '.* I was unaware at the time that I was being taught fundamental lessons in personal responsibility. I think it's called 'citizenship' or some such these days.

And, as we left, my father would always say *'Goodnight gentlemen. I enjoy your company, but can't keep your hours'.* Perhaps this does not have the elegant poetry of a true Celtic farewell, but it is both well mannered and humble. Thinking about it now, it would have been a fine epitaph.

I realise that few, if any, of these aphorisms, are truly original, but he used them so often that I still regard them as his own and I am prone to use them now as part of my inheritance. They seem eminently wise and the sort of guide to life that fathers should pass down to their sons.

There was, however, one occasion which even now moves me. It is always a poignant moment, that first time that a son sees his father as vulnerable and incomplete. We were walking past Newcastle Catholic Church, when he stopped, looked up at its front and said *'And they say they couldn't build in the Old Days'*. I remember nodding in agreement. Only in retrospect did I realise how flawed that statement was. Nobody ever said they couldn't build in the Old Days. And Newcastle Catholic Church was only about 30 or 40 years old at the time anyway. Pretty enough, certainly with its echoes of Orvieto, albeit in blue brick, but hardly worth remark. I suppose I became aware then that I was outreaching my father, that I was growing up. But I still feel curiously uneasy at the memory, well, almost of treason.

And I consider his life - the trenches of the First World War, strikes, poverty, the appalling working conditions of the Potteries, the chronic ill-health, the uncompensated injuries and industrial disease - I consider all these and feel the pain of my own self pride. And then I wonder at my own legacy to my own sons.

I have mentioned earlier that our early life was constantly punctuated by disease. The recollection of those episodes, after a life in Medicine, has its own fascination, if only to emphasise the dramatic changes in medical science and practice that have taken place over the last fifty years or so.

When dad was admitted to the Sanatorium in the late forties, we visited him once with mother. The Sanatorium was not so much a hospital, more a large village, even a small town, in the Staffordshire countryside. It must have housed hundreds of tubercular patients. I remember seeing them laid out in beds on the verandas of the wards, for fresh air, rest and good food were the only treatments, except for occasional surgery. He was there for months. Even ten years later, as a medical student, I visited a ward containing about thirty or forty children with tubercular bone disease. Yet, in the course of forty years as a doctor, I saw only two new cases of TB. It is difficult to appreciate now just how widespread the 'White Plague' was and how dramatically it declined.

My older sister, Eileen, had chronic and severe asthma which effectively curtailed her education and lasted throughout her life. As children (Eileen was twelve years senior to me), we found her treatment fascinating, especially the '*Potters Asthma Cure'*. This was a herbal powder containing, I think, a stramonium compound. A small heap of the powder was placed on a saucer and the apex of the pile was lit. Clouds of smoke were given off and Eileen would lean over and inhale it. I would recognise the smell anywhere. If we were very good and she was in a good mood, Eileen would give us a little to put in the funnel of our clockwork train. Looked quite authentic, it did. During times when her asthma was worse – and later as a routine – she used inhalers. She had one, an *Atomiser*, that was the latest in technology. It was glass and had a big red bulb which you pumped to produce a spray for inhalation. *Brovon* was another inhaler, similar but smaller. In a bad attack the doctor would give her an injection. What that was I have no idea, though I suspect it was adrenaline or something similar. Certainly, in my first practice, adrenaline or noradrenaline subcutaneously was the standard treatment for an attack, though it gave the patient a dreadful pallor and their pounding hearts were quite frightening.

Steroids were coming in as I was at medical school. We were shown a promotional film of their effectiveness in rheumatoid arthritis. They really were quite miraculous, though the full impact of their side effects was not understood for some time.

Their use in asthma followed their use in rheumatoid. Again their efficacy was dramatic, but their regular use in children affected growth, an ill effect that took much longer to become apparent.

Incorporating steroids in creams and ointments transformed the management of eczema. My brother Peter spent a very long time in hospital with what was probably eczema. Mother was allowed to visit once a week. I was not allowed in, but I could wave at him through the window. At that time everyone knew that having visitors upset the children.

My own childhood medical experience was limited to one major event. I awoke during the night with what I recall as the worst pain ever. I was taken to the doctor in the morning and found to have an 'abscess in the ear'. It progressed to mastoiditis and I was admitted to hospital. My memories of that stay are few, but vivid. Mother could visit two or three times a week. I was treated with '*M&B*', a sulphonamide. I was not allowed eggs. The nuns from St Dominic's visited me bringing a brown paper bag of biscuits, those special biscuits that nuns have always made. They are sweet and crumble easily. In the bag were also some boiled sweets, slightly sticky. They had a patina of biscuit crumbs and were indestructible. And every day the nurse would enquire how I was and ask if I had had my bowels open. I would always say no. I didn't know what she meant, but I had enough trouble already and this sounded threatening and complicated. By Christmas Eve, my ear had not improved and surgery became necessary.

The smell of the rubber mask is unforgettable. Even now, the smell of rubber transports me to that white, stainless steel theatre ante-room. When I came round, the ward was in darkness, apart from the lights on the tree. I had no pain. Through the door of the ward, half lit from behind, came a group of nurses. They wore their cloaks and their translucent head-dresses glowed. They were singing carols. I often wonder if that is what heaven will be like. And on Christmas Day, I had a boiled egg. It was exquisite.

I do not often return to Stoke now and, although there is still a sensation of 'home' when I'm there, I know I am now a visitor. Stoke remains ugly, but it is now new clean and difficult to distinguish from a hundred Northern towns. But if I wander the back streets, I can still find traces of the old Stoke. All you have to do as a visitor is follow the signs "To The Museum" and "The Heritage Trail". You will soon find the remaining bottle kilns, great avuncular figures. These true uncles of the Potteries are now respectable and proud in their Sunday best, celebrating, but celebrating only their passing. Their clean round bellies are no longer warmed by furnaces within. They no longer create the embellishment of high teas and Sunday dinners. They exist now, only to intrigue the tourist, concern the socialist, impress the historian and make the industrialist wonder.

But should a native come upon them, coughing as he goes, he will remember these uncles in their youth, fired with intensity, belching foul black smoke. And producing from within their stinking, hot foulness true beauty and art.

I have hardly mentioned my older brother, Bernard. But ten years is a big gap between brothers and our lives diverged considerably. Occasionally, when he and his friends were going to the pictures, mother would persuade him to take us with him. It was an uneasy arrangement. We walked about fifty yards behind him. And we never sat with him in the cinema. He did develop a passion for cross country running and his enthusiasm was catching; Peter and I both took it up eventually and joined

24

what was then the North Staffs Harriers. They were big in those days. Roy Fowler won a bronze at the European Championships and I'm sure I remember the club winning the European Cross-Country club title. But Bernard's main contribution to me was the part he played in my going to Medical School. It was not an easy decision for my parents. The headmaster and the priest both tried to persuade my father that I was worth it, but the thought of another wage coming in was seductive. And nobody we knew had ever been to University before. It was, I think, Bernard who swayed the argument in my direction.

Going to Edinburgh was an enormous culture shock, for I had rarely been outside Stoke till then. I was struck by the tremendously high buildings, for Stoke had few. The language was tricky for a while, but attractive. The tenements were full of foreboding. I was shocked by the virulent anti-Catholic feelings that seemed so widespread. I had, up to then, moved only in Catholic circles, school and Parish, and I felt quite threatened. Not surprisingly, I sought regular refuge in the Catholic Students' Union.

It was there that Mike Lynch and I used to call for a cup of tea and keep an eye on the talent. Freshers' Week was always interesting. It was Mike who first spotted the Blonde Bombshell from Liverpool, the one in the tiger dress. She was quite nice, but I fancied Florence from the West Indies. Her dad had a plantation and sent her a crate of oranges every month to sustain her through the Scottish winter. She was alright. I took her out a couple of times. She didn't talk much and had the habit of walking two yards behind me. I was unskilled at courtship and our relationship proved fleeting. I think it was the trip to the theatre that finished it. I had done all the things I had read about in books, but to no avail. I bought a corsage and a box of chocolates. As the overture started, I turned to offer her a chocolate. She was startled and twitched. The chocolates fell into her lap. It was a hot night. She talked to me even less after that. Most people later referred to her as Ice Flo.

I did have a mild flirtation with a beautiful Norwegian girl, but she was six inches taller than I was. She was very polite and always used to stand in the gutter when we waited at the bus stop. The relationship did not flourish. She took up with another Norwegian – a very big lad who was studying Fisheries or Forestry or something very macho. It was never really a contest.

It was in my third year that I got to know the Blonde Bombshell. I was a senior anatomy student and she one year my junior. There was a shortage of bodies for dissection that year. For the first time in Edinburgh, so I was told, men and women were allowed to dissect the same body. Julie, for it was she, was dissecting the upper limb and I was dissecting the head and neck. We met over the circumflex nerve as it travelled from the neck to arm. We discovered we were born on the same day. It was, as my mother would have said, a match. Worth going to Medical School for.

The actual medical course was great. I loved it, particularly when we moved to the Medical School proper. There, every building and monument spoke of the history, especially the medical history, of the University. I absorbed every nuance and my vocation grew. Looking back, though, the actual course and teaching would now be unrecognisable to the modern student. It was almost entirely theoretical, the feeling being that a scientific basis was critical for a life time in Medicine and that the practical skills would follow. Well, it seemed to work for me.

Certainly, by the time I left Edinburgh, I was content that I was quite ready to serve the Great British Public.

26

In at the Deep End

The two years that I spent as a junior hospital doctor were the most exhausting, anxious and exhilarating time of my life. It was the continued flow of excitement that I remember. Even in the rare quiet times, there was still anxious anticipation. Perhaps it doesn't sound so delightful, but to be at full stretch intellectually, emotionally and physically, and for so long, was totally fulfilling. It did not seem to matter that working conditions were poor, sleep continually sought for, but rarely found, and the pay a mere pittance (about £20 per month in my pocket). The life of a junior doctor then would not be tolerated now. I would not wish those times to return, but in the early '60's that is the way it was. And our seniors would tell us we had it easy compared to them.

Oddly enough, I do not now remember much of the tiredness, but at times it must have verged on the pathological. I do not remember feeling unduly irritable, nor, so far as I know was I guilty of any major errors, apart from one. On that occasion, I was rescued in the nick of time by an astute and assiduous registrar (who, incidentally, had less rest than me). These days, there is considerable emphasis not only on working conditions, but also on continuing education. When I was a junior in various district hospitals, formal education was rare. Lectures were non-existent and 'seminars' unusual events. Yet with close monitoring by dedicated registrars and graduated exposure to responsible experience, we learned rapidly. The surgical, medical and obstetric procedures I began to treat as routine are, I suspect, rarely undertaken by junior staff of the present day. Perhaps that is wise, but I'm glad that my training was what it was. It certainly sharpened my diagnostic skills. If you made a diagnosis that demanded some action, and you yourself were to be responsible for that procedure, then you made damn sure that your diagnosis was as complete and certain as possible.

I was better able to adapt to the comparatively sudden change from student life to responsible doctor by having become familiar with hospital life through doing mundane jobs in the wards during vacations. I reckon that over a period of five or six years, I did every job in the City General Hospital and the North Staffs Royal Infirmary, apart from that of mortuary attendant. I enjoyed being a Ward Orderly most of all. Under the strict eye of the Ward Sister (the capital letters are important, for they were different in those days), the hygiene was assiduous and good old fashioned nursing care was of the highest standard. A patient lying in a wet bed was an indictment of that care and a ward enquiry ensued. The Ward Sister was a dedicated professional and the post was virtually permanent; it was not seen merely as a stepping stone to higher things. For this reason, the Ward Sister was a queen in her own kingdom. Her discipline was strict. Sometimes, the rules seemed ridiculously trivial, but they all had a point. I did get irritated by the nuances of bedmaking and the obsessive attention to cleanliness, but I grew to understand it. When I became a junior doctor, I depended on the Ward Sister. Not only did she guide me in the ways of the ward, she was an astute physician. One might disagree with her opinion (just quietly and diplomatically), but only a fool would ignore it.

My first post was as house physician at Bridge of Earn Hospital, set in rural Perthshire on the edge of the Highlands. It was a rambling, widespread hospital with a large orthopaedic department. A big section was devoted to the care of miners and their diseases (we were not far from Fife). I was to rotate with two colleagues between the geriatric ward and the male and female medical wards. I was first attached to the Care of the Elderly. It was an invaluable introduction to practical medicine for the elderly have a wealth of physical problems and it was exciting to find the textbooks coming alive.

A new Consultant geriatrician had recently been appointed. He was remarkably young, had immense energy and a holistic approach that verged on the eccentric. He was very keen on the 'new' popular music. Not only did he encourage physiotherapists to use it in their group sessions, he also brought a record player to the ward and played it for ages especially, I remember, in those languorous afternoons one always associates with groups of the elderly. His particular favourite was a young rising star named Cliff Richard and when he came to give a concert in Perth (or it might have been Dundee) any patient fit enough to travel was taken there by coach. I often wondered what the rest of the audience thought. It certainly livened up the auld wifies. Yet as he bounced about the ward on the normally formal ward rounds, he exhibited that rare combination of an enquiring scientific brain and caring attitude which made a deep impression on a young, green doctor.

Moving to the care of the more acute (and younger) medical patients, had less of an impact on me. Like every doctor in every hospital in every era, I, and those about me, were convinced that we were at the cutting edge of medical science and that our treatments were up to the minute and state of the art. Perhaps we were, then. Patients with heart attacks were kept in for six weeks, two weeks in bed, immobile and doing absolutely nothing for themselves; two weeks in bed, allowed to wash and feed themselves; two weeks gradual mobilisation. All had anticoagulants. I often think back to that when I hear of new scientific approaches in medicine. No doubt many of the current doctors will, in time, look back in horror at their current practices. Because the hospital was so isolated, most of the staff lived there. This made for an active social life. Every week there would be a party somewhere, in the junior doctors' mess, the physiotherapists' mess, the staff nurses' or somewhere else. We wrote and organised a pantomime which was most ambitious and ran for three or four nights. Based on Cinderella (a student nurse), characters included the ugly sisters (inevitably), Dr Buttons (junior doctor) the handsome registrar ('Charming') and the Pharmaceutical Rep who, with his magic drugs could achieve anything a Fairy Godmother could. My memory says it was very good, but then my memory has always been selective.

Sometimes we had a trip to the pictures or the theatre in Perth and once we crossed the Forth to a Rugby International in Edinburgh. I had been to many of these before as a student, but this was the only time I ever went by car. And we opened the car boot and picnicked in the car park with tartan rugs and all, just like the toffs.

The time at Bridge of Earn was really quite unique and could never be repeated. There was one occasion that I feel guilty about though. I was one of the few non-Scots in residence and I was given Christmas off, but would be on call at the New Year. New Year's Eve came and with it the realisation that I was responsible for virtually the whole hospital. I began my evening round. I met Jimmy Shand who was visiting his very ill brother. He was surprised that we had no music in the ward and returned with a gramophone and records. By eight o'clock, the male medical ward was in some disarray. Coronary patients were singing and dancing with nurses. I tried to get round them all to wish them Happy New Year as was expected of me. Those I managed to greet reached into their lockers, "Y'll ha a dram, doctor". It was impolite to refuse, though I had rarely drunk whisky. By the time I had left the third ward, I could hardly walk down the corridor and bounced from one wall to the other. Any one I met produced a 'wee dram'. It took an age to reach my room and my spinning bed was little comfort. I prayed fervently that I would not be called. I wasn't. Sometimes God is very good indeed. I awoke still wondering what Hogmanay was all about.

I left Scotland for a junior surgical post in Stoke-on-Trent, a couple of miles from my home. There was to be a couple of months delay before the job began and during that time, I was engaged as a Casualty Officer. The department was a busy one and it is remarkable how much responsibility I was expected to shoulder despite my lack of experience. Fortunately, during the day, there were usually senior doctors about and I felt secure. Even so, the work was non-stop and immensely varied. But later, when my 'proper' job started, part of my workload was to work the night shift in casualty a couple of times a week. There was a couch in a side room for the doctor, but it was unusual to be able to sleep for more than the odd hour.

Nightshifts in casualty are lonely and exposed affairs. There was a steady stream of patients of course, the nursing staff was there and a senior doctor was on call at home, but you still felt alone. And, inevitably, it seemed, patients arriving at night were more seriously ill and complex than those seen in the light of day. I suppose much of the apparent complexity stemmed from the lack of the support of the paramedical staff. Social workers, X-ray departments and the laboratory were all 'on call' but it was always with reluctance that they were called.
Sometimes during my professional life, people have remarked how wonderful it must be to have had a job saving lives. I always

squirmed a little at that, for in truth, saving a life is, and was, unusual. There is only one occasion I can recall, when I personally prevented the death of a patient. In the mid afternoon, a young French priest, touring England, had been knocked off his motor cycle by a lorry. He was brought in in a wheelchair. Young, charming, incredibly handsome and with his French accent, he entranced the nursing staff and they vied with each other to help. He protested that his only injury was a painful wrist and admitted to no other symptom. I arranged for an X-ray which confirmed a fracture. But the radiographer remarked that he had become faint while in her department. I helped him up on the couch and examined him. There was just a twitch in his face when I felt his abdomen and his blood pressure was the low side of normal. When I sat him up, he was a little pale, but oddly, his pulse was rapid.

While the implications of all this were going through my head, a nurse arrived with a hot meal. "Poor soul, no wonder you're weak". And to me "He hasn't eaten all day, doctor". I felt mean waving the food away, but suddenly I was clear in my mind. I told him I thought he was bleeding internally, arranged theatre and staff and took blood for cross-matching. Phoning the consultant was more difficult. Adept he was, but he was also irascible and, moreover, he was dining out. He thought little of my story – there was little to go on, it was true – and made it quite clear that he didn't enjoy wild goose chases. But he came. By the time he arrived, the patient was ready in theatre with a drip running and the anaesthetist standing by.

There was still little to find on examination. The surgeon hesitated, then nodded to the anaesthetist who weaved his magic and the patient sank into unconsciousness. And then his blood pressure plummeted. It was difficult to sustain it, no matter how fast the blood was transfused. As the surgeon opened the abdomen, blood welled out and over the floor. As fast as we pumped blood in, the faster it spilled out. With difficulty, the torn splenic artery was identified and sutured. The damaged spleen was removed. Presumably the torn artery had gone into spasm and closed itself until relaxed by the anaesthetic and muscle relaxant. I don't recall exactly how much blood was transfused, but I know it was over twenty pints. Most of it was on the theatre floor.

The priest was sitting up in bed the next day, surrounded, as always by attentive nurses. I don't think he ever really understood what had happened.

Not all cases were so satisfying. A lady attended one Saturday lunch time. Her face was badly bruised and she had teeth missing. When undressed, we found she had at least one broken rib and there were many bruises on her body, both old and new. She said she had been hit by her husband. I asked if the police were called. "What's the use," she said, "They came once and didn't do anything. And it was awful when they went". Apparently these beatings happened regularly over a period of years, usually on a Friday night. She had never been to a doctor before. Why now then? "I felt I wanted to tell someone," she said. And no, she did not want anything doing. Over the succeeding years, I met many women who were subject to regular beatings by their husband. I never understood. I knew many were bound to their husbands economically and by children, but how could they stand it? The comparatively recent founding of homes for such women is a boon, temporary though they may be.

Dealing with similar situations in General Practice was always frustrating and complicated by the husband also being a patient.

I never understood them. My occasional attempts at interference – in the 'hot' situation at their home or in the neutral consultation room – were rarely successful and sometimes worsened the situation. Later still, when I first began to meet children similarly beaten – or worse – I was even more confused. How can human beings act like that? And yet the perpetrators I met and knew all seemed perfectly normal men with normal concerns and worries. Women abusers were rare, but more memorable. I remember attempting to solve a chronic urinary infection in a child. The mother was later found to be contaminating it. And several children were 'pushed' into investigations and treatment which had ill effects. All this was – and is - incomprehensible.

But now I am drifting. The talk of children does bring back to me an incident which still haunts me. A youngish woman attended one afternoon, saying her baby was ill and she couldn't get hold of her doctor. She carried the baby in to see me. She was rocking the baby and murmuring to it. He had been 'off it' for a day or two. I made a lighthearted remark about how nice it was to have a quiet baby in the department and started to move the shawl away to see. The baby was breathing his last. He was cold, collapsed and floppy. I tried to explain to the mother, but my explanation was, of necessity, short and sharp. I said, "Follow me", grabbed the baby and rushed to the nearby paediatric unit. There was little that could be done, the baby died within minutes. I gather he had septicaemia, though one of the difficulties of casualty was that often you never got to know exactly what happened to your patient after they left you. I sometimes think about that mother. But I learned a golden rule, a baby who is poorly AND quiet is a very poorly baby indeed. It would be little consolation to that mother to know that the lesson I learned that day remained with me for the rest of my life and many children benefitted.

One problem I did not anticipate. Because the hospital was quite near my home, occasional patients were familiar to me as acquaintances or friends of my parents. These were always awkward consultations and I was always aware that my performance was being strictly monitored and that it would be reported back in some detail. Not surprisingly, then, when Alice Sparks appeared, my heart sank. I had hitherto known her only as my mother's best friend. She was a formidable lady whose only Achilles heel was her inability to eat food with her teeth in. It is said that she always went to the same boarding house in Blackpool every year because she could book the table in the window for her meals. This enabled her to remove her teeth surreptitiously and rest them in the bay window bottom. This snippet of information enabled me to cope with the consultation with a degree of equanimity. Even so, it was not easy to be comfortable when faced with a large, formidable and familiar lady when she was down to her corsets. And the removal of those majestic feats of engineering did require quite exceptional surgical skills. From that day on, I always arranged to be out when she called to see my mother.

When I became a House Surgeon, my life was eased by the fact that 'my' ward was the same one in which I had worked as an orderly. I was familiar with both routine and the staff. The Ward Sister, as I have mentioned before (but cannot mention too often) was invaluable in every way, though there was always a constructive tension between us. Within a few weeks, I was operating under supervision and by my last three months had become adept at most of the minor surgery and a dab hand at uncomplicated appendectomy. I did not realise that whenever I was operating, the registrar sat in the dressing room in case I ran into trouble.

Only one operation for appendicitis remains fixed in my memory. Surgically there was nothing special about it, but the young lady and her husband were so grateful that they invited me to dinner at their home. I began to feel that I had arrived and that this was the life for me. But overconfidence rarely lasted long.

One morning, I was asked to start the operating list. The first patient had a fairly large, but benign, fatty tumour of her back. Removing it was not technically difficult, but teasing it out required time consuming dissection. As I stitched the patient up and she was transferred from the theatre back to the ward, the consultant arrived. His first patient was a lady with a tumour of her breast, again, fortunately, benign. The operation proceeded routinely, but again required fastidious dissection.

The following morning, I accompanied the surgeon and the registrar on the ward round to review those who had undergone surgery the previous day. As Sister took down the dressing on 'my' patient, it became obvious that she had developed a large haematoma (a collection of blood) under the scar. I was berated in no uncertain terms for failing to control all the bleeding before closing the wound. The next patient was the consultant's. Coincidentally, she, too, had a large haematoma under her wound. The consultant was furious and blamed me publicly for failing to check the wound on her arrival back in the ward. Sometimes, life is not fair. The registrar, pleased to be out of the line of fire, smiled benignly. Neither complication was serious and the patients made uninterrupted recoveries. My ego took a little longer to revive.

Between the medical and surgical activities, I learned to play billiards. I had never played before, nor have I played since. It filled in the hours in the mess. Only rarely did any of us have the chance to leave the hospital – usually only on what was known as our 'half-day', though it rarely was. One night in the week became sacred. It was the night when '*Hancock's Half Hour*' was on the television. The whole junior hospital staff used to gather in the mess to watch it. The evening operating list started half an hour later that night and only the direst emergency was allowed to interrupt.

After leaving the Potteries, I spent six months in Chester, doing obstetrics. I loved the job, but, my goodness it was wearing. Days stretched into nights and the labour ward became more familiar than our own rooms. The two of us (the juniors) were guided by a registrar whose dedication – and responsibility – were phenomenal. We were introduced to all the basic arts of delivering babies and never lost the euphoria that accompanied each live birth. We did all the uncomplicated forceps deliveries, most of the breech presentations and even gave general anaesthetics when they were required. The thought of what might have been is terrifying.

We worked a three night rota. One night on call, one night second on call (if a colleague needed help) and one night off duty. The person second on call, may with luck, be undisturbed, but was nevertheless expected to remain in the hospital. As I remember, the mess was not a particularly homely place, more a dining room really, so spare time was spent in your room. It was then I started to dabble in oil painting. I was never much good, but I liked the idea. And I fancied myself. I would play records and, with studied posture, apply paint to canvas. I think I once wore a beret, so freely did I throw paint about. And I remember smoking Christmas cheroots. Personally, I thought the paintings I did then showed definite promise, but later, when we were married and had our own house, they never made it on to our walls. Well, not for long any way. I've kept them, though. You never know with paintings. Somebody might discover them.

Although, my time at Chester was a happy one and incredibly fulfilling, my memory is of the disregard of the care of the junior medical staff by the hospital management. My bedsitting room was within yards of the wards. It was spacious and I was quite happy with it until a large section of the ceiling collapsed. Fortunately, there was not a lot of rain while I was there, but I moved my bed in case. The hole was still there when I left, several months later. And I'm sure I mentioned it to someone.

I spent the most miserable Christmas of my life in Chester. At that time, it was expected that a woman would remain in hospital for two weeks after delivery. As a result, the postnatal ward was a very sad place indeed at Christmas and all the jolly goings on cut little ice with the ladies who wept buckets at every happy carol. We weren't very happy either. We were informed by official letter some days before the festival that there would be no hot meals available on Christmas Day for the medical staff, but a plate of cold meats would be left in the dining room. Now since all the patients were provided with traditional Christmas fare, it seemed rather odd that the provision of half a dozen extra meals was beyond the capabilities of the organisation. In fact it was almost vindictive. I don't remember what we did with the 'cold meats', but I do know we drifted round the wards, scrounging what we could.

It was towards the end of my time in Chester that I heard of a vacancy in a practice on the outskirts of the city. It was a well established practice with a good reputation and certainly, the patients from that practice always spoke highly of it. At that time, such vacancies were unusual and much sought after. It was fairly common for the GP's to 'headhunt' likely junior hospital doctors as they drew near to the end of their hospital stint and I was invited to attend for 'interview' one afternoon. It was, however, less an interview and more a trial by conversation.

The day was miserable and wet. I did not have a raincoat in the generally acceptable sense, but I did have one of those grey plastic 'Pacamacs'. They were waterproof when new, but being somewhat insubstantial, tended to split at seams. I had repaired it with the early form of cellotape. The loss of buttons was irreparable, but an old belt closed the folds sufficiently to keep out the worst of the rain. The doorbell chimed impressively. The senior partner showed me in. "May I take your coat?", he said. He helped me off with it and, to my embarrassment, tried to put it on a hanger. Unfortunately, the hanger caught in the already peeling cellotape, which caused a problem.

We went through into the elegant sitting room, with views of an extensive garden through the french windows. Several people were sat around in easy chairs. I'm not sure who they were, but I think one was his wife. "Tea?". "Thank you", I said. I suspect that was the only appropriate remark I made through the long hour I was there. "Do you ride?" I was asked. "Well, I do have a bike, but I haven't used it for a while". "So you don't hunt, then?" I made the mistake of trying to raise my status. "No," I said, "there was little opportunity in Stoke". "Yes", he looked resigned. "Have a sandwich". They were quite small and I picked up two by mistake. His wife's upper lip curled a little. "Do you shoot?" "Well, only at the Wakes". I shuffled a little and tried to accommodate my double sandwich. I was aware of depression and disappointment permeating the room. I waited in vain for some enquiry about my medical skills and attitudes but none came. They thanked me for coming and he helped me on with my Pacamac. The right sleeve was adrift and the errant cellotape floated free. My discomfiture was complete. I did not get the job.

But I was appointed to a rural practice nearby for a three month locum. This was fortunate, for I was due to be married soon and I had little money. The promise of £30 a week was beyond the dreams of avarice and I really couldn't imagine how one could spend such money. It was an extraordinary practice. No records were kept and hospital reports not filed, but kept in a large pile. The bottom third were destroyed every month. There were no clinical notes and no record of any treatment. Tablets were, at that time, unnamed on the bottle. I was stymied when patients asked for 'their prescription'. My only recourse was to collect a selection of tablets from the chemist, stick them on a chart and hope they would enable me to identify what the patient brought in. I kept my own notebook. A further complication was that I failed my driving test just before I started the job. An elderly man was drafted in to sit with me on my rounds. It was a bind. I eventually passed my test in Widnes. I'm not sure there were any other cars in Widnes, just bikes. I missed most of them.

The final straw was the fallout between the two partners. They did not speak to each other, but left notes on the consulting room desk or used me as a go-between. It was a fraught experience. I was glad to leave. And yet, it was, potentially, an idyllic practice.

Just after I left and a week or two before we were due to marry, my putative father-in-law asked me where I was going to work after the wedding. This prompted me to look at the adverts. I settled for an 'Assistantship' for 12 months. It had many advantages, situated in beautiful countryside and among the most pleasant of people. The disadvantages took a little while to become apparent. It should have been obvious from the interview. We drove 150 miles there and 150 miles back. We were not offered a cup of tea. After that job finished, I applied for a place in a "South Yorkshire semi-rural practice".

Attending for an interview at Chapelthorpe was quite different from any other I had previously experienced. We arrived a little early, fortunately, for our young daughter was hungry. Since breast feeding in public was, at that time, frowned upon, we sought what appeared to be a quiet lane. Within a few minutes, a crowd of people walked by, leaving their work at the stocking factory. We called it a day and went on to Reed Hall.

George Wightman was welcoming. We were offered tea and a place to freshen up. The baby was fed. He apologised that he could not offer us a room for the night, but arranged a meal. I did not appreciate the pressure he was under. His wife Patsy was seriously ill and he was running the practice virtually single handed, yet he gave us all his time. Throughout my early years, his generosity, good manners and integrity sustained us. He was the epitome of the senior partner, guiding me with only the gentlest chiding.

I was appointed for six months. I stayed for more than thirty years.

Starting Off

Why I decided to become a doctor at all is a bit of puzzle to me. I rather think the credit – or blame – must lie with Dr Gamble. He was the GP to our family in the '40's and early '50's, a time when we had a lot of medical action. My older sister's asthma, my father's chronic ill-health, my younger brother's skin and my own flirtations with the knife all contrived to make him a regular visitor and a member of the family. He was blunt and monosyllabic. There were few laughs. But his integrity and care shone through his rather stern exterior. He became sanctified by my mother especially on the night he was wearing a dinner jacket when he came to see me. I heard her telling Auntie Polly about it later "Came straight away, he did. And you could tell he'd been at a dinnering".

Perhaps it is not surprising that when, at Primary School, we were asked to write an essay on 'What I want to be when I grow up', I chose to write about being a doctor. Not that it was a positive decision, but I could think of nothing else. There didn't seem a lot to say about being a miner, a postman, an engine driver or the like. And even though Stanley Matthews was at that time the Patron Saint of the Potteries, I was sufficiently realistic to know that my talents as a footballer were somewhat limited.

Eventually, I stumbled into Medicine. My 'O' levels seemed to indicate some leaning towards the Arts and when I eventually moved to the sixth form, it was Languages and English Literature that I chose. Curiously, within a month or so, my interest dwindled and, after some soul searching, I transferred to the Science side. I began to enjoy it, but with no idea of my future. I became acquainted with Jimmy McMinn who was a year ahead of me. He had decided to study medicine and had chosen to go to Edinburgh. It seemed a good idea to me and I followed suit.

Like most newly qualified doctors, once I had that special parchment in my hand, I felt I was ready and the complete package. What I had yet to realise was that illness happens to people and it is people, not just disease and mishap, who make life tricky for doctors. It all seemed so straightforward at Medical School. Patients would describe their problems succinctly and fluently. I would examine them assiduously and then, having defined the diagnosis, issue the correct treatment, which worked just as the manufacturers said it would. The patient would recover and be eternally grateful to me. Well, it wasn't to be quite like that.

My junior hospital jobs did little to dispel these dreams. Hospitals are strange places. They are communities within themselves and apparently separate from, and oblivious to, the outside world. There is an unreality about the patients, too. The junior doctor has little idea of where they come from or, indeed who they are apart from their name, address and age. During my time, they arrived with an introductory letter, were parcelled up in a pristine envelope of a bed, stamped with the diagnosis and, in the fullness of time, returned to sender. Patients who left the ward were, so far as we were concerned either better or dead. When I left to enter General Practice, I found that, in fact, most patients who returned to me from hospital were neither better nor dead, but hovering somewhere in between. I realised that one of the arts of the GP was the managing of patients who were suspended in this Limbo.

I made life more difficult for myself by choosing to practice in the West Riding. I assumed, quite reasonably, I thought, that since Wakefield was in England, I would have no problems with the language. After all, it wasn't that far from Stoke. But it wasn't long before I heard words whose meaning I did not understand. Then there were words that should have been familiar, but were so modified by accent and intonation that they meant nothing to me. But the worst of all were the words I thought I understood, only to find they had a different meaning here than they had in Stoke – or anywhere else for that matter. Chaps would open a consultation by saying something like "*A w' playin' last week an' a wanter play agin nex*". At first I used to congratulate them on keeping so active. I soon learned that we were talking NHS certificates of incapacity.

It became important to take and read the local paper. Unsuccessful consultations were often solved by glancing down the court reports in the *Express*. And had I been unaware that Wakefield Trinity were in the Cup Final, I might have thought the city had been struck by a major epidemic, so many were taken ill on the Thursday by an ill-defined 'virus'. They were all well on the following Tuesday. Well, not all. Two aged supporters died while watching the match on the television. One of the deaths took place in bizarre circumstances. During the second half, I received an urgent call to a nearby bungalow. It sounded dramatic, but the message was confused and garbled. I arrived, knocked and walked in. In the sitting room an elderly couple were sitting on the settee, watching the last few minutes of the match. Between them sat an even older man, obviously quite dead and, oddly enough, wearing no trousers. This circumstance passed without comment. I think I was too embarrassed to ask, in fear of the possible answer. I asked what had happened. "We don't know, he just went quiet" "Who is he?" I asked. It seemed a reasonable question. They looked at each other. "I don't know. D'you, Mary?" "I don't know. I

44

thought you knew him". "He just called in to watch the match". I found his name and address in his wallet in his jacket and contacted the coroner. He had no known relations. I have often tried to reconstruct that day in my mind, what happened and why, but I never can.

Gradually, I began to learn the art of communication, probably the greatest art in Medicine. And it wasn't just the way the patients spoke; my language to them was probably as opaque as theirs was to me. I might well have thought I was being honest and truthful when I talked about 'concerns over the possibility of Systemic Lupus Erythematosus', but this conveyed little to the average chap at that time. Jargon is often a doctor's downfall. I was learning that, in order to convey a message or an attitude, it was vital that you chose a suitable 'code', one which not only truthfully defined what you wanted it to, but one that could be decoded by the receiver.

Communication is not, though, simply about words and language. On the contrary, the spoken word is so often quite inadequate to describe pain and discomfort, let alone emotional stress. And not many patients have the eloquence to convey how they are feeling, especially when so many are frightened, embarrassed, ashamed or angry. So often in these complex circumstances, the patient will offer, subconsciously, perhaps, something that he thinks the doctor will be interested in, like 'headache', 'tiredness', 'can't sleep'. Unfortunately, sometimes the doctor accepts the words at face value and settles for 'painkillers' or 'sleepers'. Communication therefore is complex and subtle. Truth is as often revealed in the actions and the body language of the consultation

Even the way the patient first contacts the doctor reveals something about the illness, something about how the patient thinks of himself, something about what they think of their illness and perhaps even something about what they think of the doctor.

One Saturday morning, I received a letter from a lady who lived a couple of doors from the surgery, asking if I would call to see her, when it was convenient, as she had a bad stomach ache. I was tempted to leave it over the weekend, but since I was passing, I called in. She had advanced peritonitis.

I am still not sure how to interpret this. Did she think so little of herself – or had so much fearful respect of me –that she could only communicate by letter? Was she simply a stoic? What did her husband or family think? Did this communication tell me more about the family and her position in it?

The man who wakes in the night with chest pain and immediately sends for the doctor, thinks he has had a coronary. A man who wakes in the night with chest pain and attends the surgery in the morning does not think he has had a coronary. Now both of them might well have suffered heart attacks, but their management may be different, because of their beliefs and expectations.

I always found it difficult when someone asked me to call on someone else, usually an elderly relative "But don't tell them we've called you". Now, do people really believe that doctors drive about, looking for the poorly or 'dropping in' on people on the off chance of somebody being 'off it'. I was zealous in my youth, though, and I used to respond to such requests, but it landed me in some complicated situations. "Who are you?"

"I'm the doctor. I'd heard you weren't very well". "Ada!. The bloody doctor's here. Have you sent for him? Oh yes, you bloody have. I've bloody told you before, I don't bloody need a doctor and I won't bloody have one… " I stand and wait. And sometimes, I leave them to it, having inadvertently created discord where there had been peace. I stopped accepting such requests quite early in my career. I never did understand them. I suppose it indicated either a reluctant patient or some inadequacy of understanding in their family. I'll never know.

The problems of communication during home visits are always complicated by the life that goes on there. Not uncommonly, relatives and neighbours collected when the doctor was calling. They gathered round, listening to every word, observing every move. I sometimes felt like a cabaret turn and I regret I sometimes responded to the audience with a dramatic statement or gesture. A walk to the window and a silent stare into the street would produce a tense silence. I would swing round, my mind made up and pronounce a verdict or expound a defined course of action. Mothers and their in-laws would nod and look at each other. I had to restrain myself, lest I got carried away.

An audience was not the only distraction. The most common one was the television – which was always on. I often used to think that one of the greatest unsung skills of the GP was the ability to assess whether this was the sort of house where you saved the important statements for the advertisements or for the main programme. Why not ask them to turn it off? Oh dear, that's asking a lot. I did sometimes. It was like cutting off an oxygen supply. Parents would look shocked, children screamed. Could be nasty.

At the surgery, it soon became apparent that the way a patient entered the consulting room could indicate problems looming. The chap who swings in through the door with a merry wave and "Hi doc!" can be tricky. As he sits back in his chair, adjusting his trousers, he launches into a complex, but apparently unconcerned description of his problem. He often will proffer a diagnosis. This chap is expecting an interesting, clean disease that he can chat about over the dinner table with equanimity. He will not accept easily something associated with the poorer classes or something 'dirty' or infectious.

Such a man consulted me asking for advice about his ' neurasthenia of the scalp'. I admitted I was unfamiliar with the condition. I examined him. The diagnosis was obvious. "Actually, you have nits", I said. He was appalled and demanded a second opinion. I managed to catch one of the head lice (another useful skill of the GP and one not to be sneezed at). I put it on a slide under the microscope. "That", I said, "is a head louse". He got up and stormed out. I heard later he'd transferred to another doctor.

I suppose we're all a bit like that. Nobody likes an anti-social disease, especially "..like that lot down the road. Have you seen the state of the kids? Filthy. Never have a decent meal......no shoes on their feet..."

The other end of the behavioural spectrum is the 'poor me' patient. A small man with the top button of his raincoat fastened and his cap straight and flat on his head, shuffles slowly round the door and pauses. He is expecting the worst for that has always been his lot in life. You find yourself standing up from your chair, putting out your arms and are tempted to cry "Come, come in lad. Come in and be saved". But you will be increasingly frustrated, whatever treatment you offer. He will be difficult to cure, whatever his problem. Whether you are compassionate or brusque, authoritative or in counselling mode, serious or lighthearted, you are unlikely to be successful. Unfortunately, it is this type of patient who seems to attract tragedy.[2]

It all happened a long time ago, but not long enough to have healed the pain of my own inadequacy. There was little odd or unusual about it at the beginning. Two days before, George Foster had seen my partner because he had noticed a little bleeding when he opened his bowels. Little definite had been found apart from a small external haemorrhoid. I was not sure why he had chosen to see me this time.

He edged his way shuffling slowly into my room, pausing for a moment with his hand on the door handle. I did not understand my rising impatience and it annoyed me. "Come and sit down". I could hear an edge to my voice. He sat down slowly, his eyes averted. "No better", he muttered, "Still bleeding" I was over-bright and too brisk. "Nip on to the couch, then and I'll have a look" Perhaps the pile was a little larger than had been described in the notes. I could find nothing else. I reassured him firmly. "Can I go into hospital?" he asked, still lying on the couch. "What on earth for?" I was becoming more exasperated. "Just carry on with the treatment for a few days". As he slowly dressed, I glanced through his notes which were sparse and old. Some entries were faded and difficult to read. One remark, just after the War, read 'Concert pianist' The following day, I was asked to visit him at his small flat on the edge of the village. I climbed the short flight of stairs and rang the bell. His wife opened the door and blasted me with a stream of invective.

[2] A shortened version of *The Music Man* was originally published in *The General Practitioner* magazine 25th September 1987.

"You doctors are all the same, you don't care. Can't you see he's ill. Why isn't he in hospital?" The tirade continued as I eased my way to the bedroom. *"He's been up all night on the lavatory. He's not fit to be at home"*.

The curtains were drawn in the bedroom where he lay, unmoving in the dark. I put on the light. He looked at me then turned away. He didn't respond any more. I examined him. The piles were a little worse, no doubt from the continual straining. His wife watched me from the end of the bed, her arms folded.

I explained my findings to her. *"There are no signs of anything more serious, no cancer or anything like that"*. She exploded again. *"That's a terrible thing to say to somebody who is so ill"*. I was non-plussed. *"Mrs Foster, your husband has piles, like many other people. Why is he taking it so badly?"* She didn't reply. *"I'll refer him to hospital, but we cannot consider it an emergency"*. She was not satisfied. I suggested continuing the treatment and left. I forgot to say goodbye to George.

The following day, another visit was requested. *"He's no better. He's not eating and he keeps pulling at himself"*.

George was still in bed, looking fixedly at the ceiling. He appeared to be writhing under the bedclothes. I pulled them back. They were bloodstained. I found it difficult to move his hands from where they were clutched in and around his buttocks. The piles were much larger, scratched and ulcerated. George's mouth was open showing a half-chewed bacon sandwich.

I did not know what to do. It was like watching someone slowly wish themselves to death. I turned to his wife. The wetness of her face was now not anger, but tears. She could not cope and neither could I. *"I think we'll have to send him to hospital"*. I couldn't think of anything else to do. She nodded.

As I waited for the house-surgeon to answer his bleep, I looked at the picture of a dapper man playing a very large concert organ. He looked familiar.

I discussed my predicament with the house surgeon. It is always difficult to admit to inadequacy. "I've never thought of piles as an emergency", he said. He accepted George reluctantly. I still had misgivings. Should I have tried for a psychiatric admission? I couldn't imagine any psychiatrist admitting him.

I visited him the next day in the surgical ward. He was lying on his back, staring at the ceiling, his wrists tied to the bed frame with bandages. He did not respond to my greeting. Sister said the psychiatrist was coming in later that day.

George died the next day. The post mortem was inconclusive. He had some bronchopneumonia, probably linked to his recent immobility, and some pelvic vein inflammation related to his ulcerated piles..

I went to see his wife that evening. She gave me a cup of tea and wept a little. There was no animosity. "He's never been the same since we moved here. He lived for his music, you know. But we couldn't get the piano up here, you see. You were not to know, doctor"

There were only three people at the funeral. The music was piped.

Since I retired and now dabble in medicine only as a patient, I have become increasingly concerned that not only do I speak as a patient, but also that I act like one, steering a course between the extreme types I have noted. But, not surprisingly, I have also become more aware of how doctors behave, too. Usually, the doctor swings round in his chair to greet me smilingly. Sometimes, he or she even rises to shake my hand and welcome me. I relax and spill out the anguish of my body and soul. But there are times when it is not like that. I rehearse my story, note my concerns and fears, take a deep breath and enter. He or she sits with their back to me, grunts a 'sit down' and turns to the computer. A great 'Sod it!' overwhelms me and I ask "Can I have some more tablets please? Yes, they're fine". Perhaps I'll tell him next time. It's painful to think how often, over the years, my own patients have had the same experience.

It took a little while before I fully understood how privileged doctors were in being able to touch people so easily. I suppose touch is the ultimate in communication. It was the District Nurse who taught me.

Sister Mary was a big girl who was also profoundly dedicated – to the point of sainthood some would say. I was having a bad time that day and when she came through between patients to ask me to see a patient in the treatment room, I was quite sharp. "Can't you get somebody else?" She came over to me where I sat and put her arms round me, burying my head in her generous bosom. "I know, love" she said. "I know". That was all. It was enough.

Men have much more difficulty in touching than do women, which is a pity, but it is difficult to change our national reticence. Touching and holding though are surely essential in some circumstances. How false it seems to say to the recently bereaved, "I'm sorry" and stand apart. How artificial it is to visit the sick and especially the dying, and leave without touching. How can you admire the beauty of a baby without stroking its skin. A great gift is the sense of touch.

Despite all the reservations about the true effectiveness of speech, we still feel we depend on it. It is interesting, though, how we modify the meaning of the simplest words by the slightest inflexion or hesitation. Just think of the enormous variations in the meaning of 'yes'. It can mean agreement in all its degrees of enthusiasm; it can mean 'perhaps', 'not really', 'certainly' and even 'no' under some circumstances.

So the spoken word can mean what we want it to mean – or hear it to mean. And in the medical consultation, the patient and doctor are perhaps, emotionally and even intellectually, poles apart. The doctor may be tired, but he or she is usually well-fed, well-paid and comfortable. It is the doctor who is in the pound seats, for it is their skills and advice that are being sought. The patient, on the other hand is in the role of supplicant, seeking help, advice or relief. Often they are anxious and possibly in pain or discomfort. They may be embarrassed or ashamed. How difficult it is for effective communication between human beings in such contrasting circumstances. It amazes me that it ever works.

Sometimes consultations verge on the bizarre and farcical. Things may have improved now in our over liberal society, but there were many times in the '50's and '60's when complaints about anything to do with the 'naughty bits' were so confused and complex, that at the end of the consultation, I was unsure what we had been talking about. Heaven knows what the patients made of it. Doctors were often as bad as the patients in their reticence.

The language used was often a curious mixture of baby talk, modified dog Latin and the vernacular. Any casual observer listening to grown adults talking of *wee-wee* and *poo* and *tuppences* and *down there* and the like would have been at least intrigued. But it was the local vernacular which often threw me and women, especially, seem to have a special language of their own for their particular problems

A lady staggered into my afternoon surgery, laden with shopping and fell into the chair. "Ooh, doctor, I've come the wrong way on the bus". I was puzzled, for the 110 stops quite near the surgery. We spent a fruitless and confused few minutes discussing, I thought, the vagaries of public transport, before it became clear that she was suffering the unexpected onset of a heavy period.

Another lady was complaining of an itchy scalp and dandruff. I recommended an effective shampoo and suggested she used it twice a week for a while and then return to let me see how it was getting on. "Well, doctor, I'll not be able to use it yet, 'cos my visitor's here". I reassured her that it did not smell, nor make a mess. "Anyway, I thought your mother was going back tomorrow". She blushed. "No, not my mother, my visitor, you know, my visitor". She glanced down. I had not realised that in some parts, it is considered unhealthy to wash your hair during a period.

I think I can be forgiven for my confusion under those circumstances, but you would have thought that I would have had little trouble understanding members of my own sex. In fact, men are worse. Not only do they have their own code, they are often so embarrassed that they can't get the words out. Conversations often consist of half finished sentences and questions accompanied by grimaces, screwed up eyes and contorted movements of the head and neck. The doctor soon becomes afflicted.

"It's…er…y'know.   The   wife…   she's   a   bit bothered……y'know". He was twisting about already. I tried to help him out "Ah, women", I said wisely. He looked blank for a moment, then continued "I can understand. Can't you,

doctor?" "Ah yes", I said, not understanding at all. "It doesn't, y'know...." He tailed off lamely, rocking in his seat. It was dawning on me "Does it not y'know...sort of when you want....? I was entrapped in the vernacular fog. "You've got it, doctor". He relaxed visibly. "Can you give us something for it?" I can't remember much of what happened after that. I like to think that I was wise and caring – even constructive in a sort of a way. I hope his problem was what I thought it might be.

I don't know how they managed elsewhere at that time. I heard that in some places they had proper sex clinics. I don't know what my patients would have thought of waiting room full of bed and cushions. Especially before you've had your dinner. Doesn't bear thinking about.

Mind you, it wasn't just sex and that sort of thing which perplexed me in those early days. There were sometimes far more complex communication processes, some of which continued, and indeed continue, to puzzle me to this day. Berne has explained some of these complex interactions in his fascinating (and entertaining) book, *Games People Play*. The particular game which caused most difficulty to me - and the Practice - was *Chaos*. There are some people who somehow can transform a stable organisation into utter mayhem. Why they do it – I'm sure it is not a conscious or planned exercise – I do not know. I have always thought that it was an extreme form of attention seeking, but their very behaviour makes exploration of their motives and psyche very difficult indeed. They are, curiously, often charming and even attractive people who remain, apparently, blithely unaware of the devastation they cause.

*I had finished the evening surgery an hour ago and was dealing
with letters and administrative tasks. The receptionist had
her coat on to leave. There was a knocking at the office
window. I could hear a conversation. "Can you see this young
lady, she's in a bit of a state". The young lady was shown in
and was effusive in her gratitude. She'd heard so much about
me and my partners. Her friend said that everyone knew we
were the best doctors in the area. I succumbed to her flattery.
She'd called to see her friend – "I can't remember her name
since she married" - when she felt most peculiar. The address?
"I can never remember, but I can show it to you". I explained
I needed it for the records. "No, I don't have my Medical
Card with me". Yes, she'd had these turns before, but her
own doctor was too busy to take notice. And anyway he didn't
understand. A full examination was obviously required, but
no doctor with any sense would undertake such an examination
in an empty surgery. The receptionist had already missed her
bus and stayed as chaperone. I said I'd run her home. The
examination was normal. I said I would write to her doctor.
She said she would let me know his name and address. She
couldn't remember them offhand. She left and we locked up
and set the alarm. As I started the car, she appeared in front
of us. She had lost her car keys. We went back in and found
her keys in the consulting room. By the time I returned from
running the receptionist home, Miss Chaos had added well
over an hour to my day. We never heard anything from her
and were unable to contact her own doctor.*

Fortunately, such patients were uncommon, though there were
of course many who played a milder form of the game.
Over the years, I gradually acquired an enormous collection of
letters from patients. They still make interesting reading and
bring back many memories, good and bad. Before we established

a formal system for the ordering and control of repeat prescriptions, many of the letters were along the lines of *"Can you send me some more of the red tablets. Not the white ones. I know you said they were the same, but they're not you know. Upset my stomach rotten they did…"*. At that time we practised from a surgery at the back of my partner's house. There was a small glass porch at the entrance where we used to leave prescriptions and medicines (we never thought they might be stolen and they never were). We had a surprising number of requests for the prescription to be left *"…in Dr W's back passage…" or "…to be left at your convenience.."*.

There were many letters of thanks and appreciation. Surely no one ever gets as much gratitude as doctors do. It makes the life of a GP enormously rewarding. When I read them now, I feel humbled. After all, I was doing a job I enjoyed and for which I was paid well. But not all letters were congratulatory. After her letter detailed a long description of her lifetime of hardship and tragedy, an elderly lady went on, *"…Now can I give you some advice. You came into my home and immediately told me, in no uncertain manner, my husband had a malignant tumour in other words C.A. Don't you think it would have been kinder and more sensible to have asked had anyone else talked to me about my husband……and gone on to ask if I had any idea what was wrong and then told me, but gently…"*

Although I did not recognise the incident from her description, I had to accept her version, for her view of the occasion was more important than mine. I called to apologise. We were alright after that, but she did not want me to attend her husband. It was not the first time that a patient had taught me something about my job and the art of communication. No, not the first time, nor certainly the last.

Sometimes, patients wrote at great length to explain situations, supplement the story of their illness or ask for advice or help for a sick relative, neighbour or friend. These letters were always illuminating. Apart from the factual information they gave, they emphasised how inadequate I had been sometimes in 'reading' a consultation. One mother wrote, of her daughter who had seen me previously, "...*Helen has asked me to write down how she feels as she is afraid she will cry if she tells you herself. She is ashamed of her spots and has stopped playing sports when a short-sleeved shirt is needed. She has reduced her social activities and wears long-sleeved high-necked blouses..... She is very depressed and weepy and is convinced she has an incurable disease...*" I used to recall that letter whenever I saw anyone with a skin problem.

A patient might seek to avoid embarrassment by writing before the consultation "...*I have never spoken to anyone about this problem because I am so embarrassed by it. I have a prominent nose and my schooldays were a misery because of the teasing......it has affected my whole life...*"

Another letter began "...*I am writing this as I can explain how I am, better than I can tell you...*" Other letters were more explicit. "....*Pains in stomach. Motion loose and perforated*[sic] *appearance followed by constipation. Severe wind. No more than 3 hours sleep. Stomach rumbling...*" And, of a husband, "...*Memory and concentration becoming much worse. Abdominal pain at intervals. Sleeps badly, but stays in bed. Bad attack this morning, causing screaming...*" The most important written communications though, were undoubtedly those related to mental illness. A lady emphasised the life she underwent at the hands of a husband who was a recent convert to an odd religious sect and who strove to convert her in a particularly belligerent manner. His mental imbalance was frightening at times. "…*what a carry on this is. I'm sorry to burden you with this. Tuesday teatime. 'Explosion' came so suddenly and violently, I was shattered. I don't know what to do. He loses all reason. I asked him to sit down and stop shouting. He says he is shouting to try to get through to me. I am going to stay with a friend on Friday night, but I am terrified about what he'll be like when I come back…."*. A mother wrote about her son "…*underneath, things are seething and his fantasy life is absorbing him very much…..our normal reactions do not seem to be adequate. We don't know how to manage the situation…"*

Dementia drains the resources of the most resilient carer. Unless one has lived with such an affected patient, it is impossible to grasp the enormity of the strain. An extract from a very long letter sums it up "….*We have been going to bed at midnight. She wakes at 2.0am and gets dressed to go out. After a hot drink, I got her back to bed. She was up again arguing about going out until 5.0am. Then she rested until 7.0am when she was up and about again. Once I didn't get up with her. When I did get up after an hour she was switching all the lights on and off – inside and out. The house looked as though it had been burgled….….She complains about me 'bashing' her. She hides the door keys in strange places…if I rebuke her, she attacks me and pummels me with her fists…"*

Occasionally a letter will actually reveal the diagnosis. "….*In furie. I said hello. She said ——blady bla. 'I have just lost my dolly's clothes. Hello. Things are OK again except we have a writing illegible problem+spelling which is usual. Read gradually which is what I'd like you to do for all our sakes. Because it is Sunday. We've nearly done…"*. This was a trigger which prompted her admission to hospital. That was many years ago. She remains well after her treatment for her schizophrenic illness.

Other letters are less easy to classify. A man arrested for importuning was terrified of his wife finding out. Could I help by suppressing the court report in the local paper? An elderly lady vowed in her letter that, whatever the result of the chest X-ray, she would undergo neither surgery nor chemotherapy. A man wrote, after his mother was found to have diabetes, *"..In view of private circumstances, I will now in no way be responsible for the care of her health. I will not work out, prepare or serve any form of diet. I will not supply nor administer nor be responsible for any drug… ".* And another plea from a regular contributor *"..Would you be so kind as to arrange a gynaecological examination as well as a thorough examination, inc. throat, chest, ears, and heart. It's about two years since my last. I can have the 'flu injection while I am there. Not Wednesday as I have a dental appointment. Thank you for the linctus and ulcer tablets…"*

I suppose such a selection as these indicates the enormous variety of life in General Practice. After a decade or two, I felt I was beginning to catch on.

It is, perhaps only now, with the retrospection that retirement brings, that I can see the critical early incidents that shaped my professional life. Among these I count a consultation which took place after I had been in the practice about three years. By that time, I was familiar with the routine of the work, with the geography of the area and with many of the patients. My knowledge and skills were still reasonably up to date. I was beginning to 'coast'. Now one of the subtle threats to one's standards of practice is that the General Practitioner works largely in isolation. In particular, the consultation is never viewed by one's peers. In recent years, the advent of the videotape has allowed critical analysis of consulting technique and effectiveness, but it was not available then. It was easy, cocooned in the consultation, to become slipshod. Short-cuts, assumptions and empirical judgements gradually eroded my standards. At the same time, the power I held as a doctor had seduced me. I became arrogant. There is no greater sin in medicine than arrogance. One patient changed that and the effect of those two or three consultations was to last throughout my life.

A young mother, unknown to me at the time, brought her baby to see me, a little girl of nine or ten months. The child had a rash near her right armpit. I was quite confident of the diagnosis, reassured the mother and recommended a cream which would clear it in a few days. She returned a week later, concerned that not only was the rash no better, it was spreading. I was irritated and remember saying she was not using the cream properly. I demonstrated its application. A week later she returned. The rash was worse. I was sharp with her. She began to cry. "Can I take her to see someone at the hospital?" "Why?" I was furious that my judgement was being questioned, "it's only a rash. It would've been better by now if you'd used the treatment properly." She wept openly and pleaded for a referral. I finally agreed, with ill grace. I think I said something about abusing the service. I had a note from the hospital some days later. The child had impetigo. It had never occurred to me at any time during the three consultations that I might be wrong. Or that I had misdiagnosed a simple, common condition. She came to see me for some more of the cream the hospital had given her. She was thrilled that the child's rash had almost gone. She thanked me for sending her to the hospital.

I am not sure what was more devastating, being wrong about something simple or the fact that she thanked me for my help. Humility is the most painful virtue to acquire.

Within a few weeks, there was a vacancy in the Skin Department for a part-time assistant. I applied and made my ignorance clear – if it was not already. In working there a couple of times a week, I came under the influence of Dr Clifford Stuart. I have rarely met anyone who was as enthusiastic about medicine as he was. He assumed I read the journals regularly, so I did. He assumed I would attend clinical meetings, so I did. He treated me, a GP, as a specialist in my own right. I tried hard to justify his trust. Over the first months with him, I regained my vocation and began to love the work again. I felt that he, and the patient who started it all, had begun to shape me into a proper doctor.

Memorable Patients

I suppose that over the time I was in practice, I averaged about ten to twelve thousand consultations a year. While all of them were important at the time, to both myself and the patients concerned, most have long since faded from my memory. Some days seemed to pass with me on 'automatic', though I hope it didn't show. But there were some patients whom one could never forget. It may be because of the patient themselves or their illness or the circumstances of our meeting. Occasionally, the consultation had a profound effect on me. Patients were always the best teachers of all, provided you listened to what they said.

Many of these descriptions or anecdotes have been published elsewhere, in various books or journals and I am grateful for permission to use them again here. From time to time during my working life, I felt the need to share with others the lessons I'd learned or the pleasure I'd had from meeting patients. Or sometimes I wanted to cleanse myself of frustration or anger, though often this was best done by trying to find the funny side of a situation. And, of course, sometimes I wrote simply for the fun of writing

I joined the General Practitioners Writing Association(GPWA) some years ago. It was a curious group of doctors, for we never talked about medicine or any form of 'shop' except as a possible vehicle for an article, book or poem. We would weep into our pints over the abuse of the apostrophe and argue the relevance and legitimacy of the split infinitive. We would dream of the 'best seller' and for some the dream became reality. We would tell tales and comment on their telling, discuss the nuances of copyright and the curious minds of editors and publishers. It does not seem that long ago since a chap talked to us about the benefits of using a machine called a P.C. Few of us were keen at the time to abandon our typewriters – or our pens. Above all, though, we would share great joy in writing. Some of these anecdotes grew out of that joy.

When I have been a patient myself, it has never occurred to me that the doctor is human. I don't ever wonder if they are hungry or tired or had had a row with somebody. And certainly it has never entered my head that the doctor sometimes needed to go to the toilet

The bladder is a capricious organ. Its filling knows no emotional or intellectual boundaries and the need for its emptying is rarely entirely convenient. I knew it was a mistake to have another cup of coffee before I left the Surgery. Even so, I completed most of my visits without undue discomfort. But an ice cold Yorkshire wind over the 'tops' and a long drive to the mining village accelerated the remorseless ticking of my diuretic clock.

By the time I saw Jason Pogmore, I was in some distress. A full bladder does distract the intellect, but I summed up the situation in a flash. Jason reclined by an enormous coal fire. He was '*pumping everything back*' and reported to be '*burning up*'. He had been '*screaming all night*' and they'd had to '*fly to the Calpol*'. Just now, he was merely irritated that I had arrived in the middle of '*Saturday Superstore*'. I balanced the parental concerns against my discomfort. "Before I see Jason, could I wash my hands?" I was shown to the kitchen and I washed my hands. The running water was a torment.

I returned and examined Jason, perhaps a little briskly. "Could I use your bathroom?" Mr Pogmore looked perplexed, but rose slowly and went to the kitchen. I followed him. He removed several large bags and boxes from what I had thought to be a table, lifted a large piece of planking and revealed the bath. He looked at me and I at him. "Actually" (I was blushing.) "I'd like to go to the toilet". His expression was sad and resigned as he put the bath top back. "T'lav's out back". He flicked his head to the kitchen door.

By this time a large group of well-wishers, neighbours and in-laws had gathered at the back gate to gauge the severity of Jason's illness from the demeanour of the doctor as he left. The audible gasp and visible nods stilled as I emerged with a strained expression and moved straight to the toilet by the greyhound kennel. The silence was palpable. I tried not to break it.

I returned to the house light of foot. Mr Pogmore had lit up a cigarette and was sitting on his stool by the back door, "Some say it's better than a week at Blackpool", he said. "Aye", I said, "I reckon I'd go along with that".

Somehow, I don't think a patient really recognises their doctor as a human being, at least not during a consultation. Nevertheless, from time to time, controversy rages over what the doctor should wear and what effect this has on their influence and effectiveness. Most of the research that prompted such debates seems to me to be eminently spurious and a sort of occupational therapy for that nebulous but ubiquitous group of people known as 'researchers'. Surely it's all common sense. I always considered it good manners to be fairly clean and respectable. Mind you, what is or is not respectable does change. For me a tie, preferably 'college', was essential and I cringed when my junior partners appeared tie-less. A jacket, too, was critical, for not only did it provide copious mobile storage space, it also covered the vest that tended to show through a white shirt. I was always reluctant to remove my jacket, even on the hottest days.

There were few dress problems, though, which would prompt me to man the barricades. On one occasion, I had a rather glamorous female student 'sitting in' on my consultations. On the day she was due to leave, she was attending an interview for her next attachment. She appeared in the consulting room in a devastating dress that urged me to cover her with a blanket. My surgery progressed very slowly. Young women considered her, older women either envied her or sniffed disapproval. But the men. I could get no sense out of them, so busy were they posturing and making witty comment. I had to ask her to put a cardy on. A long one. Well, I feared epidemic apoplexy.

Dress can give the doctor important clues about the patient and their illness, but I never thought of it as helping in the identity of the patient. A famous cricketer appeared unexpectedly at the reception desk. He was instantly recognisable, but to help matters, he wore a tee-shirt emblazoned with his name. Nevertheless, the receptionist, refusing to give preference to 'class', pedantically took him through the formal routine of temporary registration. He came through to see me. He had a painful eye. "I'm batting against the Aussies in a couple of hours", he said. Now eyes were not my strong point and his remark inspired my confidence not one jot. I furtled a bit and extracted a speck of grit. I wished him good luck and followed the match assiduously. He made a century.

One Sunday morning in late Spring, a chap phoned for a visit to his wife. I did not recognise the name. It was an unusually glamorous bungalow they lived in and he was vaguely familiar.

His wife was in bed and rather hoarse. She was beautiful and well spoken. I asked her about the illness. "Well", she said, "It came on quite suddenly while I was shopping on the Champs Elysees". This is not a remark you hear very often in Crigglestone, but I still didn't catch on. I examined her and prescribed some treatment. I said it might take a day or two to resolve and it was best if she avoided using her voice for a while. Her husband leaned forward "But we're carrying the flag in Europe in a week". I tried to cover my ignorance and subtly, I hope, did my best to find out who they were. The penny dropped eventually. I watched the Eurovision Song Contest that year. In their victory speech and interviews, they didn't mention the wonderful doctor who had saved the trophy for Britain. A shame that.

There is always a new controversy over aspect of dress. One that has arisen of late is personal, for researchers (o blessed lot) have homed in on my beloved tie. Apparently, ties carry germs and in hospital that is not on. There is no reference to your average GP. Now, anyone could have told them that. I bet jackets and trousers carry lots more. Of course I'm miffed. I think it's mainly because my junior partners have found science on their side, fashion-wise. Anyway, I return to my first contention, patients don't notice.

That week in the '80's had been the sort of week that prompts you to consider your life and contemplate the infinite. It must be rare to suffer more than one lifetime first in the same week. For a start, my date stamp ran out. Now I have never heard of anyone else's date stamp running out, but the more I tried to change the year, the more it returned to 1967. I had to buy a new one. I never thought a stethoscope could wear out, but mine did. The combined efforts of superglue, cellotape and surgical plaster finally proved inadequate. It was not surprising that patients seemed to be getting on top of me. It was an effort to write a prescription and, without my distance glasses, I could not read the calendar above my desk. I slipped into depression. It was the cleaner who solved the problem. The large screw on my swivel chair was worn smooth and the chair was now permanently some six inches lower than the norm. Once replaced, I was a new man.

It was some relief to be off-duty that weekend.[3] Sunday afternoon was wet and Julie was away. I played the good father as best I could. I occupied the kids with an excellent game of *Cowboys and Indians* in the style of my youth. A six gun was slung at my hip, my shirt was open to the waist (I had one in those days) and my bandana was tied casually round my neck. My straw sombrero, a souvenir of a long ago honeymoon in Spain, was set at just the angle worn by Shane and Roy Rogers. I was pretty impressive.

So engrossed was I in defending my homestead against the marauding braves, that I had become totally unaware of myself and had forgotten how I was dressed. I remained unaware when I finally answered the insistent ringing of the front door bell. I saw before me a distraught young woman. What she saw in front of her, I have no idea, but she burst out "He's gone and left me - and taken the keys!" She collapsed, sobbing on to my chest, avoiding being impaled on my six-gun by the merest chance.

A cup of tea later, the situation was calmer and we sat in what had been a few minutes ago, Dead Man's Gulch. We discussed

[3] Originally appeared, in a shortened form, as *Cowboy GP Rides to the Rescue* in *General Practitioner Magazine*. 23rd 1995

the vagaries of men and marriage. I didn't feel very constructive and sundry painted kids milling about didn't help. I strove to be practical. First, she had to get into her house and she would need to break in. I thought of the local bobby; bobbies can break in with impunity. It was a winner. Of course he would help.

He called to collect her and accompany her home. As I said goodbye at the door, my raised hand touched my sombrero and an icy January wind searched out my naked chest. I blushed to my ankles. What on earth must they have thought?

I needn't have worried. The next time I saw her, all was sweetness and light and she was booked in for the Ante-Natal Clinic. I'm not sure how the transformation came about. Was it my unconscious counselling skills or the presence of the law that effected the change? I'll never know. I've never asked.

While the physical appearance of the doctor has, from time to time invited comment and debate, you rarely see advice to patients about clothing suitable for the consultation. Such advice is long overdue. Why do surgeries take longer in the winter than in the summer? The answer lies somewhere among the layers of clothing which accommodate the patients when the temperature drops. I once counted eleven layers covering one old lady. What began as a clinical examination became, at the end, an archaeological dig. And I find it difficult to describe the stress occasioned, to doctors and to subsequent patients, by the boots worn by the young at the behest of their then fashion guru. The incredibly long laces were slowly loosened with a care and consideration otherwise unknown outside a religious ceremony or the most delicate of neurosurgical procedures. The boot was carefully placed on the floor and the laces arranged decorously. Replacing the boot took at least as long, but curiously, the laces were never fastened. I never fathomed that. One of the most profound decisions that a GP ever had to make was whether to ask to see the other foot for comparison. This doubled the length of an already prolonged consultation.

The change in styles of shirt produced a sea change in the doctor-patient relationship. I reckon that General Practice has never been the same since the advent of the slim-fit shirt.[4] There was a time when the male physique could become totally available within seconds. Off with the jacket, slip down the braces, lift up the shirt and then, with a flick of the top trouser button, Homo Sapiens (male) was revealed in all his glory. Fat or thin, it made no difference. Now, alas, the shirt is contoured to the shape of the torso and retained in place by at least 23 small buttons closely opposed to the chest and a further two at each cuff. Many an appointment system has foundered on the impenetrable slim-fit shirt.

As if that wasn't bad enough, other tightly occlusive garments followed. Jeans hugged the anatomy - even if their physiology left something to be desired. As a result, abdominal examination became a difficult, time consuming and, occasionally, dangerous art. To make matters worse, increasing numbers of patients were wearing clothes the upper and lower parts of which were welded together or 'all in one'. Even babies were no longer easily available to the examining hand by the simple means of dividing their clothes in the middle. Now there was an outer layer that occluded them from finger-tip to toe. Underneath that was a one piece 'jogging suit' and finally there was the dreaded vest-pant combination.

[4] First published as *First Find Your Patient* in *Alimentary my Dear Doctor.* Hawkins C, editor. Oxford: © Radcliffe Medical Press: 1990. Reproduced with the permission of the copyright holder.

For a while, the impact of these garments on the GP's time/ efficiency ratio was reduced by the passing fashion in young women, of being harry starkers under their jogging suits. This not only allowed you to make up some lost time, it also avoided the risks to the hands of unwary physicians occasioned by the sudden unrolling of a panty girdle.

But then came that most obscenely inelegant foundation garment, the all in one, crotch-fastening corset. The first time I came face to face with one I knew that a disaster was inevitable and it was no surprise that that disaster, when it came, came to big Grace Wilson. 'Amazing Grace' was a walking miracle. Not only had she borne her life-long mysterious and excruciating abdominal pain with fortitude, she had borne it without any obvious ill effect on her health. She could get to doctors that other patients could not reach. In fog and snow and ice and hurricane, she would keep her appointment when others failed.

But her appearance that afternoon was unusual. There was something restrained about her entry into the consulting room. Her face was a trifle suffused and she sat down slowly and carefully. I thought I could detect with my naked ear, a creaking sound as she breathed. Her usual outpourings were more stilted than ever before and she occasionally paused for breath.

I decided it was time for another thorough examination and asked her to retire behind the screen to prepare herself. There was much grunting and panting and scrabbling of clothes. Time passed. Her efforts increased and I began to fear for her health. Suddenly - pop- pop - pop. Then a great rush of noise like the rolling up of a venetian blind, and finally a choking, strangled cry. I rushed behind the screen to find her already in the terminal stages of strangulation. Her all-in-one, its fierce tension released, had catapulted up her mighty torso, thrown her arms above her head and now encircled her neck. With dexterous aplomb, I divided the encircling garment with a handy scalpel. She relaxed, straightened her hair, climbed up on the couch and said "It's here, doctor", indicating her left side. "It's no better". The consultation continued along the usual lines.

Amazing woman, our Grace.

Although I continued to be interested in what people wore and how their clothes reflected their characters and their views of themselves, the longer I worked in the practice, the more I became involved in people's normal lives. I never ceased to be astonished at the lives people led when they were not at the surgery. Some people were there so often, I rather thought they had no other lives. When I stumbled on them living as people rather than as patients, it was often a startling revelation. Take Ferny for example.[5]

I had known of him for many years before I actually met him face to face. His sister, Mary, was regularly on our visiting list. Her prim expression and rather individual wig (never overtly discussed) were complemented by her unique collection of symptoms. Usually the complaint was of a pain in the head that came on when she sat down, sometimes when she stood up and, according to the season, sometimes when she lay in bed. She was as impeccably polite as her cottage was bright and clean. But then she was brought up in service and still (as she often showed me with pride) would occasionally receive notice of social events important in the County calendar. Her oft repeated remark *'if it wasn't for him'* intrigued me in the early days of our relationship.

[5] The story of *The Bicycle Man* first appeared in *World Medicine* in about 1980. Editor Michael O'Donell

Perhaps I was insufficiently astute or perhaps my non-direct inquiries were too indirect. At any rate *'he'* remained a mystery for some time. I should have paid more attention to "non-verbal" clues. The tidy pile of old tobacco tins were always there on an otherwise scrubbed clean kitchen table and the back door was always partially obstructed by neatly stacked bicycle frames and wheels.

Eventually, I tumbled to it. My rather precipitate entry one day, with bruised and bleeding shins prompted a rather more blunt approach. "What the hell are you doing with all these bikes?" Miss Fern's face crumpled with anger and sadness. *"It's him!"*, she cried. And then it all came out through tight lips.

She had lived with her brother for some fifteen years - but they had not actually spoken for the last eight years - well not since the fire. He had always blamed her of course, said she'd done it on purpose. Didn't call the fire brigade in time that's what she did. And when his shed was gone - well he'd brought all those bikes down home - and all the bits and pieces that went with them.

There had to be some arrangement of course - she couldn't stand him messing about all day, especially in the winter when he worked in the kitchen. And he never - ever - changed his clothes. (This last was always accompanied by opening of drawers and cupboards to show clean linen in abundance). An arrangement had been reached. For some years now he went to bed in the day while she worked and she went to bed at night while he worked. And so the arrangement had continued for the last eight years.

I cannot remember what medical reason prompted the call to Miss Fern at 8.0 p.m. one night. Certainly the most memorable part of the evening was that I actually met William A. Fern. I was not unduly surprised at his features or dirty oil-stained clothing. What did surprise me was the beauty of his voice. Soft Victorian cadences in a gentle baritone bade me welcome to his humble abode. Would I care to divest myself of my overcoat before attending to his sister's needs. All this accompanied by mannered doffing of his oily trilby, revealing a completely bald head that was a natural continuation of his plain hairless face. As I removed my coat, he confided that he personally had little inclination to doctors professionally, though he appreciated that his sister on occasion might require their skilled services.

Having dealt with his sister's problem, I moved back into the kitchen. Mr.Fern saw me looking at the rather elegant bronze statue of Sir Walter Scott on the mantle piece. By a happy chance (I was until then unaware of the meaning of serendipity) I had heard a little of a tribute to Sir Walter Scott on the car radio that evening - the anniversary of his birthday. *"Are you familiar with Sir Walter Scott, doctor?"* Mr. Fern inquired. I said I only just realised that today was his birthday.

There was a sudden relationship between us. Out came scrap books, newspaper references and books, and he, with shining face, regaled me with accounts of his great debates through the columns of the newspapers - including the Times - with leading figures of the days before the Second World War.

It was some months before I met Ferny again. Whether my counselling had achieved an end, whether they had softened or whether they had begun to realise their mutual dependence, I do not know. He began to appear in the daylight. His encyclopaedic knowledge of the bicycle, some manual dexterity and a large supply of spare parts attracted boys from all around. He made even their smallest purchase - of a nut, screw or brakeblock - an exciting experience.

I began to see him occasionally on my visits to his sister. He would always bid me welcome, remove his hat, bow, and move out of the way. They still did not speak to each other - not in my presence anyway. Should his sister be confined to bed, Ferny and I would occasionally talk on my way out. He read and wrote copiously, but otherwise he was devoted to the pedal cycle. He told me about the large garden shed nearby, where he worked-indeed virtually lived - until the tragic night of the fire. His voice broke as he recounted the story of how his hut was burned down

As Miss Fern's symptoms became more persistent and pronounced and her stamina and tolerance began to run down, so did the obvious state of the cottage. Inevitably, it was a small incident that provoked the crisis. Several upset boxes of screws and nuts resulted in an urgent call to the house. Miss Fern had "broken down". She wanted, insisted, on going into a residential home and despite the sorrow of leaving her cottage, nothing would diminish her determination to leave her brother. After some weeks of activity of ourselves and the social services, she eventually moved - taking with her what she could.

Over the ensuing Autumn weeks, the house - and Ferny - deteriorated. His eccentric appearance, now exaggerated by dirt and oil, became almost demonic. His ever open flies revealed that his social deterioration was complete. Neighbours shunned him (apart from a saintly "next door") and few boys braved a visit - most of those who did come, came to laugh. The kitchen, now inches deep in bicycle parts, old newspapers and ashes was only rarely warmed by an occasionally glowing coal.

His manners never changed; his voice always gave great pleasure. Under some pressure, I tried to persuade him to follow his sister's example. How could he? He would not leave his bicycles and he was having 'no interfering women in'. He denied the obvious chaos of the house and, I must say, could usually find within minutes any bicycle part I could name. He would accept no help.

It was no surprise when the health visitor found him lying on the rug by an empty fire grate one cold morning. He refused to move or in anyway co-operate with either of' us. Officially, I suppose he was hypothermic but he would not accept a thermometer. All persuasion having failed, I 'pulled rank' and he was carried protesting incoherently to the ambulance and thence to the acute geriatric ward.

I visited him the next day. He would accept no food, nor would he speak to anyone. He was staring fixedly at the ceiling, splendidly clean and shaved in a sparkling envelope of a hospital bed. He did not respond to me. I was rejected.

He died the next day, ultimately conforming.

Even today I think of Ferny sometimes. I wonder what happened in his life before I met him. I wonder, too, what else I might have done. And, above all, I wonder how people- and families in particular - can pursue vendettas so assiduously and for so long that they themselves become emotionally paralysed.

The central motivation of most human beings, when the chips are down, is self preservation. I had not always appreciated that and wasted considerable emotional energy on patients who seemed unable to appreciate that they were merely one small thread in the great tapestry of life. Once I was working in the surgery despite having vomiting and diarrhoea. It was an uncomfortable and time consuming complaint.

During one consultation, I was overcome by the urge to vomit. I moved rapidly to the sink and retched for several minutes before returning to my chair. Jenny was sitting as I had left her. She completed her sentence and continued. At the time, I was a little hurt that she failed to sympathise with me or to volunteer to return with her own problem when I was feeling better. On reflection, though, we do focus on our own problems to the exclusion of everyone else's and I think in Jennie's shoes, I might have acted the same. Certainly, it was a humbling experience for me. However caring and compassionate a doctor might be, he or she is still simply an agent of potential relief. But if I failed to learn that lesson from Jennie, I could not fail to be influenced by Doris.

It happened on the third day of true winter.[6] There were already three or four inches of snow and it was still falling. At 9.30 in the morning, the surgery was incredibly quiet. The telephone rang occasionally – mainly to cancel appointments or to postpone visits. Rarely had I known such lack of action. The paper work was up to date, 'snow stories' all told. Conversation was desultory. We walked about aimlessly.

[6] *When Winter Comes* originally appeared in *General Practitioner Magazine* 29th November 1985. It is reprinted here by permission of the copyright holder

Out of the window, I watched a blackbird sink in the snow, fluttering wings outstretched, lifting itself to equilibrium. " I always give them scraps", said Mary, "even chopped meat. They don't like sprouts", she confided to no-one in particular. "Is it worth clearing the paths again", asked Harold, looking at the still falling snow. No answer came and he didn't move.

Then Doris phoned. Doris had disturbed our peace often before, though rarely had she broken such peace so dramatically as then. Her strident, primeval tones pierced the quiet surgery. "Ooh, come quick", she screeched, "there's been a terrible accident in the village. He's trapped and screaming in agony". Now "screaming" and "agony" had long been everyday words in Doris' life, but we had to admit there did seem some urgency about this call. I checked that other emergency services had been alerted, picked up my bag and set off for the village three miles away.

The hilly road was not too bad and within ten minutes I was there. Two large lorries had collided, completely blocking the entrance to the village. Under the black sky, blurred figures moved about in the snow. Blue and orange flashing lights illuminated the eerie scene. At the centre of it all, the young driver sat trapped in his cab, his pain obvious. I remember thinking how terrible it must be to be in pain, in public. I made my way through the villagers and uniformed figures. With the impact, the trailer had moved forward into the cab, crushing the driver's seat against the steering column and trapping his leg. Otherwise he seemed unhurt and was conscious but pale. We slit his trousers as best we could. What part of his leg I could examine was blue, but I could find no obvious bone damage. We could not check the upper part of his leg though.

There was no immediate risk of fire and he was calmer now. Gas and air had eased his pain and my morphine was superfluous. With great care, the firemen began to cut away the seat. It was slow and difficult. We waited, tense in anticipation of what the first movement of the seat would reveal. One by one the seat's attachments were severed, each movement causing a spasm of pain that passed through us all. The Press photographer viewed it all objectively through his lens.

We neared the final act. The seat was moving. The stretcher was ready, its blanket rolled back. There was a leaning forward. The ambulance man and I slowly eased the leg free. Squeezed and compressed, it was nevertheless otherwise whole. He could move it freely. He offered to get out himself. I felt irrational anger that he might spoil the climax. We lifted him down and on to the stretcher. There was an audible "Ah" from the crowd.

I remembered I had left my lights on and contemplated a flat battery. Doris interrupted my thoughts. " While you're here, doctor, could you call in and see me? I think I've caught a chill"

It is so easy to disregard the chronic moaner, the hypochondriac and that vague entity, the neurotic. They all frighten me, for one day their significant illness will be obscured by their previous history and their present demeanour. And sometimes I have asked myself how they came to be that way and why does their behaviour persist. It is not often that I found a satisfactory answer, but I did, by accident, on two occasions. I had seen this chronically anxious mother many times. Her children were, it seemed, ever present on the surgery lists. Consultations were never satisfactory and she rarely seemed any happier at the end of our meetings than she had been at the beginning. Their records grew and hers were so large that they were beginning to disintegrate. One day I resolved to tidy them. At the bottom of the great piles of cards and papers was a crumpled carbon copy of a pathologist's report. It was a postmortem report on her first born son. Later we were able to discuss it and how it had affected her subsequent life. Our understanding did not dramatically change her life, but it had a marked influence on our relationship and, consequently, a beneficial effect on our consultations.

And then there was Brian Banks. I do not recall meeting a more pathetic creature than Brian. Everything happened to him. In spades. His speech was monotonous and he seemed never to draw breath. Consultations were prolonged and seemed interminable and pointless. He not uncommonly presented as an emergency. In fact that's when it happened. He attended the Saturday morning *Emergencies Only* surgery. I did not recognise him. He was dressed in flannels and a blazer with a regimental crest. His beret carried a glistening badge. There were several medals on his left breast. His bearing was good, his back straight. He was off to a service and reunion of the Burma Star Association. With prompting, he told me something of the horrors of the Burma Campaign. He became agitated and his eyes were moist and focussed somewhere else. He was with a forward patrol in dense jungle when they were ambushed. All his colleagues were killed. He rolled under a bush and listened to the enemy talking, searching and laughing. He stayed there alone and undiscovered for many hours until he was found by his own advancing army. He never really recovered, despite months of rehabilitation. We sat in silence for a while, then he rose, shook my hand and left. I never did know why he came to see me that day. It seemed irrelevant.

Until fairly well on in my career, there was an ingrained tendency in doctors to try to label patients with a formal diagnosis and pigeonhole them into a defined pathological entity. This often produced a false sense of security in the doctor, superfluous or inappropriate therapy for the patient and, importantly, a diagnostic tag that might dog a patient for years. The gradually acquired approach of 'problem solving' rather than 'labelling' was altogether more realistic and creative, especially when dealing with the confused life and behaviour of the 'neurotic' or 'heart-sink' patient.

Nevertheless, diagnostic labelling remained an integral part of our day to day work. The traditional clinical approach of history, examination, investigation, explanation and management remained the bedrock of our approach, particularly to physical problems. For psychiatric problems, this approach was less defined and the examination rather vague. It was many years before I realised that how you as a doctor responded to a mental problem was an important sign. I have already intimated that a consultation with the 'difficult' patient was often associated with irritation, anger or frustration on my part. Properly evaluated and analysed, this may well be an important sign in the diagnosis of neurosis. Some have gone so far as to say that the doctor's clenched fist under the desk gives an absolute diagnosis of neurosis.

The contrasting feelings hold true, too. I began to notice a rising well of compassion within me when faced with a patient suffering a true psychosis. Even in a disturbed or threatening patient, I became aware of a gut feeling of great sadness as I observed a fellow human being dislocated from their own humanity. The sadness would persist even though blurred by the frustration of trying to communicate with someone whose thought processes were distorted and whose reality was not my reality. Such major psychiatric illness was fortunately uncommon in General

Practice. I never knew how psychiatrists, nurses and carers coped with it on a day to day basis.

Not all influential patients were human. In fact, in my early days in a rural practice, it was quite common to be asked for advice on the health of animals and birds. You can learn a lot about life from animals and birds.

My close association with poultry began when the school asked my daughter to look after a chicken during the school holidays. Rebecca became deeply involved in its welfare and her interest grew to an obsession. Within weeks, it seemed, we had acquired a collection of bantams.

Her every waking hour was spent either at school or with her chickens. Each one had a name, each one an individual personality and a defined place in the pecking order. They lived in a custom made coop with a good 'run', but security was lax and they would often be found around the garden. Particular birds laid their eggs in particular places and egg-gathering was often time consuming. One September morning, Brownie appeared with eight new chickens. They became part of the family.

Then tragedy struck. One morning, Rebecca rushed back from feeding the flock. She was weeping and inconsolable. I went down to the run. The birds were all lying down. Although quite alert, they could not stand. Their legs ware flaccid. Yet they fed and drank normally if the food was within reach and two even laid.

Finding nothing relevant in the text books, I went down to the shop where we usually bought our feed. It was a traditional small shop, piled high with everything to do with animals and birds. The two elderly men behind the counter, their brown overalls buttoned high, nodded to each other as I told my story. An even older man, leaning an a stick and carrying a plastic shopping bag, leaned against the sacks of rabbit food and nodded too. "D'ye think it is, then, Jack ?" "No doubt. No doubt at all".

I scanned the faces, wondering whether I was hearing good - or bad - news. "What you've got," said Jack, pausing as he lit a cigarette, "is Leg Weakness in Poultry". Relief flooded through me at the name. He fetched some ladders and reached a bottle from the top shelf. It was a very special bottle with that sort of writing on its yellowed label that always used to adorn medicine bottles in the olden days.

He paused and read from it. "Poultry Tonic", it said, "Cures Leg Weakness in Poultry. Guaranteed since 1883". He kept looking over his shoulder to the door, as though he feared someone overhearing him. We automatically followed his gaze each time. He leaned forward over the counter, drew on his cigarette and lowered his voice to scarcely a whisper. He turned once more to the door and back. "Only two drops in four pints, mind. Morning and night. One week. No more". The hushed words just carried to me on the vapours of Craven A.

"How much do I owe you?" I was whispering too. He turned the bottle round and adjusted his glasses. One more glance at the door. "Half a crown".

I rushed back home and carried the elixir into the house and then to the hen run. With a dropper from some eye drops, I measured out the dose, divided the solution into individual bowls

83

and distributed them among the paralysed fowl. They sipped cautiously. We waited. One by one, they arose, staggered a little, then confidently strode about. I was astonished.

Rebecca thought I was wonderful. Julie was more cynical. "If it's that good, there are some people here who could do with a dose". She was looking at me at the time.

I never fully understood what was wrong with the birds and never knew how I had cured them. I presume they had some electrolyte imbalance, some disturbance of their inner chemistry. But I learned two lessons that day that were to stand me in good stead in the practice. You must recognise your own limitations and be prepared to seek advice. This is not always easy, for pride is not always easy to swallow. The second thing I learned was the importance of naming the disease. I will never forget my relief at hearing Jack give me the diagnosis, even though he couched it in self evident terms. Of course, naming the disease was the most important gift of the Medicine men of old. The 'Naming' exposed and released the evil. It is the same today. Doctors strive to name the disease and the patient is consoled. "I don't know" may be honest and may trigger further investigation, but it can also leave the patient in limbo. I think this is why you will often hear "It's a virus, there's a lot of it about". Naming the disease, however empirically, implies knowledge and familiarity. It is an important part of any consultation.

I know I have said it before, but I'll say it again, the best teachers of doctors are patients.

Technical Problems[7]

To be perfectly honest, I do not understand machinery. I never have and I never will. From time to time, I have pondered on this. Perhaps I have a genetic defect - after all, my father was pretty helpless when faced with inanimate moving parts. Or perhaps I have subconsciously rejected learning about machinery in case it uses up too much of my brain space. I have a deep fear that it might displace more important knowledge. Perhaps machines, especially the more intelligent ones, sense my rejection and, throughout my life, reject me as I have rejected them. For whatever reason, I am terrified of anything technical or mechanical

It is not surprising then, that I should choose a career far removed from the mechanical sciences. Medicine was my choice, since it was concerned primarily with a warm biological mechanism that could, through natural and spontaneous appetites, maintain and reproduce itself. This same mechanism could tell you details of its own malfunction and - best of all- would often sort out its own problems, provided doctors allowed it. Unfortunately, I entered Medical School at a time when Medicine itself was beginning to suffer from a hypertrophy of machinery.

As soon as possible, I fled from the technical tyranny of hospital life to the vital pastures of General Practice, but, even there I found I was unable to free myself entirely from the influence of the machine. I became, all too soon, aware of my naked vulnerability when practising medicine without technical support. Moreover, General Practice was improving itself and the outward sign of this inward grace was the possession of an E.C.G machine.

[7] Originally published as *Me and My ECG Machine* in *Myocardial Medley* Gray I. Editor. © Radcliffe Medical Press 1990. Reproduced with the permission of the copyright holder

"Own E.C.G." became an essential part of any advertisement for any vacancy in any practice worth its salt. It was obvious that no self-respecting GP could be without one - and I was, at least, self-respecting.

There were snags, of course, even if I could overcome my own fundamental unease with machinery. For a start, £200 was a lot of money to pay out, simply to resolve an occasional clinical dilemma and to put a thin veneer of science on the mess of everyday life. Then there was the difficulty with electricity. My attitude to this magical substance owed more to James Thurber than it did to science. I still have this gut feeling about electricity being a fluid running through minute channels in wires, leaking out of empty plug sockets and dripping from light fittings. An 'A' level in physics had done nothing to convince me otherwise. Curiously enough, I had no fears about interpreting the actual tracings. After all, I'd done my house jobs and there were plenty of books.

I overcame the potential financial handicap by the simple expedient of borrowing the superfluous ECG machine from the local cottage hospital. It was very old and covered in a real leather case. The faded gold lettering was in the Romanesque style. It was heavy - probably weighing about 30-40 lbs. At times, the weight was a disadvantage, but, at least, it provided me with some upper body exercise. It was the plug that caused me most trouble. The hospital was built in the round-pinned 15 amp era, but many of the houses in the practice had already converted to the modern square-pinned 13 amp plugs. Many an hour did I spend changing plugs at the bedside, for it was some months before I was able to acquire a 13/15 amp adapter. My electrical kit accompanied me everywhere and was an essential part of my medical armamentarium. That is providing

I could unzip the leather case. The zip had a mind of its own but no fastener. I needed pliers for that. And somehow, there was never enough jelly for the electrode plates. It was always a mystery to me where the jelly went. Fortunately, I came across a timely article by a Bedfordshire physician in which he had scientifically explored the efficacy of various household commodities as substitutes for electrode jelly. Mayonnaise (H.P. variety) was undoubtedly the best, so I always carried some of my own for one cannot always trust patients in matters of taste.

Being somewhat heavy laden as I went about God's work, I found it some disadvantage to have a broken handle on the case. I solved that problem easily enough with a length of washing line, cunningly fashioned into a carrying net. Thus equipped, I set out to deliver the science of modern medicine to the lucky people of Crigglestone. It was not long before I had earned a reputation as a "turn himself to anything" type of doctor, though remarkably few complimented me on my cardiology.

It was soon pretty obvious that there were more mechanical and technical problems in using an E.C.G. machine than even I had imagined - even after I had gained access to the machine itself and the electricity. Most of these problems could be classified roughly under the heading of the "AC Problem".

To tell you the truth, I never did fathom the "AC Problem", though, of course, I had my theories. The books were vague when describing the cause, but explicit in describing the effect - very rapid regular oscillations on the heart tracing which distorted the essential picture. They were even more detailed when describing how to solve it. They reckoned it was all to do with electricity in the air and the Earth's magnetism and similar scientific things. I followed their advice to the letter. First I would turn the machine clockwise. If there was no improvement, I would then turn it anti-clockwise. This exercise proved a useful diversion to the patient with acute chest pain and distracted them from contemplating the imminent infinite. Should these simple measures fail, then the books recommended that the bed be similarly rotated, thus adjusting the overall position in relation to the Earth's magnetic field. This was an exhausting exercise, damaging to carpets, injurious to my back and provided an unnatural end for at least two elderly double beds of my acquaintance.

Overall, it seemed to me that the writers of these books had little day to day experience of E.C.G. machines in Crigglestone. Even when we bought our brand new, up to date, battery driven model (circa 1965), the daunting problem of "AC" remained. I was forced to evolve my own theories and a suitable practical method of solution.

First, there was the lead. Coming from exposure to the searching, cold Yorkshire north wind into the roaring, overwhelming heat of a miner's fire, there was an obvious hazard from condensation. Cleaning the lead with a spirit-soaked rag, drying and then warming the lead, became an essential preliminary ritual before one could even contemplate the clinical problem. Should the interference persist, then I was forced to face the problem of the plugs.

Is the electric blanket still plugged in? Whether it is switched on or not, a plugged in electric blanket can provide a nasty shock to even the most modern ECG machine. It leaves a layer of static you can cut with a knife. Not only can such a layer prove detrimental to things electrical. An unwary doctor, used to examining his patients, can get a nasty shock from a patient lying immersed in static. I know. It has happened to me on more times than I care to remember. That's why I always made it a rule to wear Wellington boots whenever I attend a patient with chest pain. I once wrote to the Agony Column of the British Medical Journal about this difficulty I was having. There was little help forthcoming, indeed, nor very much sympathy. The letter stimulated only a stream of literature from manufacturers of electric blankets. At any rate, I always unplugged the electric blanket - and anything else in the vicinity. And I always switched off the plug sockets, in case any electrical fluid seeped out.

There have been times when even these diligent steps have proved ineffective and I have had to switch off the whole electrical supply at the mains. This almost guarantees a perfect tracing, always supposing that you can find your way back to the bedroom and then find your ECG machine. You must also be prepared to cope with the inevitable trail of domestic havoc following such a dramatic manoeuvre in the shape of ruined freezers, stopped clocks, imperfect videos and the like. Apart from the effect on the electrical impedimenta of life, it goes without saying that you will be deprived of light.

Because of this, in my later years and with more experience, I used to send the spouse down the cellar to disconnect and reconnect the supply. Unfortunately, muffled cries in the darkness became a common complication of the procedure and, on occasion, I have had the embarrassing experience of having to ask the ambulance, taking my official patient to coronary care, to drop off the spouse at Casualty to get their leg, ankle or arm fixed.

On four occasions, my routine was unsuccessful. Each time the patient was a woman in the later stages of her youth. All were wearing glamorous nylon nightdresses. Now, while I have been aware for some time of my own susceptibility to electricity - I have been shocked on several occasions by nylon nighties - I had no reasonable doubt that I had stumbled across a fundamental scientific fact. Whenever the "AC Problem" persisted in the presence of these garments, all other causes having been excluded, I would ask the lady in question to remove her nightie. It usually cured the problem. But, on one occasion, the lady's husband returned from his journey to switch off the electricity in the cellar, to find his ailing wife harry starkers, lit only by a single candle (I always carried one in case of power cuts). I found it difficult to explain to him the scientific nature of the exercise. Perhaps the mayonnaise smeared over her body distracted him from my explanation. I did reassure him of the health of his wife's heart, but, somehow, it didn't seem to cut much ice. It is difficult to be convincing under such circumstances, especially when dressed in Wellington boots, even the green ones.

Now, I may have misled you into thinking that the management of things electrical is a simple matter of logic and the correct course of action is based on scientific principles. Unfortunately, this is not so for there are other more subtle electrical forces at work in our atmosphere. I need only mention radio waves. These became apparent during my management of what came to be known as the "Briggs case".

I was, in my early days down south, haunted by Ernest Briggs. He'd had more episodes of chest pain than I care to remember. I could never sort them out. No one ever could. He was a clinical enigma.

At 7 a.m. one morning, the telephone announced another episode in his ever unfolding history. I was determined, as I climbed from my bed to a frosty day, that this time I would sort him out. ECG in hand, I hunted him out to his retreat in the back bedroom and, with unparalleled efficiency, set up the machine. There was no interference, no hiccups and no abnormalities until I reached the early chest leads. Suddenly, from the machine came a voice, "Five to eight. Time for '*Lift up Your Hearts*'". Then solemn organ music. Exactly what happened next was the blur of a racing pulse, a collapsed, whey-faced wife and the incessant ringing of ambulance bells. I hastily constructed a referral letter, which sounded vaguely clinical and included my ECG tracing. This latter was a cause of considerable interest in cardiac circles for some time afterwards, especially the chest leads. Perhaps a skilled musician may have been able to discern in them the musical outlines of "*O God Our Help in Ages Past*".

I do not wish to dwell unduly long on other practical aspects of electrocardiology. I will merely note that there have been several excellent papers on how you stick electrodes on the chest of the hairy male. Moreover, "Electrocardiology in the Female" shows agreeable understanding of some of the difficulties of electrode placement in some female torsos. It is an excellent review of the "under/over" debate, which has dominated cardiology for some time.

There are, though, important philosophical and behavioural aspects even in this technical area of Medicine. For example, why, when you choose to reassure that most neurotic of patients with an ECG, do you inevitably find a minute but inexplicable abnormality? And why does the most classical myocardial infarction sometimes fail to produce changes in the trace? Life is simply not fair.

91

In reviewing all the cardiographs I had done over a period of three years, I found that half of them were done for reassurance. Moreover, half of those done for reassurance were done in married couples. This is an interesting fact and reassures me that even in today's uneasy state of marriage, it is not uncommon to find two hearts beating as one. But, just occasionally, this phenomenon can go to extremes.

The couple who most typically exemplified this interesting sociological aspect of cardiology were Norma and Frank Worthington. Frank requested a visit because Norma had been up all night with an upset stomach. There was no apparent urgency. I called around midday, heard the story again from Frank then went upstairs to see Norma. She was her usual bright self, but somewhat pale. She'd felt cold and 'trembly' all night and had been sick a couple of times. I felt nothing untoward in her over large tummy and I started to chat about gastric flu and related topics. My hand naturally strayed to her pulse, but registered little. As I was writing the prescription for a stomach soothing mixture, it occurred to me that I had actually been unable to feel any pulsation at all at her wrist. I tried again. There was the merest flutter. I listened to her heart and could barely count the rate. The E.C.G. recorded a ventricular tachycardia of about 200 plus, a very serious business indeed. I gave her I.V. Lignocane - a risky business, but it was all the rage then - and arranged her transfer to the Coronary Care Unit, where she was effectively cardioverted.

Thelma, the daughter, phoned the next morning to ask if I would call to see her father since he was most upset and shocked by the previous day's drama. He was sitting by the fire, agitated. "That hospital drive nearly finished me", he said, "I could hardly breathe, when I got in". I felt his pulse. It was rapid and totally irregular. He admitted his chest had been tight. An E.C.G. confirmed a myocardial infarction with atrial fibrillation. I chatted to the receiving doctor about the availability of double beds in the Unit, but he did not seem particularly amused; in fact, I don't think he believed me. I visited the Worthingtons that evening. They were lying side by side in single beds, discussing the day's events. Apart from the wiring and the somewhat repetitive pictures on their individual t.v. monitors, they might have been in their own bedroom. Funny thing, marriage.

But even the most technical aspect of Medicine must, eventually, be applied to the individual and it is in this application that the science of Medicine becomes an art. Life does not begin nor end with an E.C.G. recording - well, not often anyway. More commonly, the E.C.G. is the beginning of what is now called an 'ongoing situation'. The handling of such a situation requires tact, understanding and not a little nous. Some people would say it might also require a degree of counselling skill. Personally, I am less adept at counselling than I am at managing machinery. I did try it once but failed. Generally speaking, I resorted to 'telling'.

The story of Fred and Vera Benson epitomises for me the sheer helplessness of machinery when faced with the biology and psychology of the living human being – especially when I had complicated that interaction with my own brand of counselling. It began simply enough. Fred came to see me and gave a history typical of angina. We discussed the implications and I was able to show some supporting changes on the E.C.G.. He wished to continue working as a senior clerk in the NCB. His main stress, he admitted, was the hassle of travelling to and from work, what with the traffic and everything. I suggested that he might rearrange his travel by leaving home earlier and return from work a little later. I still do not consider this to be extravagant advice. As he was leaving, he asked me not to reveal his condition to his wife - for she worried unduly.

A week or two later, Vera came to see me and, as was her wont, burst into tears as soon as she sat down. "Its me husband", she wept, "He's got another woman. He goes to work much earlier than before and he's always home late". I suggested that there may be other reasons and that in my experience, few love affairs flourished only from 8 a.m. to 8.30 a.m. and from 5 p.m. to 5.30 p.m. She was not consoled. "But why should he suddenly change his habits?" she asked. I could not tell her the truth. When Frank returned for follow-up, I suggested that it might be as well if he put her in the picture. There was no chance. What about doing something to ease her loneliness? I felt sure this was the root of her chronic unhappiness. Perhaps a dog might help - I had read of the value of pets in rehabilitation. He would think about it. I had in mind a cosy Yorkie or a Peke.

Some days later, while out on my visits, I was struck by the sight of a middle-aged lady travelling at an admirable speed up the steep hill of Clifton Road. As I passed, I realised that she was being pulled along by a fearsome pair of young English Setters. She tried to wave, but couldn't. Her smile was not, in fact, a smile, but rather the fixed grimace of the trapped. Later that week, both the setters appeared in the 'Pets for Sale' section of the Small Ads. Frank told me she had phoned the advert in from the ward as soon as she got over the repair of her fractured tibia. The dogs had spotted the hole in the pavement, but she hadn't. He went on to tell me that he had decided to take early retirement on medical grounds, so that he could look after her. "It suits me as well", he said.

My relationship with the E.C.G. machine was forged over the years in the twin fires of expectations and disappointments, but eventually settled to a wary companionship born of reality. The machine itself soon lost the shining cover of its youth and the corners became scuffed and worn. The hinges became rusted and cracked and the lid needed opening gently. It ran down more easily than before and consumed batteries faster than it used to. Some days, if the wind was cold or the humidity high, it produced a curiously wavy trace. There were even days when it would not work at all. I sensed it did not take kindly to the authoritarian approach of the Practice Nurse. It required cosseting a little to produce a good performance and, above all, it needed time.

We grew together, me and my E.C.G. machine.

Beginnings – and Endings

For much of their history, family doctors were judged by their effectiveness, their dedication and the gentleness of their care. In particular, their reputation was often earned by how well they looked after the woman in labour and the patient who was dying. Perhaps the first three criteria still hold with most patients, but of late, few GPs have much experience of home deliveries and though many people express the wish to die at home, only about a quarter do so. Undoubtedly, the technical and pharmacological advances in Medicine have played a major part in this sociological change. And with such advances, expertise has become concentrated in the specialities. Increasingly, too, patients' expectations have grown and with that growth has come a growth in litigation and a culture of blame. Soon, only the best man could have bad results and the generalist was rarely perceived as 'the best man'.

Obstetrics has become, almost entirely, a hospital based speciality, and, as more babies were born in hospital, so the obstetric skills of the GP have diminished through disuse and there are now few who would risk caring for a home confinement. For the most part, a GP's involvement in pregnancy has now been reduced to the mundane organisation and overseeing of ante-natal and post-natal care. This is not to diminish the importance of such contributions, but, to be honest, they were never my favourite activities. I know it was nice to have a surgery full of happy (for the most part) mothers to be, but it was so hard making each routine consultation 'special' and 'exciting'. And while it was always pleasant to visit mother and baby after a successful delivery, I was always left feeling I'd missed out on the main event.

I would not like to give the impression that the days when home births were common were always happy and beautiful in their fulfillment. They were not. As you heard that a woman was 'starting', your pulse would quicken. The 'midder bag' was checked. Your day's work was examined to see how it could be adjusted to accommodate perhaps hours at the confinement sometime during the day. Labour starting late in the day often meant a sleepless night, either in anticipation or in activity. The tension would build as the labour progressed and the relief at the delivery of a normal healthy baby would be euphoric.

If I have intimated that the doctor was the mainstay of the care of the delivery, I have done a disservice to the district midwives. I never ceased to be in awe of their dedication, expertise and, above all, their stamina. How they could spend nights on end monitoring labour, chatting interminably and consuming great volumes of tea continually filled me with awe. And then they would continue working the next day. Their importance was emphasised on one night when every midwife in the city was occupied with home deliveries. On that night, Susan's 'twinges' grew to a crescendo. When no midwife answered (there were no 'bleeps' or 'mobiles' then), they sent for me. I felt completely lost. Oh, I managed the delivery all right, though I left them a major washing problem and a damaged mattress, but it was the organisation I couldn't cope with. By the time nurse arrived, I was bathing and dressing the baby in some confusion. And the bedroom was in chaos. The midwife smiled. A little wryly, I thought.

But I like to think we usually worked as a team. I always felt I had, like the midwife, a personal responsibility. For most of the time we were able to share our skills constructively for the benefit of the patient. Only rarely did we disagree and then it was usually when the midwife and I were strangers to each other and unsure of the other's mettle. Sometimes, if I felt that things were not going as well as they might, the suggestion of transferring the patient to hospital would arise. Occasionally, this must have seemed an insult to the midwife's competence, but it is essential in any medical activity that one is aware of one's limitations of skills and knowledge. As often as not, of course, the anticipated or potential problem did not arise and I was always pleased to accept the blame for messing up a happy domestic confinement. No matter. We could not risk the health of either mother or child. Happiness and fulfillment could follow later.

At that time, when our practice was handling about 40 or 50 confinements a year, our skills remained well honed and our acumen sharp. We, the doctors, and the midwives became familiar with each other. Most of the midwives at that time were of Celtic origin, a fact which added a certain flavour to the procreative activities of our community. At first, I did wonder if the language used during labour was Gaelic or not, for I had led a fairly sheltered existence. I gathered later that it was not, but a curious mixture of the 'vernacular' (I am ever polite) and what the Church used to call 'pious ejaculations'. It seemed to work, anyway and babies would usually appear fairly briskly, but with a startled expression on their faces.

There were times of course when things did not go to plan. Very, very rarely, thank God, did this result in tragedy or mishap, but it did sometimes lead to farce with just a touch of drama. At that time, it was normally accepted that before a patient was 'booked' for a home delivery, her home was visited to check that the accommodation was suitable. Sometimes, one could be misled; at other times the patient would insist on home delivery, whether her home was suitable or not. There was nothing you could do about it if persuasion failed. There was no way that one could withdraw medical or nursing services.

The caravan was a 'static' on a caravan park out in the country served by a single track, one way, circular road. Each van was allocated a single parking space. The 'van was quite smart and had mains electricity and water. It was clean and roomy. Unfortunately, its suitability was assessed with the double bed folded away neatly in the wall. When labour started and the double bed was lowered, it was apparent that there was only 12-18inches clearance on each side.

I arrived at about 2 am as labour was progressing. The midwife was parked in the parking space. I left my car on the road. When I entered the caravan, the husband was at the head of the bed and the midwife at the business end. I stood, a bit spare, at the foot of the bed. I thought it would be a good idea to check her pulse and blood pressure. We could not pass each other, so I went out, followed by the midwife and then by the husband. We re-entered in reverse order. This left the husband in the close catching position and the midwife merely at long stop. I checked the blood pressure and paid my respects to the mother. There was a hooting outside and then a bang at the door. "What stupid bugger's blocking the drive?" From the head of the bed, I said I would move my car. We filed out, midwife, then husband, then me.

There was no room to turn the car. I drove round the circuit to the exit on to the main road, a dual carriageway. In the dark, I missed the obscure entrance to the caravan park and was forced to drive a further mile before returning. By the time I re-entered the 'van', the labour was reaching a climax. The husband was holding his wife at the head end, the midwife was now in the close catching position and me at the bottom. I felt the need to check the pulse and blood pressure again. We filed out – rather briskly now – and back, with me leading. But the midwife did not have cord scissors to hand. She reversed to get them. The husband moved up. His wife pushed. The midwife at the bottom and I at the top could only watch as the husband, in the vital position, delivered the baby with remarkable panache. I have never felt such an absolute berk. Heaven only knows how he described the event to her mother – or his mates

As I have mentioned, lack of proper assessment of home conditions was sometimes taken out of our hands. If a patient insisted on having their baby at home, we were snookered. Similarly, there were patients who, for whatever reason, concealed their pregnancy and labour came out of the blue. Remarkably, there were patients who did not know they were pregnant and called the doctor because of abdominal pain. When I was a house surgeon we admitted a couple of young women who had been sent into hospital with *'Abdominal pain ?appendicitis'*. Such a provisional diagnosis said little for the efficacy of the GP's examination. Surely, even a nincompoop could diagnose pregnancy. I was, at that time, scathing about such doctors. Only when I became a GP myself did I understand how such errors could occur.

I was once called to such a patient. She was in a double bed, on the far side, nearest the wall. Not an insurmountable obstacle to a proper examination you might think. The trouble was that her husband was also in the bed (with 'flu) and on the near side. He showed no inclination to move. My examination assumed all the features of a French farce. Even kneeling on the bottom of the bed and slowly inserting myself between them gave me only limited access. I could make neither head nor tail of her pain and was starting to think in terms of 'gastric flu' when my guardian angel stepped in. I began to develop cramp and was forced to ease away from her. My hand was still on her stomach. Suddenly, something struck my hand. Unmistakably, a baby's kick.

It was not easy to break the news, but it worked wonders for her husband's flu

It was not always the patient's ignorance that caused problems. Even doctors and midwives can make mistakes. Inevitably those mistakes come home to roost and continue to niggle years later.

During one Saturday night, I was called to a difficult home delivery. We eventually delivered a fine, but smallish little boy. Then we waited. It was a shock to find there was still another one to come. Fortunately, the second twin, though a breech presentation, was easily delivered. It all took some time not only for the delivery, but also to get over the shock. By the time we had organised further care and tidied up, it was approaching 9 o'clock. I suddenly remembered I was due to read the lesson at church that morning. I got there just in time and approached the lectern. I became aware that my pyjamas were showing at the bottom of my trousers and slowly folding over my slippers. I left church early that day and slowly backed my car out of a crowded car park. I scraped the front wing on the gate

It was Mothering Sunday

There is no defence against innocence – or ignorance. But when someone steadfastly holds out against orthodox and informed advice from all quarters, doctors, nurses, family and friends, it is infuriating and frustrating. I'm not sure if those women who insist on a home delivery in the face of such advice were truly

101

convinced of the beauty of natural means or whether there was an inherent fear of the hospital and its medical 'interference'. I could understand such an insistence when circumstances were good, the doctor and midwife competent and with practised skills and when hospital back-up was near. But when Tracy stuck out for a home delivery, my heart sank.

She lived with her parents in a mining village. The house had two rooms downstairs, both carpeted with a material of indeterminate colour and a damp, spongy consistency. Her dad bred whippets. Their extended family lived close by. Tracy was young and prone to drama. When labour started, it seemed as if the whole village had moved into the front room. The fires were stoked. The women sat around the bed in the kitchen, talking of labours past. As time went on, Tracy's shouts and screams reverberated around the village. We ushered the 'audience' out, but we could do little about the dogs. The bitch was tethered on a longish lead to the leg of the bed and her pups scrambled around her.

I knelt at the head end, encouraging Tracy to push in some constructive mannner. The midwife knelt, trying to control the bottom end. I could feel wetness soaking through the knees of my trousers. An errant puppy was near my foot. The bitch peed near me. The delivery seemed to take for ever, but the baby cried immediately, setting the dog barking. I lifted the baby to examine it. It was a boy. He peed accurately over my tie – my new college one - completing my day.

As we stood there, wet black kneed, Tracy's mother offered us tea. It was in enormous, cracked mugs. Joy emanated from the front room and people spilled into the kitchen, smiling.I suppose there was a certain primitive beauty about it, but I wouldn't recommend the experience.

Distractions and complications did not always stem from the obstetric situation itself. The trouble with home deliveries is that they took place, obviously, in the home and were subject to the vagaries of home life. Moreover, the home was set within a non-medical community, a community which had its own life. Kids often wandered about, for instance, and power cuts were not uncommon. Because the doctor and nurse were often in a house for some time, they were available to neighbours who, not uncommonly, would pop in for a *'while you're here'* consultation.

For nearly an hour we waited for the second stage to progress to completion. The head was tantalisingly near to delivery, but the mother was tired. I was at the time, fairly competent and I decided to lift out the baby with forceps, using a pudendal block (a deep, but local anaesthetic). I might shudder at the thought now, but, in the event, everything went smoothly. A splendid young chap came into the world, crying his heart out. As I sat awaiting the delivery of the placenta, I heard a knocking at the back door and agitated conversation.

Simon, next door, had fallen and had a badly cut head. I already had the suturing materials sterilised ready to stitch up the episiotomy. While the midwife stayed with mother and baby, I gathered up my instruments, chose a suitable suture and nipped through the gate.

Simon was quite a disabled lad and he looked a sorry sight with his bloody head. Stitching him together was pretty straightforward. I returned to my first patients. All was well and celebrations had started. I interrupted them for a few minutes to stitch the episiotomy. We tidied up and shared a small glass of bubbly. It had been a neat sort of evening.

The care of pregnancy, labour and delivery always demanded the very best of a doctor in every regard. Looking back from the comfort of retirement, my greatest regrets stem from the realisation that sometimes I did not give of my best for a variety of reasons, some outside my control, but others stemming from my own inadequacy. Not that I can do anything about it now, but those occasions still trouble me.

Caring for the dying is different, but shares with the care of pregnancy the fact that it is the sternest examination of a doctor's skills and attitudes. In the care of these two defining times of a human life, any doctor may, with even a modicum of sensitivity, rediscover his sense of vocation. Every medical and social fibre will be strained.

There is, of course, a difference in mood during the two events. Understandably, the care of the dying prompts a sombre tone to the relationship as independence is gradually lost and death approaches inexorably. My attitude was modified by hearing Leonard Cheshire's opinion that death should be viewed more as the culmination of life than simply its ending. Certainly this produces a more positive, dare I say creative, approach. Not that this is always possible. The nature of the illness, the personality of the patient, their family – and the doctor – together with their beliefs about the nature of life and death all influence the 'mood' of the terminal phase of life. And, however 'positive' the process, there is always the sense of impending loss.

Oddly, though, dying is not entirely without its lighter moments. A chap who was visited by his parish priest told me about the visit "He told me he wanted to hear me confession. Ah said 'What for like? Ah've bin nowhere an ah've done nothin' So he asked me if ah'd a good tip for the Gold Cup".

As the beginning of April came in with a touch of Spring, an elderly, retired businessman was now largely bedbound. After discussion with the tearful family downstairs, I went up to see him. I could hear the wireless and what sounded like chuckling. He certainly looked happy when I went in. "I'm just listening to the Budget", he said. "And you know what, I couldn't care less. It's not going to affect me!"

In the context in which they occurred, these were not just merry quips. They exemplified humour of such depth and poignancy that they revealed the very essence of the human spirit.

In the days before long acting morphine became available, it was quite common for the doctor and district nurse to alternate visits to the dying to administer morphine by injection, especially at night. Although the traditional Brompton Cocktail (a mixture of morphine, cocaine, gin or brandy and flavouring) was effective, it was comparatively short acting and one of us would call at about 10 or 11 o'clock to see if they needed anything more to see them through the night. These visits were always very special to both us and the patient and their family.

I was a bit late getting to Arthur that Saturday night. As I started to prepare the injection, 'Match of the Day' started. He asked me to" hang on a bit 'til the Leeds match had been on". It was the last match on the programme. We sat and watched for an hour, engrossed in the football. He showed no evidence of discomfort. But as the final music started, he began to squirm. "Ah think ah'll have it now". Distraction can be an excellent pain reliever.

Albert was cared for by a wife who looked nothing like the Saints whose pictures I had been brought up with. Short and square in her pinny, there was always a sparkle of perspiration on her moustache. She spoke little. She didn't need to. Her eyes, behind her glasses, were intense. The looks that passed between her and Albert spoke of a love that was tangible. They had no family and she was the main carer.

They had lived all their lives in the village, well known, but quiet. Their only holidays were an occasional week on the East Coast. Just before the cancer gripped, Albert decided they would holiday abroad. They had a week in the Italian Lakes.

As we chatted, waiting for the morphine to work, he would talk about it. Usually, he would reach down the side of the bed and lift a bottle of Campari. We would sip a little and live for a while in the warmth of the sun. He sometimes said that after tasting Campari, he regretted spending his life supping ale. His wife did not survive him for long. She had a severe heart attack while hanging clothes out on the line. I admitted her to hospital, still in her pinny. She died shortly afterwards.

You can learn a lot from a patient who is dying. Focussing down on the ultimate reality leaves little room for the mundane trivia that concern us when we are well. How rarely do we have the time or inclination to consider how fortunate we are to live in our particular human body.

I had been seeing Graham for some months. The tumour that was killing him was an unusual one and the medical management of it was complex and difficult. Visits tended to be prolonged. They lived 'over the shop' and there were many distractions.
Graham had many physical problems and we were having difficulty controlling them. For some time, the constipation,

106

nausea, headache and dizziness had made his life a misery.
His wife was ageing before my eyes.

One day we had had a fairly fraught discussion, for she was
approaching the end of her tether, so I revisited the next day.
She was in the kitchen and radiant, her hair done and make-
up on. "He's wonderful today", she said, "his bowels have
moved, he's had some breakfast, had a shower and he's reading
the paper". She was right. He was sitting up with his glasses
on, always a good sign. I thought about it as I left. I too had
been to the lavatory, had a shower, eaten breakfast and looked
at the paper. Why was I not 'radiant'?

But for insight into what life is really all about, I need only
remember Sally.[8] I had seen little of her since her husband died.
And then, soon afterwards, she had a cancer of the breast and
underwent a mastectomy. After that, she attended for her hospital
reviews. All had been well for a while, but then she was found
to have a recurrence. There was a flurry of medical and surgical
activity.

By the beginning of November, I was visiting her. The years of
doubt and anxiety and technical activity were over. The cards
were on the table. She was dying.

Her most distressing symptoms had gone with the withdrawal
of the cytotoxic therapy. Her pain was well controlled and
she slept well. Only her constipation was a nuisance, but I
think we were coping with that. As one might have expected,
this most beautiful of people, quiet and easily smiling, had a
caring family. She had attracted to her a group of people to

---

[8] The story of Sally originally appeared as *What I Learned from the Dying*
in *Pulse Magazine* 21 June 1986 and is reproduced here with their permission.

whom the Sermon on the Mount was a list of privileges not duties. She and her "team" grew in, and from one another. We, Sally and I, did not often talk overtly of her dying. It seemed unnecessary. Formal counselling implied being objective and I could not be that. Her dying was, though, implicit in all our meetings. I use the word "meeting" deliberately. They were hardly consultations, apart from an enquiry about her pain or her bowels, that is. Somehow, other things seemed more important. Christmas was approaching. She was to spend it with her son and his family. We talked about presents and Christmases past. And families, hers and mine. We talked of joy and of being together.

We talked about the future. How she might best use it and how might I help. What if something happened while she was at Pontefract with her son and his family - might it spoil their day? Oh, it wouldn't spoil hers of course, but what about theirs?
I reassured her

Sometimes, we talked about her late husband and his death, ten years ago. She was so pleased she was able to look after him at home. I remembered his death well.

From time to time in life there are rare moments which hold within themselves true and total realisation. Such moments are awesome in their clarity even though they are fleeting in their time. There was such a moment during my caring for Harry, Sally's husband. He was in bed when I called, but while I was there, he wanted to sit out. "We can manage," she said, "We have a system". She moved his thin legs to the edge of the bed then lifted him up to sit. He put his arms over her shoulders, loosely around her neck. Her arms held him firmly round his back.   Then with her knees braced against his, she lifted him.

They stood there, clasped together for, it seemed, an age, but was only a second or two. He'd trapped one leg of his pyjamas under his foot. They staggered slightly, then he grinned, "You silly bugger!" She laughed and they fell, still laughing, on to the bed.
In those few moments, I knew and understood.   Knew and understood about love and its completing man and woman.   I knew and understood about depending, and being dependent. I understood marriage and how such unions should be perpetuated in new lives.   I realised the bleakness and arrogance of selfishness and the obscenity of hate and mistrust.

The dying, and Sally is no exception, carry the burden of being dependent. If only we could tell them how much they give.

Not all deaths were as peaceful as that of Sally. And in many deaths, the doctor, nurse or carer plays no part.   Sudden and unexpected deaths leave behind them a trail of dramatic, devastating loss that is difficult to accommodate. The sense of guilt and 'if only', present in all deaths, is grossly exaggerated. Bereavement is prolonged and painful.   Perhaps counselling helped, but I am uneasy about how heavily our modern society seems to depend on it and how inappropriately is so often applied. I attended an elderly man who had suffered a mortal heart attack. He and his wife had been married over 50 years. She was leaning over him, weeping, when I arrived. We sat for some time with our arms about each other. A well-meaning neighbour came in. "She needs counselling", she said.   "I'll give you bloody counselling", I thought, but I didn't say anything.

The lonely death has a sadness all of its own. There is a very strong sense of an ending.

A policeman called at our house one Saturday lunchtime. It was a hot midsummer's day. A widower who lived alone on the nearby estate had not been seen for more than a week. We could get no reply at the back or the front of the house. The policeman broke in the back door. We were assailed by the smell of death. Opening the sitting room door released a dense cloud of flies. The heat was overpowering and the electric fire was on.

He was slumped in his chair. There were two or three bottles of tranquillisers and anti-depressants nearby. It was difficult to estimate how long he had been dead. Around him and on the sideboard and coffee table and on the settee were hundreds of opened letters, all written in the same handwriting. In the hall were more letters, recently delivered. We glanced at a few. All in the same handwriting, his own handwriting, so far as I could judge. He was not my patient and I knew nothing about him. I missed the inquest and received no report.

I sometimes think of the depth of loneliness that prompted him to write so often to himself. And I shudder.

Among the most difficult patients to manage, especially when they are dying, are those in whom you feel you missed the original diagnosis – or in which the patient or their relatives feel you have missed the diagnosis. However hard you try and however diligently you care, your original error – or perceived error – is built into every consultation and visit. Your every action, prescription and advice is treated suspiciously. Any new development demands a second opinion.

One of my erstwhile acquaintances saw me several times with a profound depression. There were obvious reasons for it. A psychiatrist agreed and slowly he responded to treatment. He then developed 'indigestion'. An urgent barium meal revealed a large ulcer. It did not respond to orthodox treatment. A gastroenterologist suggested endoscopy. It confirmed the ulcer, but the biopsy revealed that the 'ulcer' was malignant. Looking back, it is difficult to know what else I could, or should, have done, but the fact that he had been under my care for nearly three months before the diagnosis was confirmed was perceived to have been negligence or incompetence. Throughout his last weeks, I was never able to speak to him alone. His wife always sat next to him on the bed, often between me and him. When his dying became imminent, she asked for his transfer to hospital. We had little to say to each other when I called after his death. I could only say that I was sorry he had died. Explanations seemed neither appropriate nor welcome.

Death is always preceded and indeed followed by the onerous task, expected or not, of breaking bad news to the patient, to the relatives and to those who are left. There is no easy way of doing it. From time to time I had attended lectures and seminars on the subject, had studied videotaped consultations of myself and others and had partaken in role play assessments. But nothing prepares you satisfactorily for the reality. It's always painful and always leaves you feeling quite inadequate. Words alone are of limited value, unless accompanied by the right attitude. Sometimes, words are almost superfluous. Simply holding the bereaved says so much.

Yet, ironically, I sometimes had more difficulty breaking good news. So often a patient with persistent symptoms and understandable anxiety required further investigations. They came for the results, half fearing the verdict, but also hoping to find an explanation for their ill health. A report of '*no evidence of disease*' may seem like entirely good news, but it was almost invariably followed by the question, "*So what's causing it then?*" This was always much more difficult to answer. Often the patient construed my explanation as meaning "*There's nothing wrong with you*" which was palpably untrue, or "*It's all in your mind*" which seemed insulting and certainly took us no further forward. I always tried to explain that we didn't always understand what caused some pains and used to quote the example of muscle cramp. Everyone knows it exists and that it is very painful, but only rarely is a cause found and you could investigate till Kingdom Come and you would find nothing abnormal. I'm not sure whether this helped a lot, but perhaps it did, a bit.

The most gross example of the difficulty in breaking good news occurred many years ago.

I was called to an elderly lady at about 5 o'clock in the morning. Her chronic heart failure of the last few months had suddenly deteriorated. She was fighting for breath and blood stained froth covered her purple lips. Her blood pressure was barely recordable and her pulse too weak to feel. I gave her a morphine injection to help sedate her and a diuretic to drain off the excess fluid in her lungs. My small cylinder of oxygen helped for a while until she settled into a deep and more restful sleep.
I waited for an hour or so. The daughter, who had some nursing experience, and her husband were adamant that she would not go into hospital. I explained the seriousness of her condition. I arranged to call back before starting the morning surgery.

Just as I was about to return at about 8.30 am, the family phoned me to say my visit was unnecessary, for she had died a few minutes ago. I said I would call after the surgery.

Before I left, I made out the Death Certificate. The relatives were gathered in the sitting room, discussing funeral arrangements, the will and the legal impedimenta of death.

I went upstairs to examine the body. She was lying flat and unmoving. I did not notice perceptible breathing. I unbuttoned her nightie and put my stethoscope on her chest. To my horror, she twitched and opened her eyes. "What's up? Oh it's you, doctor". I calmed myself and continued the examination. She sat up. "Ooh, that was a lovely sleep". She was quite remarkably better.

I went downstairs to the relatives, wondering what to say – and how. I stood there as they faced me expectantly. I started "Look, I'm terribly sorry to have to tell you...." I could have kicked myself. They sat down and tried to rearrange their emotions before going up to see her

She lived for several years after that. I had given her her death certificate. She had it framed. Quite a talking point that was.

In recent years, the care of the dying has improved out of all recognition. Development of new drugs, and new approaches to their use, have enabled many of the dying to spend their last days with their pain and other symptoms eased. The Hospice movement has not only demonstrated what can be achieved in the holistic care of the dying, it has been in the forefront of an educative movement which has benefitted patients in general wards of hospitals and patients dying at home. The demands for legalised 'Euthanasia' still continue, but the Hospice movement has surely obviated the need. I often used to wonder how the proponents of 'Euthanasia' (such a bad term) envisaged it being achieved. I suppose they expect the doctors to do it. I just can't imagine it. Perhaps they'll invent a 'Euthanasiast'. What a job. Not much future in it, I should think.

There is no doubt, though, that however much we have improved in the care of the terminally ill, dying is always a sad affair. It remains, despite all the surrounding love and sadness, a very personal journey. I'll cling on to Leonard Cheshire's idea of a *'culmination of life'* rather than an end. And, for myself, I'll bear in mind J.M. Barrie's concept, *"To die will be an awfully big adventure"*

Outside Activities

When I was young, people had a 'Vocation' to become a doctor. Perhaps it is the same now, though the concept we had then, of romantic and dramatic caring for the sick, seems blurred of late by such distractions as computers and contracts and managers and the like. I entered medicine somewhat nakedly, cloaked only in the ideals of Hippocrates, the dedicated martyrdom of Semmelweis and the romantic drama of Cronin.

I retained all this throughout medical school, becoming steeped in the medical history of Edinburgh, history that pervaded every stone and desk. By the time I graduated and then completed my junior hospital jobs, I was, I considered, a complete doctor. I could not wait to find a community that deserved me as their GP. When I did find such a lucky area - in the West Riding – I did anticipate that there was medicine to be practised. I looked forward to sitting in my consulting room, full of science and understanding; I could not wait to visit the bedside of the sick, dispensing care and compassion. What I was completely unprepared for was what one might call the 'Community Commitment'. It dawned on me only slowly that a GP was much more than a medical man. I had become a sort of figure in the community. It became obvious that not only was I expected to provide a medical service, I was also expected to contribute to the area in ways I had never dreamed of. And since these commitments inevitably involved mixing closely with my patients, I soon found that 'consultations' became far less formal than I had anticipated. My medical knowledge was often tapped in a shop, over the bar, during dinner and even in the 'Gents'. These situations diluted my science no end.

Early in my practice days, I felt obliged to attend the local Amateur Operatic Society's performance of the *'White Horse Inn'*, mainly because the local postlady gave me two complimentary tickets when I guided her through a funny turn. In retrospect, I suspect that had I been less caring and effective, she may well have given me four - for all three nights.

Now I'm fairly lukewarm so far as such musicals are concerned. Frankly, I can take them or leave them alone. And, to be honest, exposed often in my youth to school and parish concerts, I find it difficult to cope with the tense embarrassment of 'Amateur Operatic' performances.   But this performance was by my patients and, as such, demanded some loyalty and even curiosity. What were people like when they were not being patients ?
It was not as bad as I thought. The orchestra was a little thin, but the soloists were acceptable and the chorus enthusiastic.   We reached the interval without appreciable distress and were enjoying a cup of tea and the story of Albert Rowbottom's hernia, when a somewhat flustered lady approached me to ask if I would see Gretchen. I was puzzled at first, until I realised she was still in *White Horse* mode.

I felt acutely embarrassed as I followed her into the ladies' changing room and was aware that I was blushing. No one else seemed to mind. "It's alright luv, he's the doctor". My heart sank when I saw who Gretchen was. The alpine blouse and voluminous dirndl skirt over multiple taffeta underskirts could not disguise the formidable figure of Muriel Hitchin, a figure that had accommodated more symptoms over the years than you could shake a stick at. When she lay down, her skirt arose like a giant parachute.   It was, of course, her abdominal pain again. Why it had started now was a bit of a mystery.   Perhaps it had something to do with the rebukes she had suffered as a result of

116

her demolition of the balcony supports during a flamboyant, but unwise, pirouette during the dance of the village maidens. Finding her within her merry Alpine dress was exceedingly difficult. For my examination to have been truly effective, I really needed X-ray control - and perhaps some bone forceps to achieve access through her heavily boned corset. I did manage a modicum of contact, but soon switched to counselling.

She went on again after the interval. There were no more incidents. She stayed at the back of the chorus and her dancing and singing were altogether more restrained. I saw her again after the show to see how she was. She was still unwell and now, since she had changed to her normal clothes, I was able to examine her more effectively. By now the signs had become more definite. I felt a diagnosis of ectopic pregnancy was possible and arranged for her admission. She underwent surgery that night. In fact it was an ovarian cyst that was the bother. The show managed without her for the next two nights. Understudies they had who could take her part, but none who could fill her costume.

The episode changed our relationship. Beforehand, consultations between Muriel and I had been somewhat fraught. I had found her a difficult patient and always felt dissatisfied when she had gone. After the *White Horse Inn* episode, consultations with her were easy and even enjoyable. Many years later, when she was dying, we often talked of her blighted stage career. And we were able to laugh about it.

Despite the rawness of life in mining Yorkshire, especially during the bitter winter of '62-'63, I still retained my innate naivete. At the beginning of my first spring in the Practice, I was thrilled to receive a letter from the local cricket club asking if I would consent to be Vice President. I swelled with pride, but I was a little puzzled. I had not, hitherto, established much of a cricketing reputation, except with my two- year old son. I had, you see, been educated by the Christian Brothers. Now, I have a lot of time for the Christian Brothers at St Joseph's College and I am eternally grateful to them for their efforts to educate me, but cricketers they were not. Their expertise and enthusiasm involved most sports, but certainly did not extend to cricket. Dear me, no. For the sake of tidiness and speed, they had always insisted that I bat right-handed even though I knew I was a natural lefthander. I was immediately and effectively deprived of any aggressive shot and reduced to being merely a 'stopper' – and an ineffective one at that. I sometimes wonder how good I might have been had they left me alone. Makes you think, you know.

Anyway, I wrote to the cricket club accepting their invitation and looked forward to their first match. I enjoyed it, though, despite getting there early, I was not asked to play. The Committee was a little reticent, I thought. On Monday, I shared the news with my senior partner. He asked how much I had sent, "It's usually about a fiver", he said. I cringed inwardly. So that was what they thought of my expertise. I sent then £3. I didn't watch much after that, but my name appeared in the programme, under 'Vice-Presidents'.

Summer was always pretty busy, what with Fayres and Fetes and Shows and the like. I became reasonably adept at opening things and, with my cricket club experience behind me, realised that important aspects of my presence were a) to give a donation, b) to buy something from every stall and c) undertake a wide variety of informal consultations. I managed to avoid judging anything for some time, but it was inevitable that this freedom would not last.

I cut my teeth on the Fancy Dress at the Parish Summer Fete. This was a gentle introduction, for organisers of such competitions are the epitome of diplomacy. There were so many prizes, in umpteen categories, that upset was, I gather, rare. In any case, there were loads of jelly babies and other delights available for the odd mite who slipped through the prize net. It soon became obvious that judgement was best based on the appearance of the mother rather than that of the toddler. The more heavily corsetted, the blonder the hair and the higher the heels, the more likely is a woman to have produced a winner. In recent years, big shoulder pads often gained winning points and, if the father was present, off sick AND had a video camera, success was assured. It isn't entirely that I am a moral and physical coward, more I think that I have acquired wisdom in human relationships.

But, wise though I became, I was never able to cope with Best Baby contests. As a matter of fact, no human being is, unless they have a pathological longing for pointless martyrdom and an innate desire for social isolation. Solomon's problem was trivial compared to mine on the day the thunderstorm hit Kettlethorpe Summer Fete. Some 200 people fled the torrential downpour to take refuge in the church. Steaming men moved benches, stallholders regrouped and the Maitresse de Fete wiped her face, combed her hair and announced through an overloud tannoy that the babies should be brought up to the front for the judging. "Moreover," she added, "Dr and Mrs Mulroy look forward to announcing the winner shortly." But Dr and Mrs Mulroy certainly didn't. Look forward, that is. However they accepted it as their duty. The babies - about twenty of them - were laid out along the altar steps, their mothers, fearsome creatures they seemed to me, stood close. From the outsider's point of view, I'm sure it was a beautiful sight, some might say allegorical. To Julie and I it was terrifying. Whatever we decided, we were aware that our chances of giving joy were 20:1 against. All recently fed and changed, despite the storm (mothers are marvellous, aren't they) the babies gurgled and smiled as one. All were at least plump, some bordered on the obese. (Best not to dismiss them on that score, what with their mothers and all). Their dress was impeccable. None of your modern dungarees and tee shirts. These were proper babies with dresses, satin shorts and lovely tops. How I shrank. Julie smiled with pleasure - we had produced only a few of our family at that stage and Julie was still feeling benign towards children.

I have already stated that, by then, I considered myself a man wise in the ways of the world rather than a coward. It was this virtue upon which I called. Only one of the babies was not my patient. What better, or more egalitarian winner could there be than this. Of course I wrapped it up a bit in my speech about the future of England and the glorious days of the Tykes that were promised by the wonder of these children. But it cut little ice with mothers. I was not exactly hounded out of church, but my presence was certainly not required thereafter. I have never judged a baby business since. I think such competitions have evolved into abeyance. This is one of the few major advances achieved by our post modernist society.

But beauty contests continue. And who better, you may ask, to judge such an event than your friendly GP and his lovely wife. So it was that Julie and I joined the Mayor of Wakefield and the Lady Mayoress at the Working Men's Club to choose Miss Crigglestone. We sat in front of the stage. Once my embarrassment had settled a little, I became increasingly astonished at the appearance of the candidates. Were these the tired, depressed and anxious patients I was familiar with in the surgery? I knew the names, but they were unrecognisable in their spotlighted finery. I tried to be objective, but it was difficult. We all conferred at the interval. It was tempting to be flippant and jocular, but I was soon brought to heel by the Mayor. We reached our decision and handed in the result to the Chairman. He made the announcement to an audience, silent but with bursts of applause. As the winner was announced, the applause was deafening (we had obviously chosen well). Then silence. No one moved. Where was Tracy? The Chairman repeated the announcement of the winner's name. Still no one moved. "'As anybody seen Tracy?" he asked. A loud voice from the back broke the silence "She's in t'lavvy". The laughter slowly died down and in the quiet that followed, we heard the welcome flush. The day was saved. Tracy smiled, collected her trophy and kissed all the judges. I had another pint.

Fortunately, the next judgement I was asked to achieve was altogether more scientific. This was not surprising, given the growth of litigation, insurance cover and the like. When Big Stan was organising the Summer Fete, he had the idea of insuring it against rain. The contract demanded that someone officially respectable should be responsible. Magistrates were somewhat distant, the Vicar was otherwise involved and Stan knew no headmasters. I was next in line. In due time, I received a large package containing a complex measuring gauge, piping and a funnel. This was to be set up on the site of the fete for an hour before starting and it was to be supervised by the committee and myself. All to observe the rain collected and measured.

The day was still and hot, the sky cloudless. The six of us stood around watching and looking up to the sky. Conversation was desultory until we were joined by some of the chaps on the way home from the 'Nelson'. For a while we were quite convivial. I can't remember who first said he was busting. But with the pavilion not yet open, eyes turned to the inviting funnel. "Pity to waste it". "How much are we insured for ?'. I shuffled uncomfortably, aware that such lighthearted thoughts, once expressed may soon turn serious. Images of ' *The Lavender Hill Mob'* drifted across my mind. I wondered how the General Medical Council would tackle such a scandal and was mentally constructing my defence when the clock struck two. "Right lads. That's it", I tried to sound professional and packed up the equipment. The crowds began to move through the gates and Drum Majorettes struck up a march on their kazoos. "Waste of a good fiver", muttered Stan and set off for the beer tent. I went home, my honour still intact, the funnel still dry.

As the summer drew to its close and the nights drew in, clubs and meetings and societies began to resume their activities. Secretaries had been arranging 'speakers' for months before. There must be a very close relationship between secretaries, with much exchanging of opinions about the efficacy and popularity of 'speakers'; who was good, who wasn't and whether they were cheap or not. If you were any use at all, it was inevitable that after one appearance, you were 'on the circuit'. GPs are common on the circuit. I suppose they are usually articulate, are known, and their common topics are likely to be of interest and promise a bit of spice.

I suppose my 'career' as a public speaker[9] began many years ago when, just after I had completed my houseman's year and was appointed Casualty Officer at the North Staffs Royal Infirmary. I was approached by a seriously bespectacled and uniformed gentleman who informed me that the First Aid Lectures began on Thursday. As an afterthought (thank God), he handed me the St. John's Manual and said he would write to confirm the time and place.

The first butterflies fluttered when I saw the venue. I had not unduly worried about it till then - certainly not about the medical content. After all I had been a Casualty Officer a whole week and was experienced in these matters. But the Victoria Hall, Hanley, seat of local government in the Potteries, host to the Halle Orchestra and Colosseum of wrestling! I was not yet, however, destined for the large central arena that housed these illustrious events. Still I was in the Mayoral Chamber, just off the large main corridor, which encircled the concert hall. Here was my first test. The First Aid lectures were held on the same night as the orchestral concerts. The interval, when the audience spilled out into the corridor outside our room, came just as I was three-quarters through my lecture. At this stage in my presentation, attention was, at best, flagging. The distracting noise of the concert-goers threatened to be the last straw. I learned to time the dramatic climax of my lecture for this moment. I perfected my Risus Sardonicus. I produced my Grand Mal seizure. I demonstrated, with panache, how to correct a pneumothorax using a bicycle wheel spoke and an inner tube.

It's a funny thing though, First Aid. When Harriet, a second year cadet, really did break her metatarsal coming up the stairs, everyone thought she was a 'demonstration' and rushed to practice their art. Overall I felt the best thing to do was to get her to hospital as quickly as possible. It was not quickly enough. By the time the ambulance arrived, her First Aid colleagues had 'treated' her for a full half hour. My colleagues in Casualty had little difficulty with the Thomas splint, but the head bandage and broad arm sling puzzled them a bit.

[9] These recollections of public speaking are substantially derived from two articles which appeared originally in *General Practitioner Magazine*. *Never Be Rendered Speechless* appeared 20th December 1985. *Excuse me, Doctor* appeared 24th may 1996. They are incorporated here with the permission of the copyright owner.

Forays into the field of public speaking were, for some time thereafter, sporadic and, for the most part, eminently unmemorable (though I still cringe at the memory of addressing the pregnant ladies at the ante-natal class).

As a GP assistant, I was once asked to talk to the village ladies about cancer. Word got round that I was an expert on the subject. Neighbouring GP's complained about advertising (it was in a long ago rural practice) and the posters came down. Only Mrs. Rogers and her friend Polly came anyway.

The breakthrough (I'm not sure that's the right word since it implies striving) came when, after several years in the practice. I was asked to address the local Women's Institute on subject of "Drugs". I was assiduous in my preparation, not only of the subject matter itself, but of how I was to do it. My wife, showing an interest and enthusiasm not previously obvious, bought me an American book on public speaking. It told me where to put my hands, how to place my feet and how to give my speech SPARKLE! Now this may all have been sound advice for your average American junior executive addressing his Masonic Lodge in downtown Chicago, but it had little to offer a red blooded Yorkshire GP taking on the Bretton WI. I began at 7.30 p.m. in the committee room of the village hall one hot July evening. My audience was too small for me to give you an average age. Sarah must have been all of eighty even then, but the other two were younger I think. It became obvious that they didn't sleep well - at night anyway.

Within a few minutes, all learned talk of sedatives and tranquillisers was superfluous. In a desperate attempt to attract attention and to give my speech 'SPARKLE', I switched to the natural sources of drugs. I discoursed, with much scholarship, on the poppy, Morning Glory, Deadly Nightshade and the like. I noticed more people coming in and some were young and some were male. I blossomed and grew. They sat, at first attentively and then , after a few minutes, they shuffled restlessly. They began to whisper out of the corners of their mouths. They were in the wrong place (it transpired that they were the Flower Show Committee - in the wrong room). They were polite and I enjoyed a few minutes watching and waiting for their nerves to break. It wasn't fair though. I gave them an opportunity to leave and resumed my delivery to the beaming, chained President and her restful companions,

It was enough, however. I had appeared on a WI programme. Inadvertently, I was 'on the circuit'. Within a few months invitations came from as far afield as Kettlethorpe and Kippax. My subjects varied, as much to avoid boredom for me as anything else. I tried to find areas that might pass as educational (what a grand word) and found that. "Drugs" and "Communication" were the most popular. Why was it, though, that whenever I talked about the problems of tranquillisers, an awful lot of the audience seemed to have been told "never be without them".

It was the Townswomen's Guild that provided my largest and most enraptured audience. There must have been two hundred or more in the Community centre. I was at my ease sitting informally on the edge of the stage. I was talking on the subject of the Doctor-Patient communication. I repeat, the audience was enraptured. It was the entry of a latecomer that defused my ego. I was suddenly aware that the draught she caused by opening the door was reaching areas that were normally draught free. I glanced down surreptitiously. I was right. My flies were undone.

Now the ability to think on one's feet combined with the judicious use of (intended) visual aids must be an essential part of any public speaker's armamentarium. I sauntered over to a friendly blackboard to illustrate a point and, by controlled chance, dropped the chalk. With a dexterity I have not had before or since, I rescued the chalk and adjusted my dress in one fluid movement. There are more reasons than the fear of road accidents for changing one's underwear regularly.

As I have inferred, the roles of doctor and speaker usually fit well together. In my case, the roles are inseparable and interdependent. Never was this better exemplified than on the night I was the after dinner speaker at the Annual Dinner of the Worsborough Dale Flower Arranging Society. It was an all female evening and the occasion was to be covered by the *Chronicle*. It was all very pleasantly formal and the meal was splendid until we got to the pudding. The lady half way down the centre table seemed to take a long time to slide gracelessly off her chair, taking with her the strawberry mousse. Usually at such times, I assume that the responsibility is that of the organiser, but I was the only male, and a chivalrous one at that. Moreover I was known to be a doctor. I moved calmly to the scene of the action, lifted her and carried her out to the bar. She had, I was told, a 'Bad Heart'. I had no doubt that she had had a coronary. The ambulance was arranged, the relatives informed and the hospital contacted. I leaned over, felt her pulse and reassured her. She vomited over my suit and college tie. There was a tap on my shoulder, "We're ready for you now, Doctor". Wiping myself as best I could, I strove to entertain them with merry tales of life and death - and those grey areas in between.

I was conscious throughout of my delegated duties lying in Limbo in the bar. I told myself the show must go on. I warmed to my responsibility to the remaining guests. As I approached the humorous climax of my speech, a lady who I now know to be a nurse, beckoned me vigorously. "She's gone again", she said. I must say my patient looked bad, but I think the problem was her being lifted to the ambulance. She came round when we lowered her head. I returned to the waiting audience still facing the front. It was difficult to pick up the threads of humour. At least they smiled and I did get a bouquet! The *Chronicle* didn't do me too badly either. My suit and tie cost £2.50 to clean.

There is, I have to admit, usually something odd about speaking after dinner though rarely is the situation so bizarre as at Worsborough Dale. I've often wondered at the point of an after dinner speech apart, that is, from giving the diners the opportunity to digest their food. Sometimes, it is necessary that the speech is straight and informative. Usually, however, it is intended to be light in tone and of a length compatible with the diuretic clock of most of one's audience. This question of length is delicate. Apart from the limits of both intellectual and emotional stamina (on either side), there is the question of "books" and bets. There are times when the organisers of such "books" will chat to you before the meal. They may even buy you a drink. Now, if there is any morality or ethical ambience to public speaking, then this is the crux. Should one give to one's friends an indication of anticipated length? Should one deliberately mislead those low in your favour? I try to smile, I hope inscrutably, and remain non-committal.

Microphones are a boon but may distract. They occasionally produce a whine that is a potential cause of epidemic tinnitus or even widespread mania. There are microphones which are sensitive to only narrow arcs of sound and, with movements of the speaker's head, can convert the best speech into the sound of sirens, with Doppleganger.

Even the stands of these fiendish instruments are, I swear, alive. The telescopic types are often ill-fitting and tend to slide slowly down over a period of two or three minutes, taking with them the unsuspecting speaker. With luck, he may become aware of the gravity of the situation before he disappears behind his menu, out of view of his audience. The 'bendy' type of stand is splendid, providing there is no doubt about its potency. If the flexibility is greater than its strength, though, the resulting slow detumescence may be in a direction impossible to forecast. I once got a nasty attack of sciatica from one of those.

So why did I do it? I put it down to my Gaelic ancestry combined with a hysterical personality and a frustrated Thespian urge. All catalysed by an awareness of the great wisdom within me. I forgot to mention something. An essential gift of the public speaker is an ego greater than anyone else in the audience.

Public speaking did lead you into tricky situations. I was appointed to the newly founded Younger Disabled Unit to oversee the day to day medical care of the residents. Almost inevitably, one of the roles implicit in the job was that of 'front man', responsible for any votes of thanks and the like that were usually required at social functions. It should have been obvious to me when I was appointed that one of my most important duties was to rehabilitate patients socially. This truth dawned on me quickly. Within a few weeks I was leading a hectic social life and with patients and staff, visited more pubs, clubs and Church halls than I can remember.

I soon became familiar with cabaret and bingo and achieved gourmet status with pie and peas. I was a connoisseur of British ales. But the night I still remember, however hard I try to forget, was the night we were entertained by the Yorkshire Federation of Ladies Auxillary to the Licensed Victuallers. It was in the Christmas season and the occasion was to be a Medieval Banquet.

For those of us on the Top Table, fancy dress was obligatory. I was appointed to be Court Physician and Apothecary and to propose the Vote of Thanks. What better character could I choose to be than George a Green, the Merry Pinder, after whom our hospital was named. My costume was in the best of Medieval tastes. The dark green leather jerkin over an oatmeal shirt was complemented by what I can only describe as puce tights, the whole illuminated by sundry chain belts and medallions. My cap was of fine green velvet with a most elegant feather, plucked from a pheasant.

The big snag was that I had an evening surgery that night, due to finish at 6ish, and the coach left at 6.30 p.m. It was obvious that I would have to change, partly at least, before my surgery. Tights, particularly, are time consuming. Although I wore trousers and jacket on top, I felt less than sartorial. Apart, that is, from my feet, for my black, silver buckled shoes, with 3 inches of puce tight above gave me an ecclesiastic air.

I was briskly efficient through the surgery and rang for my last patient at 5.55 p.m. There was a pause. A small man edged his way in. He was nervous, there was no doubt. He was sweating profusely, twitching uncontrollably and would not sit down. I found it difficult to follow his staccato speech and soon I, too, was beginning to twitch. As I twitched, my trousers edged further up my legs, exposing more puce.

"It's me lad. Coming in next. He's very nervous. He's gone deaf and .... he's very small down there". We both looked down automatically "He doesn't know what he's coming for. Be kind". I was firmly reassuring.

Young Tom came in slowly, more pale and twitchy than his dad. In an overloud voice, I asked "Your dad says you're deaf. Can I look in your ears?" He grew visibly more pale. I discussed glue ears with them both in slow, stentorian tones. "Now then, young man, what about the other?" He turned greenish with perplexed agitation but didn't move. "You know. Down there.". My voice was becoming strident. "Drop your breeks", I bellowed, aware that I was not behaving as I should. There was a long, empty pause. Then there was an explosion of vomiting.

On the way to the sink, he hit the floor, the desk, the phone, but, most of all, he hit me. I was aware of my diminishing puce.

I cleared up as best I could. I ran the tap in the sink until it became obvious the sink was blocked. I rang home to ask if one of my sons could nip over the wall with a plunger. Within minutes my son appeared with the biggest rubber plunger we had. Lacking refinement, he burst into the consulting room without knocking and came face to face with young Tom. Tom looked at the plunger, glanced down at his nethers, turned green again and vomited over the couch.

We missed the bus. My wife (a Medieval Queen crowned in gold) and I drove conspicuously through Leeds with the window open lest I bend my feather in the cramped Mini. People in other cars passed comments to us, especially at traffic lights.

The night passed in a great feast of wines and madrigals and wines and tumblers and then more wine. When I eventually stood, uncertainly, to speak from my poetic scroll, it was after midnight. My scroll kept re-rolling itself and played havoc with my skilfully constructed iambic pentameter. My tights, shorn of elasticity by the emetic assault of hours before, began to concertina down my legs. Slack tights ill become a Court Physician. My feather had become bent in the course of the festivities and drooped sadly over my right ear. I did not feel like the Merry Pinder.

As the formal proceedings ended, I sought relief in the toilet. The ambience was different to the usual. Most of the chaps were having a little difficulty with their tights, except for those who had incorporated modern aids into their costumes. Oh what joy there was in the sound of the ripping open of a Velcro codpiece (apart from one unfortunate, who wore inadequate underwear beneath).

The following morning, a senior Nursing Officer visited the Unit to review its progress. Her report noted how quiet it seemed and suggested that a little more social activity would not come amiss. Oh, had she only known what life was like in Olden Times.

I am not sure whether accompanying a pilgrimage to Lourdes[10] as a doctor can be classed as an outside activity. But since it was work outside the practice and undertaken in my own time and at my own expense, I think I can consider it 'extracurricular'. Pilgrims at that time travelled in a variety of ways, car, train, bus or plane. But there were some who were too ill or too disabled to use standard transport. For this reason, a specially designed bus/ambulance was designed and built by the Across Trust. Known as Jumbulances, they were capable of carrying 24 passengers and included eight couches for the sick, oxygen and

---

[10] This is an extract from an article *To Lourdes-by Jumbulance* which appeared in *Yorkshire Medicine* Vol 3. No 1. 1990.

a power supply to sustain sundry medical equipment. The in-built kitchen was capable of providing hot meals and drinks.

Despite increasingly improved design, I found it no picnic to travel a thousand miles in a bus and with responsibility for patients. The tiredness and continual movement made nursing and medical procedures a unique art form. I once was obliged to administer a drug rectally to a patient with repeated epileptic fits. Talk about moving targets? Anyway, wherever it went, it worked.

Lourdes is an strange place, nestling in the foothills of the Pyrenees. It has three distinct parts. One is the usual small French town, a mixture of old and new. Another is the commercial aspect of a pilgrimage centre and surrounds the sacred area known as the 'Domain'. Some complain that Lourdes is 'commercialised'. It is. It has to be. Six or seven million pilgrims a year need food, drink and lodging – and most want to buy a memento of their visit. The Domain remains unsullied. No money exchanges hands there, apart from payment for candles and Mass offerings. There are no collections there. I reckon that the preservation of the Domain from development and commerce is one of the miracles of Lourdes.

Most people associate Lourdes with miracles. Yet there have been only about 70 cures recognised as miraculous during nearly 150 years. I have never met anyone in the twenty odd times I have been who admitted openly that they hoped for a cure. I once did know a paralysed young woman who felt odd during a church service and panicked that she might be being cured. She wasn't. Most people I met came for a mixture of holiday, good company and a hope for spiritual refreshment; perhaps, too, to put their own illness or disability into a different perspective.

For myself, I was always grateful when the group remained free of new illnesses or complications of their established problems. There were some problems, fortunately minor, which happened on most trips. Constipation was common, insect bites a hazard and sore throats almost invariable. And it was not uncommon (in our groups) for someone to suffer a fracture. Our nurse slipped in the high Pyrenees and broke a leg. It became an oft repeated joke that Brigid got plastered in Lourdes. I have to say that my several trips to the hospital were always a delight. The place was quiet, the staff charming and the nurses devastatingly beautiful and efficient. Investigations were immediate and the results were incorporated into a typewritten letter before the patient left. I have never seen such peace, cleanliness or efficiency in any UK hospital for the last fifty years.

It was always odd, living with one's patients. At home I would see someone, treat them and arrange to see them again in a day or two, by which time they were usually better. But living with the patient is different. You see them frequently during the day and feel they will never recover. And a dozen helpers will tell you repeatedly, that 'Gladys is no better' – every half hour. I suppose it's the 'watched pot' syndrome.

Most of my time I seemed to spend talking and listening. Many people who are elderly or disabled are isolated and love to have the opportunity to talk. And wow, can some people talk. Sometimes I had to go to lie down to rest my face, cramped by continued smiling. My other duties were variable. Being a respectable sort of chap, I was usually appointed wine waiter. Not an onerous job, I admit, but demanding a certain amount of panache and a modicum of responsibility. How I became a Bingo caller, I do not know. I think it was one of those evenings when storms raged and spirits were dampened. At any rate, it became part of my duties. Not an unpleasant one. Despite the interspersed humorous quips and asides becoming tarnished by age, their familiarity had its own attraction. And, of course, the doctor, like the priest, has to be a fool on party night.

It was hard work though. The most strenuous part was being a proper Christian for a whole ten days. No wonder Chesterton remarked that the Christian ideal has not been tried and found wanting; it had been found difficult and not tried.

My flirtation with the radio was intermittent and attracted no media moguls. My first appearance was some years ago. I was asked to take part in a 'round table discussion' with some illustrious medical chaps. The subject was the ill effects of medical treatment and I was asked on the strength of a paper I had written for the British Medical Journal. To my surprise, when I arrived at the Leeds studio, I was shown into a little cupboard with a microphone. The presenter then interviewed me, mainly to clarify the contents of my paper. And that was it. When I heard the programme later, excerpts of what I had said were cunningly inserted between the comments of the others. Clever chaps these BBC men. It really did sound as though we were sitting round a table.

On the other hand, an interview for *'Home Truths'* was immensely enjoyable. The subject was my hobby of making Christmas Cribs. It was edited of course, but perhaps it was as well. It is all too easy when being lighthearted about the sacred to stumble into sacrilege and even heresy. I am always grateful to the editor for saving me from perdition.

My longest stint was *'Problem Page'*, a phone-in programme on Sunday evenings, between 10pm and midnight. Not an easy programme. Many problems concerned difficulties in interpretation of medical advice and treatment. But the trickiest ones were what one might euphemistically call 'personal'. Now, I've always been a little reticent about such matters and I was worried when my family threatened to phone in to hear what the birds and bees were really all about. They never did, thank goodness.

An odd thing about that episode, though, was the attitude of the BBC. There was no pay. I understood that. There was an assumption that an 'expert' would be only too pleased to appear just for altruistic motives. Now, that's fair enough, but I do wish that when I left the programme, someone might have written to say thank you, especially as the organisation of those late night visits was often abysmal and rarely resulted in an apology. On one occasion the sound engineer did not appear at all. I had to drive back home and conduct my interviews on the telephone. Doesn't encourage loyalty at all.

I must say that, although I enjoyed all these diversions from my 'day job', it was always a relief to return to my home ground. After all, it's what I trained for.

Anger and Violence

It should surprise no-one that anger and violence are common in a doctor's surgery. After all, most patients who attend a doctor have some degree of concern and anxiety. Some are unhappy that their problem was not solved at a previous consultation and are determined to 'sort it out'. Many have pain or discomfort. Some have slept poorly. Frustration is frequent, for normal life has been interrupted and the problem is beyond their control. And asking for help is an admission of this inadequacy. Perhaps the patient's feelings have been exacerbated by the surgery staff and organisation. Perhaps it's taken a while to get through on the appointment line; perhaps the receptionist was unhelpful or brusque; perhaps there has been an unacceptable wait; all these factors can raise the ire of someone who is not on their best form. And if the doctor is unwelcoming and dismissive it might prove the last straw.

A patient's anger is often justified, especially following an omission or error by the doctor. This has to be accepted, but since General Practice is a long term commitment, there is no room for continued personal animosity. Apart from the chronic unease it causes, it will lead eventually to further clinical error. Unresolved anger is dangerous. There are times when you have to bite the bullet, admit your mistake and say you're sorry. This is to fly in the face of commonly accepted legal advice, but it is just and it is creative.

I had spent a long time that Sunday evening with a patient I did not know well. His history was complex and his symptoms confusing. I listened well and examined him thoroughly. I recommended treatment and arranged follow up the next day by his usual doctor.

Unknown to me, something went wrong with the phone. I never knew what. They had tried to phone during the night, but failed to get through. When my partner visited the next day, the patient was seriously ill and required emergency surgery. He survived. Just.

So far as he and his wife were concerned, I had missed a straightforward diagnosis and, I suspect, they also felt that I was responsible for the phone problem. I went to see them. "I didn't want to see you again" was the greeting, but she let me in. There was no point in a complex, self protecting explanation. I said I was sorry and took what was thrown at me. It was an uncomfortable half hour. When I left, she said "I'm glad you called".

Doctors themselves are, of course, not immune to anger. Sometimes it is understandable; occasionally, it is justified. It is, however, likely to be a negative emotion, especially when directed at a patient. A consultation with an angry doctor is rarely fruitful. Yet anger arises unbidden and must be dealt with. It is possible to suppress it, but difficult and more often it remains, simmering and unresolved. On a few, admittedly rare, occasions I have recognised it and used it to creative effect. I remember a patient who was pleasant enough, but who attended the surgery frequently with a variety of complaints. I never felt I grasped her underlying problem. Every time I saw her name on the consultation list, my heart sank, but each time, I vowed I would be positive, listen keenly and be understanding. Yet within a few moments of any meeting with her, I would feel my hackles rise and hear my voice getting sharper. It was not that she was aggressive or unpleasant. On the contrary, she was always ultra polite. It was just that she was impenetrable and her misery was remorseless. One day, in frustration, I heard myself saying *"Why is it that you make me feel so angry?"*. She started to cry.

"*That's what they all say*", she wept. Now this exchange did not solve all her problems, but it took our relationship to a new level. We could become more positive.

A more frequent way of resolving anger is to recognise it, accept it and, importantly, analyse it. This is easier said than done, for it demands understanding yourself and being honest. Such virtues are not easily acquired. On those occasions when I have managed to analyse my anger constructively, I have usually revealed some inadequacy within myself. A patient may ask a question I can't answer. Unbidden within me rises the response "*Stupid question!*". Someone requests yet another visit for a problem I thought I'd solved yesterday. More often than not, it was not that they were being a deliberate pain in the backside, it was that yesterday's consultation was inadequate and perhaps the diagnosis – or the treatment – wrong. Whenever I read of another doctor being brought to task for an error of clinical judgement, I wonder how big a part anger played in the situation.

Needless to say, it was a patient who taught me all this.
It was about 8 o'clock in the evening. The surgery was over and the paperwork complete and tidied. The phone rang. A stumbling female voice asked if I would visit her because she had had a bad headache for two days. I pointed out the time. I was angry and remained so as I arrived at the house
The house was a bit of a tip. She lay on the settee. Some members of her family were sitting round the table, eating. There was no greeting. "Why didn't you phone earlier? I was visiting next door earlier today. And anyway, the chemist's shut now. Why didn't you take something for it…" I was suddenly aware that I was standing above her, ranting and bullying her. She began to weep. "Doctor, I'm sorry. I'm sure you've had a bad day and I've had this headache since

Wednesday. Can we start again?" We did. She was the breadwinner in a dysfunctional family damaged by mental, physical and social disabilities. It was she who sustained them. Her illness, perhaps minor in another context, produced a crisis in her family. She had simply had enough.

I often think about that young woman and how courageously she spoke and of her unsung devotion to her family.

Not that I have handled anger well ever since. On some occasions, I have forgotten every lesson I've ever learned. Care and understanding have been displaced by a great explosion of fury which may have been cathartic at the time, but never left me feeling anything but cross with myself and wishing I'd been better controlled. For hours, sometimes days, afterwards I have gone over what I should have said or done.

The telephone call that Saturday night was, at best, peremptory. "If that's the effing doctor, get down here quick". It was not easy to extract the name and address for any question produced another flow of expletives.
He met me at the gate. His vest was stained, his baseball cap belligerent. He poured obscenities into my ears as I entered the front door. His wife, plain and impassive, sat on the settee next to a blanket covered child in front of the roaring fire. "Effing disgusting. That kid's bloody ill and you effing lot don't give a sod". Curiously, 1 felt quite unmoved by all this - surprising myself with my calmness. My partner had seen the child yesterday and the Trainee had been called early that morning. "Lot of effing use they were". I deduced that the child had been feverish, but with no other definite signs. I asked to examine the child. The mother slowly pulled down the blankets. His stream of invective continued "Fat lot of use

that is. I want him in hospital. I haven't forgotten what you effing well did to her". He nodded at his wife. I vaguely remembered she'd reacted to some skin cream I'd prescribed some months ago.

My examination was thorough. His rant went on and on. Putting my stethoscope in my ears dampened the sound a little. As he drew breath, I explained that the child had measles. It proved pointless explaining that early measles is not always easy to diagnose and that young doctors nowadays rarely saw it because of immunisation. The word 'immunisation' triggered another verbal explosion. I explained that there was no 'cure' and outlined how the child was best cared for. "So it's Eff all then. That's what you're saying. Get him off to hospital". Further discussion was useless.

The house physician was puzzled and understandably reluctant to admit a case of uncomplicated measles. Social and psychological reasons seemed irrelevant to him. I had rarely insisted on admission before, but I did then. I gave the parents the necessary directions and wrote the introductory letter, couched strictly in clinical terminology and containing no personal comment. He snatched it from me before I put it in the envelope. "Bloody lawyer'll want that". I remained calm, shrugged and wished then goodnight.
As I left, he shouted "Eff off you effing fat bastard". From deep within me, the souls of my bog Irish ancestry arose in fury. I turned to face him. "Never, ever, speak to me like that again", I shouted. No one had ever called me 'fat' before.

Inevitably, anger has sometimes led to threats and physical violence. At those times, I did not consciously feel afraid. Perhaps disbelief at the reality of the threat blunted my natural reaction, or perhaps I was so engrossed in my role as 'healer' and my striving to seek a solution to the situation that I had no emotional room for fear. Only afterwards did it come over me. But while I rarely felt fear when face to face with physical danger, I often felt my pulses race when I anticipated the possibility

There was something about the call in the early hours of that morning. Something that made me wake my wife and tell her that if I was not back within the hour to phone the police. The caravan was, I was told, parked up a farm track in a country lane about half a mile or so from a large housing estate. I did not know the caller.

There were two 'vans parked on the track. A young man was waiting in the lane, waving a torch. A lad of about eight years old opened the door. I was shown a ewer of hot water, a basin and a clean towel. His mother was sitting on the edge of the double bed. "I'm sorry not to get up, Doctor, but my boy needs me".

There were two sick children. One had heavily bandaged arms. The younger one lay quietly in his mother's arms. He was breathless and moaned a little when he coughed. He was ill and had an obvious pneumonia. In the circumstances, I felt it wise to admit him. While I wrote the introductory letter, I asked about the other child. "It was the fire", she said, "they set us on fire". Her husband had died during the attack, only a week or two before.

I took the young boy into the hospital and phoned to reassure my wife. The mother came with us, her oldest son (living in the other caravan) looked after the others. While at the hospital, I arranged for the dressings of the burned child to be changed the next morning.

I visited the hospital the next day and was astonished to find that the child had been taken 'home'. The child with burns had attended and his burns had been redressed. I called at the caravan on my way home. It was not there. The track was 'sealed' with police ribbon and a constable was standing there. No, he didn't know where they'd gone, but they'd no right to stay there in the first place. And they'd received complaints. I never saw them again.
All this took place about a week after the first screening of 'Cathy Come Home'

All the violence to which I have been exposed has arisen unexpectedly. And all of it has involved knives. It is true that I once viewed a gun in a patient's hand, but I never really believed he intended using it. But the knives were different.

I had been in my first practice – a prolonged locum – for only a few weeks and was unfamiliar with many of the patients. This call was well out into the country, a house standing alone and back from the road. The front door was half open and the house was in the disordered state one would expect when people had just moved in. The child was lying on the settee and the mother sitting nearby, half leaning on the dining table. She indicated the child. "He's got earache". She looked disinterested.
I examined the child's ears. I always use my right eye. Out of my left eye, I saw her lean across the table. She picked up a largish knife and fingered the blade. I completed my examination and sat down on the settee next to the child.
"I can't cope with this any more", she said, half to herself, "and he's driving me mad". She stood up and moved towards us, her face expressionless. I became matter-of-fact and reassured her that he would be fine soon with some antibiotics.

She paid no heed and stood above us. I had the drugs in the car, but daren't go for them. "I'm going to finish it", she said. Perhaps my voice was a little higher pitched than usual, as I made some inane remark about that being a somewhat extreme solution.

Somehow, I persuaded her to sit down, but she did not let go of the knife. I talked, but got little response. I looked at the phone, but at my suggestion of seeking help, she half rose again.

In a long interval of quiet, I heard the crunch of footsteps on the gravel of the drive. There was the sound of merry whistling. The door bell rang. She did not respond. I offered to answer it and rose slowly, edging my way backwards to the door.

The milkman greeted me cheerily and enquired about my arrangements for milk deliveries. I whispered tersely "Phone 999. The police. Now". He looked a little perplexed and left, somewhat briskly, but still whistling. I think it was something from 'Oklahoma'.

The bobby arrived an age later and parked his bike. Within minutes, it seemed, he had defused the situation. How he did it, I am not sure. He had the knife and we had a social worker and a policewoman in attendance. The mother was admitted for psychiatric assessment and the child cared for until his father could be contacted.

My locum had finished before she came home, but I gather she did well.

When I realise that daily milk deliveries have now virtually ceased, I think of that occasion, and several others, when a milkman has saved my bacon. And it was not just their intervention in crises that proved so valuable. Their regular daily round kept them in touch with so many people. Failure to take in yesterday's milk was an important sign that all was not well and it was quite common for them to alert us, or the warden, to some potential need.

The other 'knife' incident was not dissimilar. Again a routine call, this time to the mother of a large family. They were not an easy family. I always felt that they thought they were a cut above their neighbours on the estate, though there was little obvious justification for that. She suffered from an unusual condition. Every few months her heart rate would double or even triple its rate. There was rarely an obvious trigger factor. Usually, it would revert to normal spontaneously after a short time, perhaps an hour or so. Drug treatment of various types did little to prevent it or to modify its course. Nowadays, she may well have been fitted with a pacemaker, but they were not available then.

On this occasion, the heart rate had been up to about 180/min for about an hour when I first saw her, but she was otherwise well. Nothing I did made any difference. I returned an hour later at about midday. Her condition was the same, but now she was feeling tired. Fearing the onset of heart failure, I suggested she be admitted for cardioversion. She demurred, but agreed to go once her husband returned from shopping. I arranged her admission, organised the ambulance and continued my visits. When I returned to the surgery at lunchtime, I was told the Ambulance Service had phoned to say that they could not get in, the house was locked.

I revisited and after some delay, the door was unlocked and I was allowed in. Her husband was in a fury that he had not been consulted and refused to let her go. I tried to explain the risks of leaving her at home, but it had no effect. She said nothing and her three youngest children sat around her. He stormed out of the room and I heard the key turn in the lock. He went into the kitchen and returned with a knife. He launched into a tirade at me then turned to the children, telling them that I was going to send their mother away to die and that he wanted 'all of us to die together'.

Rational argument was useless. I did not take his threats seriously for he was prone to histrionics. I got up from the chair slowly and said I would leave. As I unlocked the door, I palmed the key, hightailed it back to the surgery, alerted the police and asked for the ambulance again. They were understandably reluctant, until I told them of the escort.

I was relieved to return to the house and find him still in a state, still with the knife, but with no blood spilled. In the presence of the police, he calmed a little, but as she was taken into the ambulance, he threatened me with 'every court in the land'.

I saw her later in the hospital. She was back to normal. As I left the ward, I heard his voice again from the consultant's office. He was threatening the consultant this time, again with 'every court in the land' unless he let his wife home. I slid by, surreptitiously. It was all too familiar.

Psychiatric emergencies were sometimes associated with violence, which was a pity. It is not always easy to communicate with people whose thought processes are disturbed or whose view of reality distorted. Under such circumstances, one was sometimes obliged to defend oneself against violence or use restraint to enforce treatment. It was never pleasant. I learned a lot from social workers and police under those circumstances.

I had spent more than a hour trying to persuade a lady to accept admission 'for her nerves'. She remained cowering in a corner of the room and neither I nor her husband could approach her, for she struck out viciously if we came near. When we retired some distance, she would hum to herself and the doll she held. The tune was familiar. Her husband said it was a Shirley Temple song. A young policewoman arrived in reponse to my call for help. I explained the situation. She approached the patient and doffed her hat. "Miss Temple?", she asked. The young woman nodded. "Your carriage is here Miss Temple". My patient stood, tossed her hair and walked out to the police car and into hospital.

Whenever I have discussed the management of the psychiatric emergency with others, especially young doctors, there were always some who disapproved of the various strategies we employed. Violence was universally abhorred, though I never had a solution to the problem of the irrational attacker. Many felt that entering into the patient's delusion and using it was patronising and demeaning to another human being. Yet it was often very effective. When Henry adapted the washing machine to undertake space travel, my offer of transport in my 'shuttle' was accepted with alacrity and the transfer to hospital was uneventful. I still wonder about the ethics of it all, though it was infinitely better than forceful removal.

I suppose that I was fortunate in practising in the area I did. Certainly, we suffered little in the way of chronic violence and threats of the type suffered by some of my inner city colleagues. I rarely felt concerned about being out alone and carrying drugs. There was a sort of law-abiding atmosphere in those years. After a late night visit to a pretty tough mining village, I emerged to find a couple of chaps leaning on my car.

'Everything OK then Doc? We thought we'd keep an eye on your car. Can't trust some of the buggers round here these days'.

There was of course little problem with drug abuse in those days, though LSD was fashionable for a while. While it produced occasional bizarre situations, the main problem was the chronic psychiatric disturbance that sometimes followed its long term use. Only in my last couple of years in the Practice did consultations about heroin, 'Crack' and the like become common and violence and crime escalate. In those early days, crime was largely confined to pinching apples and the like. There was some graffiti about, though it was rarely obscene or vicious. One chap did spray the walls of the new surgery, but since he included his name and address in his writings, he was soon brought to justice.

We did have some excitement in the village once. There was a chronic epidemic of milk being stolen from doorsteps. The crime wave never made the national press, but it caused some local distress. One Sunday morning, a young detective constable came to see me with a plan. Why not introduce some non-toxic substance into the milk, a substance that would produce an obvious, but harmless symptom? When someone presented with that symptom at the surgery, hey presto, we'd got him.

The plan appealed to me initially. We, too, had suffered occasional milk deprivation, and dry cornflakes do not kickstart the day with any great joy. There was a substance, commercially available, which coloured the urine bright blue, but had no harmful effects. In fact, the advert promised all sorts of health benefits. Then the legal implications occurred to me. There was probably a law somewhere about the contamination of foodstuffs. And there is always the likelihood that somebody would react adversely even to the most innocuous substance. My enthusiasm began to cool, but it proved difficult to curb the zeal of the detective. He looked quite hurt when I would not co-operate.

It seemed in those far off days that crime and criminals had about them a sort of innocent naivete, though that is a retrospective, romantic view, for I also remember all summers were beautiful and sunny and winters were snow laden. There was always, though, that special violence which people directed at themselves. There were several patients who saw us regularly because they had deliberately injured themselves. I never understood them. I did not understand why they cut or burned themselves. Nor did I understand why they would then come to see us, or attend casualty, to have their wounds treated. The official line was always that it was a 'cry for help', but no offer of help or empathy seemed to make any difference. Perhaps they required a different type of help, but what? Some eventually stopped the practice, but even years later, the only explanation I ever received was by one young woman. She recalled the feeling of inadequacy she had felt at the time and of how undervalued she felt. She needed status. I still found it difficult to follow the logic.

The most extreme form of self harm was, of course, suicide. There is something uniquely tragic about suicide. Not only does it give us a glimpse into the mind of a fellow human being so tortured by depression, so arid of any hope. It leaves in those remaining behind immense guilt and inadequacy and a tainting with the shame of their association. I used to look back through the notes of the patients who had killed themselves, looking for potential reasons and searching for ways in which I might have prevented it. Occasionally, there was an obvious cause. A lady was convinced she had cancer and I had seen her several times.

Every examination and test had been negative, but I failed to reassure her. She left a note explaining that she could not face dying of cancer. As in this case, I found that reassurance often had limited value if someone is convinced they are ill. So often, at the end of such attempts, they would ask the question "Then why do I feel like this, then?" It was often difficult to answer them and any mention of depression or any obsessional trait would produce an angry response "So you think it's all my imagination, do you?"

Another patient, a youngish man, had attended surgery regularly to have the dressing changed on a minor finger injury. He usually saw the nurse, but I had seen him a couple of times. He gave us plenty of opportunity to delve beneath his minor injury and uncover his depression, the real reason for his frequent attendance. And so I, too, shared the guilt and the shame when he hanged himself.

I have not enjoyed recalling anger and violence. The 'feel' of my time in General Practice was overall one of friendliness and mutual trust. Most patients seemed generous and forgiving and now, in retirement, it is usually a pleasure to meet them. Mind you, if the talk gets round to their problems, I am delighted to be able to suggest "*I should pop down to your doctor about that*".

Doctor as Patient

It is not easy for a doctor to become a patient. For a start, there's the illness itself. Illness is not at all pleasant, but when it strikes a doctor, it is also accompanied by embarrassment and guilt. Embarrassment because, well, it just doesn't seem appropriate somehow and it is difficult to own up to. And guilt stems from the realisation that this is what patients have when they come to see you and how often you have dismissed their complaints as trivial. I was always a more sympathetic doctor after I had suffered myself.

Then there is the difficulty of consulting a colleague. One strives to be normal and to behave and speak like the average patient. Above all one dreads being thought to be 'neurotic' whatever that may mean. It is all too easy too, to slant the story of your problem to the diagnosis you yourself have made. And, when a name is given to your illness and treatment is recommended, I am prone to show a blasé attitude to cover the turmoil within. As for attending hospital, well it doesn't bear thinking about, especially when your problem is located 'down there'. And, unfortunately, most of my problems were 'down there'.

I have come to the conclusion that I regard my body as a private, inviolate temple. I know it may not look it to the casual observer, but that's the way it is. As a result, I am reluctant to share it. For example, I cannot abide buying clothes. I can hear the chaps critically assessing my body, a poor thing they might think, but mine own (I regret I can't remember whom I quote). I bet they have a right laugh about me over their coffee in the back room. "You ought to have seen what that old chap bought this morning. He wouldn't listen. Look a right sight, he will, especially with those shoes. And that shirt! You'd think they'd have more sense, at their age".

But if outer garments are difficult to buy, underwear is utterly impossible. I simply cannot buy them for myself. I refuse. Only on one occasion have I relented. With all my underkegs in tatters, I rebuked my wife for her neglect. She refused to accept any blame and told me to go and buy them myself. She pointed out that I could buy them in shops. I said I was shocked that she didn't seem to mind shop assistants, many of them women, having an insight into her personal husband's body. I didn't quite catch her last remark apart from the last few words which were along the lines of "..for heaven's sake, you're 56..". It was a Sunday morning.

I stormed out of the house and managed to get to ASDA just as it opened. There were only a handful of customers. I snatched a packet of underpants and looked for a male assistant. Though all the tills were open, they were all manned by women. There was no way out. If I tried to do a runner, the bleeps would sound and I would be arrested. In court they would hold up my underpants and the Prosecuting Counsel would be snide and the jury would laugh. I had to face the feminised check-out. I disguised my goods with a large packet of Phostrogen Fertiliser, an odd choice, but the packet was big enough to cover my underwear Size XX or some such. I slipped sideways into the checkout as soon as it was clear. I think I was whistling a little, but quietly. I spoke fast, very fast. And in a high pitched voice. I was very polite. The cashier tried to read the bar code on the pants. She couldn't. She picked up the intercom and announced to the world "Could Mrs Jones come to the check-out please to check the bar code on a gentleman's underpants?" The whole of ASDA, Kettlethorpe, Crigglestone and beyond turned and looked. I crossed my legs and my face was fierce red. I knew it was. Mrs Jones arrived and smiled "I'll soon sort them out", she said. I involuntarily took a step back. "Where did you get them from," she asked. "Here", I said, my throat dry. She smiled again, in a mothering sort of way now. "Show me". We processed slowly to "Underwear. Mens". I pointed. Quite mute now. I followed her back to the check out, looking neither to the right nor to the left. I paid and left. I forgot my Phostrogen and didn't respond to the calls of "You've forgotten something". I ran through crowds of grinning faces, got into my car and drove off. I didn't speak to my wife when I got back, not for a while. Well, women don't understand.

Curiously, though, I don't mind going to the barbers[11]. Not that I go very often, but it is usually a place of peace. The conversation is usually desultory. I have never got used to talking to a mirror image. I keep trying to turn my head to see him but all I manage to do is to provoke ire in the barber and patchy deforestation of my scalp.

I have always assumed that cutting a man's hair was a man's job and I was horrified to hear that one of my sons, an heir to my fortune no less, had actually had his hair cut by a woman – in a UNISEX establishment. I thought I had imbued him with more self respect than that. And yet I was recently trapped into a similar situation myself. The world is turning and it is not turning in the right direction, in my opinion. Not that I have anything against women. Many of them are very nice. In their place. But their place is not in a Gentlemen's Hairdressers.

That's one of the reasons I go to Indian Joe's for my haircut. Let me say at once that his nickname is nor snide remark or racial taunt. Joe is of and by Yorkshire, of Saxon stock with, I think, the merest hint of the Celt. His nickname is founded on

[11] A modified version of this account first appeared in a letter to *Medical Monitor* 26th July 1991 and is used with permission.

affection with just a touch of anxiety. I think it derives from his habit of circling the client who sits ceremonially bound and immobile in his chair. He carries a sharp instrument and mutters incantations. His music is the insistent beat of Radio Aire. Moreover, those leaving beneath his striped totem pole bear some resemblance to the early settlers out West who, too, suffered tonsorial mishap.

When I visit him, I feel and behave very much as I think my patients did when they used to visit me. And Joe's behaviour and techniques educated me.

The waiting area is not unlike ours was, though we did not have hair on the floor. Like doctors, he has dispensed with the green curtain hung uncertainly across his window. His advertisements were at least as exciting as ours from the DSS and the Health Education Council. I noticed from the rack of pastel coloured packets near the till, that he was well into anticipatory care and at the sharp end of the Community's battle against AIDS. I looked around the waiting room and wondered how long each would take and what style they would adopt.

Once I was in the chair, Joe did not wonder silently why I was there. He was direct. "How d'you want it then?" I nervously repeated my usual humorous rejoinder for the umpteenth time. "Just so I can see and hear." It never raises a smile, but then, it never did. Then a careful examination as my needs are identified and the treatment planned and discussed.

He explored my psychological and social needs and concerns with an open statement. "This weather gets you down...." Pause. How do I reply? "It's bloody miserable" (Am I depressed?) "I blame these bombs myself" (paranoia?). "I hope it picks up for the match" (anxiety?).

He considered my family background. "And the wife ....?" How do you answer that? He assessed my social status and expectations. "Where are going this year then?"

Small group sessions were held most Saturday mornings. They had different styles. The gardening group had a formal leader, Harry Drewitt. We all respected him. You should see his carrots, big as tent poles they are. But we knew he was a man who, in his time, has looked disaster in the face. He has suffered many a blackfly on his rudbeckias. Harry understood the common man and led the group with humble authority, wit and empathy. Joe himself led the Sports therapy group. The subject was usually Wakefield Trinity. Alas, it seemed that only the defence was any longer holy. It had been a sad group of late and, like all bereavement self-help groups, soon left the painful present to extol a more joyful past. The Holiday therapy group was usually leaderless. The aims varied. Some meetings were aimed at rehabilitation after a good holiday. Others aimed at honing to a fine edge the stories of drama and disaster. (I was amazed at what happened to Frank in Florence).

During a recent consultation, when I was feeling more than usually morose, I became aware that Joe was having difficulty communicating with me. He trimmed the hair from my ears and I sensed a psychoanalytical turn as he 'scanned' my interests and worries, gardens, house, family, work. He talked of bars, theatre bars in particular. I responded, hesitating. And mentioned the bar at the 'Grand'. "What do you go to see?" he asked. I glanced round, the waiting room was empty. "Opera", I admitted. A great flash of understanding and companionship shot between us. He stepped back, his scissors pointing to the sky, a smile splitting his face. "I love opera", he beamed. Our two souls joined in tales of *Traviata, Boheme* and the like. We enthused over Donnizetti and wept over Wagner.

I left the consultation exhilarated and elated, sensations dimmed only when I regarded my shorn locks in the mirror. I sighed. The trip to artistic highlands was worth it though.

I don't like going to the dentist, not even now when they have put lovely peaceful pictures on the ceiling so that you may remain tranquil and reposed as they plough their furrows. Mind you, a funny thing happened last time. I was recommended to buy some of those little brushes which firtle bits of food from between your teeth. And do you know, today I was able to whistle for the first time for years.

But what I hate most of all is going to the doctor. I hate having to play the role of patient and I play it very badly. So you can imagine my state of mind, taking into account my psychological baggage, when I finally decided that I should tackle my 'fundamental concerns'

It had always been known as 'Dad's Problem' and had caused me much tribulation over the years.[12] It had been a continual distraction from matters intellectual and had frustrated a promising sporting career. It had wreaked havoc with my singing, for my upper register had been severely curtailed by the uncertainty of my base parts. Moreover, I had developed an air

[12] This account originally appeared as *Fundamental Concerns* in *Alimentary My Dear Doctor.* Hawkins C editor. Oxford: © Radcliffe Medical Press; 1988. Reproduced with the permission of the copyright holder

of concern earlier than I could have anticipated. It still puzzles me why, after so many years, I should have decided to have something done. But decide I did, anticipating a quick, clean, painless job with minimal inconvenience. Alas, it was not to be. Somehow the matter escalated to a formal, planned admission for the ultimate in cold surgery.

So long as the decision remained an intellectual one, the prospect caused me little worry. As a matter of fact, the whole business generated many a merry quip and much witty conversation. Friends and acquaintances who were aware of my impending appointment with fate dipped eagerly into that vast genre of humour that is poignantly familiar to anyone with my problem. There was rarely anything original in their jocular conversation - everything to be said on this subject has been said. Many times.

As the time approached, though, I grew uneasy and felt people were talking about me. I began to dread, not just the admission and operation, but hospital visitors. After all, my complaint was hardly the stuff of which tea time chats are made. My son, a personnel manager in the making, counselled me frequently. "But think of the chocolate and grapes, dad.... (can I think of anything else) "There'll be piles of things to talk about ... home and that," he finished lamely.

For days I considered what book to take in with me. A friend of mine, a Trappist monk, fell heavily while cleaning windows at the monastery. As he was transferred to hospital for repair of his extensive lacerations, the Abbot slipped a book under his blanket. It was entitled *"To Heaven Through a Window"* by St. Gerard Majella. I suppose my obvious choice would be *"The Grapes of Wrath"* by Steinbeck, but I had read it. In view of the expected treatment, perhaps a treatise on Arctic exploration may have been appropriate, but my outlook seemed bleak enough without that. I eventually chose, in hope, *"I Can't Stay Long"*, by Lauric Lee.

My wife, being somewhat devout, suggested that I should be included that week In the Parish Sick List which was published every Sunday. I demurred. It's not that I lacked faith in the prayers of my fellow Christians. Oh no. But it is difficult to imagine just what prayers they might say. So far as I know, the Saints and Doctors of the Church have not concerned themselves unduly with my particular problem. Holy Writ has had little to say on the subject. There were other worries too, about the Sick List. Every Sunday, it reminded me of my failures. I could not recall, offhand, anyone who, once included, ever left it, except by one, rather final, route. Moreover, the curate who usually typed out the Parish Bulletin had many gifts, but included in those gifts were neither spelling nor typing. Misprints abounded. One poor soul had Mass said for her mother's "recovery from silliness". Got talked about for ages, she did. I did not dare imagine what they might make of my infirmity.

On that fateful morning I was brightly unconcerned. I rejected my wife's offer of help with the packing. I was quite capable of doing it myself. As soon as she had left for work, I sought out all that was necessary. The pyjamas and toothbrush were easy. My dressing gown, so rarely used, had lost its cord in some long forgotten game of Cowboys and Indians. It gaped alarmingly and revealingly at the slightest movement. It was difficult to know what to put soap and things into. The only available toilet bag I could find belonged to my daughter. It was pink and fluffy and had lace trimmings. It did not seem to me to adequately represent the macho image I had of myself but there was nothing else. I stuffed it to the bottom of the bag, out of sight.

157

On my way out, I looked in on my greenhouse. I gazed upon the trusses of swollen red tomatoes and wondered. I snipped off the ripest and tears came into my eyes.

The grey wetness of the morning complemented my inner mood. Unconsciously, I over asserted my own identity. With my College tie in place, wearing a tastefully monogrammed sweater and carrying a carefully chosen light, overtly medical textbook, I walked jauntily to my fate. As I entered the ward, I became, immediately, that five year old boy on his first day at school so many years ago.

I tried so very hard to be the perfect, all accepting patient, but my underlying anxiety continually revealed itself in slightly hysterical humour. Being clerked in was a tense procedure. I found myself assessing the significance of every 'Mm' and 'good' that the nurse muttered. Some questions obviously embarrassed her and I became tongue tied. Other questions I could relax with. "Nothing to worry about on that score", I would announce confidently. When she had finished, she fastened a small plastic bracelet to my wrist. It had my name on it. Paradoxically, as I read the label, I felt my identity ebbing away.

My next visitor was the girl from the laboratory, come to take the inevitable blood test. I felt a rising panic. In my mind, I totted up quickly the number of glasses of wine I had consumed in the last few weeks and prayed that it would not show in the laboratory. I could almost hear the conversation. "Have you seen this?" "Oh, him. I'm not surprised". The technician and I chatted as she drew the blood. Our talk was, at best, desultory and I tried to enliven it. I was aware that my voice was curiously high pitched and my humour flat and unoriginal. She smiled, thinly 1 thought, and left.

And then the long wait. It had been a long time since I had sat quietly alone for hours, with all responsibility gone. I read, then I read some more. I drank a lot of water and then went to the toilet. I combed my hair. I then had another drink of water and went to the toilet again. I looked out of the window to a now sun bright day. It was no distraction and, in fact, served only to exaggerate my imprisonment. Out there were people who were not in here. Some seemed to have a purpose in their lives, others were just walking about. I saw colleagues coming and going to and from the Staff car park. They were talking to each other. I bet they were telling funny stories and swapping anecdotes about patients. Of whom I was one.

By 7 o'clock, a long evening still lay ahead. I had not yet changed into my pyjamas, lest I lost the last vestige of my identity. Even so, my eyes still strayed frequently to the band around my wrist that told me who I was. In spite of the fact that it was still only Autumn, the bellringers at the nearby church were practising *0 Come, 0 Come Emanuel* - and getting the last note wrong every time. I meditated on the problems of being a new bellringer and wondered how you made a start. It seemed to me that however one started, that first bum note would resound throughout the City. I must have been emotionally fragile, for, before I knew what I was doing, I was silently weeping for apprentice bellringers. But the wrong note was repeated so often, that my mood gradually changed from empathetic sadness to a great anger and, by 8.30 I was ready to form a society for the abolition of bellringers. Especially apprentices.

I was aware that some medical activity that night was inevitable. I could not bear to define it in my own mind, but I knew it would be pretty basic. All the old jokes surfaced from my memory and failed to amuse me. I debated within myself how best to greet the nurse and her stainless steel trolley. "Hello. Are you a friend or an enema ?" No. My hysterical laughter would betray me. Besides, she's probably heard it before. Best be formal. "Good evening, nurse, I await your pleasure". Perhaps I'll forego the last bit. And any comment on the weather would be bound to be misconstrued.

I was, in the event, as formal as can be expected under the circumstances and took the administration almost without qualm. Alas, I found that it was not only my memory that failed to retain. My feeling of inadequacy deepened.

By now I was totally unsure and indecisive. Switching on the television took a great effort of will and much looking over my shoulder. It was not worth it for all that appeared was an electronic snowstorm. The sound was clear enough though. While I was fiddling with the controls, a benign and reassuring anaesthetist visited me and gave me 4 mg. of lorazepam. Full of trepidation at their likely effect, I took them, rushed to clean my teeth, changed and leapt into bed, expecting to be poleaxed any minute. Nothing happened. Or perhaps something did, for when the night nurse came in, I asked about the television and explained the problem. I would not have dared to do so before the lorazepam. He brought me another set. The picture was fine, but the sound was distorted, no matter what we did. I settled for both on at the same time. though changing channels was a complex procedure and the two sets were not always compatible. This confusion, combined with the increasing effects of the drug, produced some curious and bizarre effects.
So far, I have not mentioned my multifocals. Very few people do, I find. There are times when the claims for their excellence and convenience seem to me to be overstated. I admit that they

are fine for watching television while sitting square on, in a chair. But lying down, with one eye necessarily above the other, eliminates clear vision in all parts of the picture apart from the central one square centimetre. And anyway they pressed painfully into my head.

Gradually, I became calmer and more relaxed. I began to prepare myself mentally for the morrow, for on tomorrow morning I would be going over the top. In a manner of speaking.

I remember little of THE DAY other than smiling faces, jocular rejoinders and no pain. My son tells me that I had all the benefits of being drunk, but none of the disadvantages. I am assured I was convivial, though a trifle uninhibited. Those operating gowns do little to restrain one's inhibitions - or anything else for that matter.

I think one of my trainees visited me. I can vaguely recall a stubbled, tieless man with intense eyes expounding on the novel he had left me. It was all about the Devil visiting Moscow once. I believed him and took it as read.

It was the next day when, with a nearly normal mind, my fundamental concern became apparent. Gradually, that concern grew to a painful obsession. There was no avoiding the denouement. I strode manfully to that small room for my moment of truth. Ten painful minutes later, I returned, aware that another milestone had been passed.

The headline In the Sunday Paper announced that another Union had suffered sequestration of their assets. I knew how they felt.

Overall, I think that my visitors had a pretty raw deal. My room was not the place to be if you wanted stimulating conversation, spiced with heart rending, blood curdling tales of the sharp end of the National Health Service. In fact, my news had about it a repetitive inconsequence that bored even me. Nor could I evince anything other than disinterest in the news from home. I had hoped that the natural euphoria that follows the completion of a trial would be sufficient to carry my visitors along, but it wasn't. I was aware of a feeling of disappointment in the air. Several remarked, somewhat sharply I thought, on how well I looked. There were one or two who had, I am certain, a similar problem to my own. I could tell by their sheepish entrance, the obvious discomfort of their posture and, most of all by the yellow pallor of their faces as I described again the technical details of the operation.

There was no doubt that the turning point in my hospital stay was the coming of the Lucozade. You can't argue with Lucozade. It gives a chap status and I was, at last, a proper patient. People began to pay me proper respect and asked me how I was feeling. Chocolate and magazines were not long in their coming and a rather fine Beaujolais enlivened the menu no end. I became relaxed with the staff and joked and grumbled as the season declared. The routine of the hospital day dominated my every thought and action. Each event was keenly anticipated and timed. There was a major crisis on the fourth day. For reasons I could not understand, the spirit did not move me as easily as it might have done and the subsequent delay resulted in my missing the morning paper round. I panicked. What could I do between coffee and lunch? The day crumbled about me. I sank into a profound depression. So deep was my despair, that I read the Sunday papers again.

Later that day, the surgeon came to see me to ask how I was. Suddenly and miraculously all my symptoms disappeared. No longer did I suffer from all those terrible afflictions I had endured through my slough of despond. "Absolutely splendid" was my answer to his every query. I was terrified in case he kept me in any longer or, heaven forbid, did the job again.

The great return home was a little disappointing. An important badge of illness in our house has always been the inalienable right to lie on the settee if you are feeling in any way poorly. This right takes precedence over all others, including the strength of emotion generated by mother's varicose veins. But I could not get comfortable and those damned multifocals didn't focus properly. I resigned my rights and sat on a chair, losing all presence in so doing. The other major problem was more subtle. Illness needs to exist in its own right to be properly enjoyed. There is not room in any family for more than one illness at a time. Certainly this is the case in our house. Imagine my chagrin, therefore, when Grandma went 'off it' as soon as I got home. She even had the doctor calling to see her. Never noticed me he didn't, even though I'd got a special short dressing gown for my convalescence. I went back to work early.

I have often wondered since then why I had it done at that particular time. I suspect I needed to try myself out, to see how I could cope with the gentle ripple of symptoms that heralds the onset of middle age. Well, I did survive. Actually, it wasn't all that bad.

Alas, my trials were not over. You would have thought that I had had enough of illness, but just as I was coming down from the euphoria that follows survival of a crisis, I was struck down again.

Months of misery[13] began when I lost the filling during an ante-natal clinic - possibly as a result of over enthusiastic cleaning of my mouth with a resistant mint. The pain was barely noticeable at first, simply an odd sensation, but within an hour I was distracted and distraught. Using a stethoscope became a torment and I abandoned the left ear-piece. A one eared stethoscope has limited value and diminishes one's status. Conversation was out of the question; even the touch of the tongue on the affected tooth produced exquisite spasms of pain.

I rang the dentist. The receptionist noted 'toothache' and asked if I had taken anything. I explained that of course I hadn't, the pain was far too severe. She offered me an appointment for the next day. I panicked and demanded immediate attention. The receptionist tried to explain about the full list and the other patients waiting. She attempted to place my problem into the perspective of the great tapestry of life. I was not mollified and my desperation turned to anger.

Within an hour, I melted into the delight of a local anaesthetic and the healing surgery. I smiled at the receptionist on my way out and thanked her for her help. Her reciprocal smile was reserved.

My next physical trial was the tenosynovitis of my right wrist, which developed during the annual pruning of the roses. I've never had a bad wrist before and was devastated by its far-reaching effects. Mealtimes were humiliating. Unable to use a knife effectively, my meat had to be cut for me and my bread buttered. Adjusting errant underpants had to be carried out unsatisfactorily with my left hand. Steering a car also proved

[13] Originally appeared in a modified form as *I Want to be Seen Right Now* in *Medical Monitor* 18 October 1995

difficult and I was forced to avoid sharp turns. I needed to plan my route along straight roads so home visits became even more prolonged.

Then, as spring became summer, an increasingly painful throbbing of my fundament (oh not again) distracted me and disturbed my sleep. Acrobatic examination of my nethers revealed an enormous (my description) perianal abscess.

I was unable to sit comfortably, until that is, I discovered the art of sitting on two chairs, with the painful bit in-between. Although this curious seating arrangement raised a few eyebrows, patients are, by and large, oblivious to doctors' predicaments and there was little comment.

By this time of the year, what with all my medical dramas and all, I was beginning to get into the swing of illnesses. Which is probably why I went for a nap hand and decided to get my rupture sorted. While patients suffer from hernias, I have always felt that I suffered from a 'rupture'. I prefer the term myself. It has a history behind it and the word is almost onomatopoeic. Mind you, I can understand why ordinary patients don't use the expression - many just can't take it.

I had nurtured my rupture for more than 30 years and it had reached the stage where measuring the inside leg had become so delicate an operation as to threaten feasibility. And besides, recurrent abdominal spasms promised impending drama.
1 do not care to dwell on the process of repair - I did not get a badge for being brave at the doctor's, I promise you. As a matter of fact, two things irritated me. When did calling patients by their Christian name become good practice? Why is it assumed that it will create a friendly atmosphere and will allay any fears? I don't like it. I wanted to say "Look. I have never met you

before. I prefer formality". But no. "Shall I call you Dr Mulroy? Or should I call you Ronnie?" No one had called me 'Ronnie' since I was five years old. But I didn't want to be thought churlish and accepted it in case they thought I was pulling rank.

And secondly, it is self evident that even a minor operation has some pain attached. I asked for a couple of paracetamol on the first day after the operation. I was told that the doctor was busy, but he would come at the end of the operating list to 'write me up'. Why is there such a performance? Most nurses seem quite sensible and would, I think, he capable of dispensing them. But they all seem to be regarded as idiotic potential drug abusers and are not trusted. After a couple of hours, I rang my wife. She bought a packet at *ASDA* and brought them in.

I think it is unlikely that this account of minor illnesses will stir much sympathy, especially in my fellow doctors. After all, the illnesses were transient and did not threaten life. They are the trivia of medical practice. Yet all the incidents were painful or, at least, uncomfortable; each affected my life at the time and impaired my function. I had wanted each one gone and as soon as possible. I expected immediate treatment and effective relief. I did not give a damn that the dentist was fully booked or that the surgeon was tired from his long operating list. It mattered to me not one jot that there were others worse than I was - I didn't believe that anyway. If this is how I felt, can I blame patients for feeling the same? Much has been written about 'unreasonable' demands. I no longer know what 'unreasonable' means.

Perhaps I was getting used to being ill. Perhaps I secretly enjoyed all the attention, but I started to need a regular 'fix' of the NHS.

I had not had my eyes checked for a while and my glasses were in some need of repair so I thought I'd pop in to the opticians.

You might think that to a man whose medical history had hitherto been almost entirely encompassed by his underpants, the thought of a routine visit to the optician would cause few qualms[14]. What possible embarrassments or privations could it hold for a man who had recently suffered so much?

On further reflection, however, I realised that there were a few potential pitfalls. So I cut down on the garlic and red wine for a day or two beforehand lest I misted his vision or disturbed his objectivity. And, I have to admit, the state of my glasses did imply neglect. So I soaked them in detergent, which was sufficient to remove the obvious surface grime, but was not enough to clean the cracks.

Once dry, I renewed the old Sellotape. This was trickier than I expected for, by the nature of things, it was done 'blind'. To add to my difficulties, one of the arms fell off when I tried to put the spectacles back on. I was forced to come to the conclusion that I could carry out the repair accurately only while I actually wore them. Which meant using a mirror. Not a simple procedure. No matter how I concentrated, my hands moved the wrong way. Co-ordination was never my forte.

And then there was the Sellotape itself. Sellotape is capricious stuff at the best of times and within minutes I had inadvertently trimmed an eyebrow, plucked the hairs from my left ear and avoided stripping my cornea only by the merest chance. Anyway, the repair was now complete and, once I had pencilled

---

[14] This account originally appeared as *It Was No Sight for Sore Eyes* in *Medical Monitor* 18th September 1996 and a shortened version in *Triangle* the same year.

in an eyebrow and remembered to keep my head tilted a little to the right, I looked almost normal. At this point my wife decided that she would not, after all, come to town with me. Strange that.

I made sure I had everything I needed. The old student mantra never fails *'Spectacles, testicles, wallet and watch.'*. Self doubt crept in as I approached my destination. Was it really simply a checkup? Why had I chosen now? Was it that Modigliani's faces are chubbier of late or that Rubens' ladies had changed from the erotic to the merely obese? And is my increasing reputation for friendliness simply related to many mistaken identities rather than the benignity of increasing age? A tremor ran through me as I noticed that the optician had become an optometrist. When did that happen - and why? What did it mean and what were the implications?

It was not easy to enter the premises. Like most 'optometrists', the shop was completely glass fronted and the door, also glass, could not be easily identified by the poorly sighted. I pretended to study the bespectacled glamour in the window as I edged along, gently pressing the glass until a slight 'give' indicated I had found the way in. Others have had this problem and I suspect it is a marketing ploy. Few things convince you of failing sight more than the inability to find a door.

The young chap who examined me was enthusiastic, but paled at the sight of my spectacles. We worked our way through the lenses without a problem. The pressure test was different. Of course, I knew what to expect, but a slightly raised pressure in one eye resulted in him firing repeated blasts of air through his machine. I started to go mazy. I have to admit that I am prone to go mazy at any hint of assault on my body. I have fainted in some well-known establishments in my time. Not only in surgeries, outpatient departments and dentists, but also in the barber's where once I went all sweaty while having my sideboards trimmed.

But I have never heard of anyone fainting in the opticians and I had no wish to he the first.   Fortunately my Celtic steel and Anglo-Saxon sang-froid saw me through.   Still misty eyed and unsteady, I was asked to select a set of frames from several hundred identical pairs on display.   I chose the nearest one.

Newly visioned, I strode out through the exit and into the sun. But too late.   A traffic warden was there first, pen and pad in hand.   I told him of my suffering and how I had become a new man with the revelation of clear sight.   His face remained expressionless.   'You'll he able to read the notice in future then, won't you?' he noted and turned to put pen to paper.

It is generally considered that if all doctors had to suffer the illnesses that their patients endured, then they would be better doctors. Well, perhaps.   Certainly, I became a more sympathetic doctor after all my vicissitudes, but was I a better doctor?   It's a moot point.

Keeping Up To Date

It is not surprising that one of the things most valued by patients is the reassurance that their doctor keeps 'up to date'. Especially since the advent of the Health Service, strenuous efforts have been made, by the ruling medical bodies, the government and by the doctors themselves to maintain clinical standards, hone doctors' skills and help them keep abreast of advances in medical science. This is all very laudable, but I was never sure whether the formal continuing education that was available ever really got to the nub of the basic problem.

General Practitioners usually work alone. They may be in a group practice, but most of their working day was, and is, spent alone with the patient. It is unusual for one GP to observe another's consulting style and skills and indeed it is rare to be observed oneself. During a period of some 15 years when I was in a two man practice, I never sat in with my senior partner after the first week, nor him with me. We could only deduce each other's standards by written records or patients' opinions. In the loneliness of the consulting room with a remorseless parade of patients bringing with them common and repetitive problems, it is all too easy to cut corners.

Habits are acquired in those first few years, habits which may be good, bad or simply expedient. Whatever the quality of those habits, they do tend to persist throughout one's professional life, unless you critically appraise them. It is easy, too, to spend so much time explaining the nature of a problem or its treatment in lay terms that slowly one begins to think in those terms. Clinical sharpness and scientific thinking become eroded and fuzzy. The deterioration is gradual though offset by experience, by having 'been there before'. But if the deterioration is gradual, it is also inevitable, unless checked. I used to hear two compliments commonly voiced by patients. One, of a young doctor, 'he always gives you a thorough examination'. The other, of an older doctor, 'he doesn't need to examine you; he just takes one look at you and knows what's wrong'. There may be elements of truth in these, but they are only elements. They do indicate, though, the change in a doctor's approach as time passes.

One of the problems arising from a GP's professional isolation is that the GP can easily remain unconscious of his own deterioration. Oh, I know that patients may convey something of their opinion, but they can be ignored if they trouble your conscience. Even when errors occur – and everyone makes mistakes – you can persuade yourself of mitigating circumstances or, better still, blame the patient.

Consciously striving to maintain your clinical standards requires great effort and it is a lifetime's work. Some inadequacies and failings are difficult to recognise and even more difficult to correct. Concentration and listening skills are critical for effectiveness in the consultation and stamina to maintain them throughout a two or three hour surgery session is vital. Yet none of these are easy to acquire or maintain.

Of all the aspects of medical practice, the most easily defined, and therefore the easiest to keep up to date, is the appearance and value of new drugs. Yet of all aspects of maintaining standards, this seems to me to have the least urgency about it. New medicines that work need little advertising. No-one had to promote penicillin, it sold itself. There is however an advertising tendency to hail new drugs as 'breakthroughs' and it is a curious fact that when one first used a new drug, it always seemed very effective. Sir Deryck Dunlop used to observe cynically that it was important to use a new drug quickly, before the effects wore off. He might have added 'and before their side effects become too obvious'. Looking back on the many times that I used a new drug for the first time, I am sure that my enthusiasm and understanding of the new substance conveyed itself to the patient. The placebo effect of any chemical compound is well known.

So how did you come to know of new drugs? There is no doubt that the commercial drug companies were usually first with the information and I suspect too little credit has been given to them for that. But it is self evident that they had an interest in selling the drug and that interest made them prone to hyperbole. It is also true that in the less controlled days of my youth, bribery in its various forms was rife, though often subtle. The 'promotional research' deceived me for a while. Although I rarely went out to 'drug lunches', I did once. I was flattered to be asked to 'trial' a new form of an established drug for hypertension. I was given a new sphygmomanometer and a stethoscope and asked to measure the benefits of the treatment on six patients. Only later did the penny drop. Most of the patients did well, as one would expect, but once established it became obvious that they would probably remain on the treatment for years. And the cost of several patient years of therapy obviously racked up profit which more than paid for my lunch and presents.

But their 'gifts' were sometimes useful and some of their non-promotional meetings were technically superior to the standard 'lecture' that GPs were often served up.

I was always a little slow to adopt a new drug and usually grateful in retrospect. I always thank God that I never prescribed Thalidomide, though it was the 'in thing' when I first entered practice. Especially it seemed ideal for some reason, for pregnant women. I remember reading the first letters in the British Medical Journal raising questions about its effects on the peripheral nerves in some women. And then the full truth gradually emerged. I shudder to think of what might have been.

Reading the journals was an obvious way of keeping up to date in drug treatment as well as other fields of medicine. But often, full assessment of a drug and its potential side effects took months, even years. I tended to become dependent on the opinion of specialists in that particular field. I cannot speak highly enough of the guidance and support I received from consultant colleagues throughout my professional life. It began in my first practice. Left solely in charge of the rural practice for six months, within two years of qualifying, I was totally isolated. I acquired so many bad habits. Panic and ignorance were my constant companions. Sometimes I asked a consultant for a domiciliary consultation in part for his advice, but more often for someone to talk medicine with. They helped me to preserve my medical sanity.

I often think about that first practice. The area was beautiful and the people welcoming and appreciative. It should have been an idyllic start to my career. Yet some of the working conditions were almost primeval. In that first practice we had two large garden sheds, one for the consultation and one for the waiting patients. There was a gap of a couple of yards between them. In heavy rain, patients would enter the consulting room at a run. Yet no-one complained and the process of the consultation was the same. At that time I was prone to accept things as they were. It's a little different these days with the burgeoning growth of the new emporia of primary care. I'm sure that the shining wood and chrome of the new premises impresses patients and should make General Practice altogether more professional, but I am not sure that it does. It depends what you're used to.

In those early days, there were few distractions. The consultation was far simpler. There was you, the patient, the handwritten notes and your prescription pad. Later in my career, life became far more complex. With the dramatic improvements in premises came a growth in administrative staff, appointment systems, concerns about lifestyles and health promotion, anticipatory care and computers. I found the advent of the computer a great bind. Of course it should have been a great help. From its bowels we could, at the flick of a switch, extract all sorts of epidemiological information, but somehow we rarely did; the computer simply added on work – and demanded more staff to run it, more paper to feed it and more room to house it. It became a third party in any consultation and a distracting one at that. It spoke its own language and, terrifyingly, I started to think and speak in that language. It posed problems of confidentiality that we had never considered before. And yet we slowly became dependent on it and when it 'crashed', the practice crashed and we were paralysed. Nevertheless, having a computer became, inevitably, evidence that we were 'up to date'.

But I digress (see what I mean about computers). Elsewhere, I have described how, after a few years in practice, I felt I had cracked it. Then a gross error of diagnosis revealed how slack I had become. The error was not life threatening, but an error that a junior medical student would have been ashamed of. It was a turning point in my medical life. I was saved from acute embarrassment (and the patient from prolonged discomfort) by a diplomatic consultant. I determined to improve and applied for a part-time job in Dermatology. It was the best thing I ever did. Becoming part of a team – an enthusiastic team – changed me. My performance was observed; I could discuss patients with senior colleagues; I was expected to read the literature; above all I was treated as someone whose opinions were respected. And because of that, I tried to make sure that my opinions were worth respecting. It was the beginning of a truly professional life.

There were other spin-offs too. Sometimes patients of the practice would see me in the hospital in my white coat. The word got round that I was a 'proper' doctor. I quite liked that. And I acquired new skills. A latent interest in minor surgery was rekindled and I was able to use it in the practice. I met other consultants. I enjoyed discussing X-rays in the radiology department and laboratory results with the Pathologist. I could attend postmortem examinations – and I learned so much there in the 'House of Truth'. Sometimes I could contribute important clinical details. But perhaps the greatest benefit was that by being in the hospital regularly, I could drop in to see the patients I had admitted. I could follow their progress as the confused clinical picture that I had seen when I admitted them gradually clarified. My visits to practice patients was seen as showing interest and any patient who feels their doctor is interested in them is a reassured, even 'special' patient. The whole experience of a defined hospital link was of immense value to me, to my patients and to the practice.

It was during that time that I heard rumours of the impending opening of a new unit for young people with severe physical disability. Now the management and care of people with severe disability is not a major part of most GP's work. Much of the day to day care tends to be in the hands of family carers, district nurses, social workers and specialist units. I don't think I was the only GP who was unaware of the special needs of this group or of the daily commitment of their carers. Since there were changes in the dermatology department at that time, I decided to leave and take over the day to day running of the new unit. Never have I learned so much so fast. I developed not only new skills and knowledge, I underwent an enormous change in attitude. I learned humility. I remember discussing admission with a young man who was seriously affected by neurological disease. His speech was slurred, his vision blurred, his legs unsteady, his hands uncontrollable and his bladder and bowels uncertain. I tried to focus on his prime needs. "What would you say was your main problem?", I asked. He thought for a while and gathered his speech together. "I don't know", he said, "I don't seem to have one at the moment".

The effects on my General Practice of this period of several years were interesting. My attitude to the disabled patient and their carers had, understandably changed. I could empathise and make allowances, especially of time. I found saints all over the place and was in awe of their endurance. I hope my new found skills benefitted them too. But I became intolerant of the young fit layabout who had had no appreciation of how fortunate they were and what potential they were wasting. Many a time I had to bite my tongue in case I used 'unprofessional' language. I still get angry when I see people lying down under life, especially as I know I am prone to do it myself. But my lasting memory is, and will remain, of those patients and their carers who pursued their tortured Calvary road with such equanimity.

It was nearly ten years after I entered practice that I first became aware of the existence of the Royal College of General Practitioners. The College had been founded to improve the standards of general practice by a group of GPs. It was not, curiously, a particularly popular move and I have often wondered why. I suppose many of my colleagues considered that this was a self-appointed 'elite'. Perhaps they saw the College as a rival to the medico-political bodies already in existence. Or could it have been that the existence of a body to improve the standards of practice was an indication that practice did indeed need improvement. For whatever reason, many GPs turned their backs on it, certainly locally.

I have to admit that I was a reluctant recruit. It had become increasingly obvious that Postgraduate Medical Education was in a bad way. It consisted largely of five or six hour long lectures each year, the statutory number to attract the Postgraduate Education Allowance. The lectures were given by consultants to unenthusiastic GPs. I remember their desultory nature and chaps sitting at the back reading the paper or worse still, signing the attendance sheet then disappearing. The lectures were always clinical, but the application of the subject to the particular needs of general practice was never aired. I remember only one lecture which affected (and improved) my own standards. And if education doesn't change your professional behaviour, then it is of limited value indeed. For the first 10 or 12 years of my professional life, I never heard a GP talk about the problems I faced. It was against this background that the College became relevant to me.

It had been decided that each postgraduate education centre (and they were springing up by the early '70's) should have attached to them not only a Clinical Tutor in overall charge, but also a GP tutor who would initiate education aimed specifically at GPs. I was invited to apply, but an obligatory qualification was membership of the College. The problem was that admission was by examination only. Because the appointment was imminent, the examination was taken quickly and I had little time to prepare. I remember thinking that if this test was relevant and if I was as good a GP as I thought I was, then I should pass. I did, though I sometimes shrink at my self confidence at that time and wonder if my success authenticated me, or the examination, or neither, or both.

Trying to get GPs interested in listening to or sharing with other GPs proved unpopular and difficult for some time. Few of us, I suspect, understood just how much expertise was required of a good GP; expertise was to be expected only from a specialist. But I was inspired by the College and its members, who gradually came to produce an academic aspect and an educational analysis of the content of family medicine. Among the many initiatives was an interest in research and the use of clinical audit.

Research in general practice was and is different to that in academic departments and hospitals, for the patients are unselected and our records were less useful as a research tool. But wherever it takes place, research is hard work. Having the idea is exciting; it adds spring to your step and enthuses and informs your daily work; drawing the conclusions is exciting too as you start to discover something previously unknown. The big problem is the mundane, routine grind of collecting the data.

My first paper was about an epidemic of cattle ringworm in the practice. Tracing the spread through families and school classes was fascinating and tracing the source – to a single heifer – eminently satisfying. It had an entertainment value too; I found a young lad who was selling it at 6d a rub – it got you off school. And I learned a lot. A more exhausting project about the ill effects of doctors' treatments took me on average about an hour a day for a full year. It was a thrill to see it in the pages of the BMJ. Because it publicised 'bad news' about doctors, the article was quoted in the national press and I appeared for the first time on the BBC. I enjoyed my few minutes of fame, but it soon passed.

While research had its own pleasures and benefits, clinical audit was a quite different kettle of fish for it was devoted to measuring exactly what you did and what you achieved. It was, at times frightening to discover that what you thought you did was often far different to what you actually did. Unfortunately, this valuable method of improving standards proved unpopular and, in some quarters, even became a dirty word. I think the independence of the GP was felt to be threatened. I used to attend hospital audit meetings for inspiration, but was bitterly disappointed. It seemed to me that everyone studiously avoided anything that might be considered critical and focused instead on the bland and easily measured. Such audit as I did personally did indeed have some depressing results, but all were beneficial.

The College initiative which I enjoyed most was undoubtedly the introduction of the video camera into the consulting room and into the lecture theatre. My first experience was at a College weekend in Huddersfield in the mid '70's. After a theoretical instruction, we were asked to script, act and film an educational programme for use in General Practice. The finished products were shown on Sunday afternoon to everybody for their critical appraisal. Looking back, the fuzzy black and white images of hesitant actors were often hilarious and embarrassing, but at the time we thought they were brilliant and we had the added bonus of knowing we were pioneers.

Video, over the next thirty years or so, grew to be a valuable educational tool and a vital means of assessing oneself and others at work in the consulting room. The first effect it had on my consulting was that I stopped picking my nose, but of course, many more lessons were to be learned. It is interesting now to look back on my consultations. Throughout a whole series of about thirty episodes, I seemed reasonably effective, but never once did I raise the question of life style; not once did I 'promote' health nor did I, for example, check a blood pressure unless it was specifically indicated or asked for. The change of content and scope of the consultation was to change dramatically in the next five years. It was not always possible to film real patients, but suitably primed actors proved more than adequate substitutes. Some of the best educational films I ever made were using gifted actors from the Dewsbury Arts Group. That they were largely unscripted gave them, I think an air of reality. And the making of the film was always exciting, one-take stuff, warts and all.

Training specifically for General Practice had been in existence almost from the beginning of the Health Service, but it was only used sporadically and it languished. It took the form of a year as a trainee in a recognised practice and the trainer was recompensed the cost of the trainee's salary. Officially, the trainer was to train the young doctor, but the content of that teaching was often ill-defined and poorly monitored. It was all too easy for the trainee to become an extra pair of hands at no cost. It seemed to many influential GPs and the College in particular, that formal training for Family Medicine was essential if standards were to rise. And so Vocational Training was born.

There were several aspects to the programme. It was eventually to become a three year period of which, generally speaking, two years would be spent in hospital posts particularly relevant to general practice and a year in recognised practices. I always reckoned that one of the greatest benefits of such a scheme was to the 'recognised' training practice, for, to qualify, the practice had to achieve high clinical and organisational standards. The GP trainers themselves were trained in teaching and the organisation of teaching and the practice regularly inspected. The trainee should be, officially, supernumerary, though having a reasonable clinical workload. It was this last that always proved a difficult and delicate balance. A further essential part of the training was a weekly formal training session, run on a district basis by the trainers themselves. The effect of all this on a practice was often devastating. For the first time, the competence of a practice, its doctors and staff, was assessed by peers. It was a most dramatic shift in the whole 'independent' culture of General Practice.

I was fortunate that my first trainee was a most splendid chap and an already competent clinician. Even so, that first year was revolutionary. He asked why I did things and sometimes I didn't know. His fresh intellectual and scientific knowledge stretched me and hoovered out corners of my mind that had lain dormant for years. I am not sure whether I taught him much, but I know I learned a lot. He seemed a ready made GP and I would have liked him as my partner, but it was not to be. So far as I could see, his only disadvantage was his jumpers. He wore a different one every day and often discarded it if the day was warm. Our collection of his jumpers proliferated at an alarming rate and for months after he left, we would stumble over them in the most unlikely places. Another trainee, also a competent and caring doctor, was so enthusiastic that he followed me everywhere. I liked to think he was frightened of missing a pearl of great wisdom. I didn't mind that, but the trouble was he always walked by my side. This made the simple process of going through a door a most complex procedure and going to the toilet required formal planning and discussion.

I don't remember any trainee who was incompetent, but I remember especially one who was arrogant. He could be charming, but my goodness he was arrogant and would admit to no errors or omissions. He never showed remorse. Now arrogance is the cardinal sin that doctors should avoid at all costs. There was little I could do to puncture his self esteem. In fact he brought to me a great doubt in the efficacy of the whole training scheme. What hope was there if I couldn't change an attitude? Perhaps he, though, did at least show me the error of always being certain.

As time went on, there were an increasing number of female trainees. It is self evident that they were different to their male colleagues. They were all resilient, but their softer approach convinced me of the value of women GPs at a time when there were comparatively few about. They brought with them a new approach and their increasing numbers changed the style and organisation of family practice. They changed me too. At the time I was living with five daughters, a wife and a mother-in-law. I was somewhat surprised to find that I was considered to be a male chauvinist. And there was me thinking I was the last word in chivalry. It took me a long while to understand that chivalry was at the time considered merely a patronising form of chauvinism. I still hanker after it, though.

The College, therefore, had an immense influence on my professional life in all sorts of ways. I would like to think that I was able to put something back into it, but I found that aspirations to join the upper echelons demanded too much commitment. It was such a pity that my association with the College ended in rancour. Having been retired from practice for some years, my interest in Medicine gradually diminished, my knowledge faded and my skills deteriorated. I wrote (politely, I think) to the

College, tending my resignation and thanking them for all they had done. To my astonishment, some weeks later I received a legal statement forbidding me to use FRCGP (Fellowship of the Royal College of General Practitioners) after my name on pain of legal action. Were I to use letters, I would be guilty of dishonesty, misrepresentation and all sorts of heinous offences. Now, I could understand that by not paying my annual subscription I was not a bona fide member though it seemed hard to have the credit of passing the requisite examination and achievement of a demanding standard dismissed so summarily. What I could not stomach was the way it was done. No (even routine) thank you letter and best wishes. Nothing personal at all. It was almost vindictive. I did write after my anger had cooled and did get a conciliatory letter back. The episode still rankles though.

Acquiring new skills and knowledge and constantly trying to improve is laudable, but, like all human activities, such a quest may have good or bad effects. The balance may be tilted for the worse when altruistic zeal is seduced by self interest, public opinion and the lack of understanding or consideration of the consequences. All human beings are susceptible to these distractions. It is self evident that human behaviour, and that includes medical human behaviour, needs some guidance and control. A glance at the insults, cruelty and deprivation sometimes inflicted by doctors on patients will demonstrate that this is essential. And external control, though necessary, is not always sufficient.

I was fortunate in my early life to have had a good grounding in the theory and practice of ethics[15]. At school, much of our religious education was ethically based, most of it derived from Catholic writers and thinkers. Later at University, discussion of medical ethics was an informal, but integral, part of my education. The Dominican priests at the chaplaincy provided a wealth of support and constructive conversation and debate as my progress through medical school exposed me to new and difficult dilemmas.

These 'Ethics' became my guide and control, a code of behaviour evolved objectively by the profession and its advisers over a couple of millenia. They incorporated several sets of values. The generally accepted initial formulation was the Hippocratic Oath. Many of these humanistic rules of behaviour have long since gone. *"I will give no deadly medicine to anyone if asked"* is under threat; *"I will not give to any woman a pessary to procure an abortion"* disappeared in this country in 1967. The full Oath is no longer used. For many medical graduates, their only formal undertaking is a somewhat bland assurance that they will try to do good rather than bad.

I always felt that a doctor must have good manners for good manners indicate respect for others. A caring attitude oils the wheels of treatment, but true and complete caring demands hard work, discipline and organisation. Ethics are practical - *'Do unto others as you hope they will do unto you'.* In addition medical ethics draw on Christian morals. Not only did Christianity cover most of the humanistic principles, it developed them and provided a positive approach to care and to the dignity of human beings.

Our professional ethics are all these, adapted to encompass our special duties and privileges. They relate primarily to our care

[15] This discussion on medical ethics is a modified form of *Ethics and Science Need to Shake Hands* which first appeared in *The Physician* in August 1988

of patients, but also to the relationships with individuals within the profession. But doctors are human and for such a code of behaviour to be effective, acceptable and enduring, we need some imposed obligation to comply, by self-regulation, government legislation and public opinion. This is essential if patients are to have trust.

The fundamental principles of ethics are well defined. The big difficulty I found was in seeing their relevance in a particular clinical and behavioural situation and then applying them, for it is in their relevance and application to particular circumstances that most debate and controversy arise. Moreover that relevance and application has been repeatedly modified by scientific development throughout my professional life. Take the principle that we are obliged to use '*ordinary*' means to maintain life, but we are not morally obliged to use '*extraordinary*' means. As scientific medicine progressed, what constituted '*ordinary*' and '*extraordinary*' changed and became blurred. In the First World War, blood transfusion was extraordinary; in the Second World War it had become ordinary. By the turn of the current Millenium, parenteral (by drip) supplements had become routine in most surgical procedures. One could say the same about much of Intensive Care, heart, kidney, lung and liver transplants and a whole host of other procedures.

Now many of these potential dilemmas were and are, outside the immediate province of General Practice and outside our control even though they happened to 'our' patients. There was one area though, that of chemotherapy, where I felt the GP was intimately involved. Most chemotherapy, though traumatic, was aimed at cure or control and, by and large, chances of success outweighed the disadvantages of the treatment. But there were some malignant processes which were well known to respond poorly to either chemotherapy or radiotherapy. Despite these doubts, the physician might still feel obliged to try anything on the off chance of improvement. Yet it often it made the last months miserable. If it became obvious that the treatment was proving more troublesome than the disease and if the hoped for benefits were failing to materialise, I would consider stopping it after discussion with the consultant and the patient. I can understand the decision to try the treatment, though and every patient accepted the offer, even though they appreciated the likely limitation of benefit.

It is obvious to me that ethics and science are interdependent. The various controversies that surround the concept of 'Life', its protection, quality and development exemplify that. Until fairly recently, we knew what we meant by the 'Sanctity of Human Life'. Now, with increased knowledge and expertise, we have doubts and qualifications. Our ethics still dictate to us respect for human life, but science defines who is alive or dead. The debate over defining death is largely resolved, though there are still instances where this is unclear. I had limited experience of the Persistent Vegetative State, but always felt that giving food and water was an ordinary means of sustaining life, even though this was often through artificial means. But if hypostatic pneumonia (traditionally known as the *'Old Man's Friend')* supervened, as often happened, I would not feel obliged to use antibiotics to treat it, unless the patient was distressed. I felt the same about the severely damaged babies with very limited life expectancy. I could never, though, understand the witholding of water and 'ordinary care', unless giving that water or care involved significant invasive surgery.

While the timing and nature of death, and one's actions during the period when it is impending, continue to raise ethical problems, the nature and timing of the beginning of human life remain more contentious and contribute enormous and frequent ethical dilemmas to everyone. It is unfortunate that the debate is swayed as much by ignorance, self interest and blind emotion as by scientific fact, deep thought and careful consideration of the implications. As an obvious example, consider the assumed 'fact' that the baby in the womb is a biologically an intrinsic part of the mother's body. Yet, though the baby is so intimately connected to and dependent on the mother, the baby is a separate human, perhaps of different sex or blood group or many other biological characteristics.

The crucial fact, which remains unclear, is when does life begin? There is no doubt scientifically that the fertilised egg is, at least potentially, human. What else can it be? But when is it truly alive? The moralist has discussed this in terms of the soul; the scientist has talked in terms of the development of the nervous system or the ability to live outside the womb; and involved laity are swayed by the baby looking 'like a baby' on the scan. Upon the scientific and theological resolution of this dilemma depends so much. And it is insufficient to simply have good intentions. The history of the human race is littered with good intentions that were deformed and degraded later. When abortion was legalised (with strict criteria) in 1967, it promised hope of an end to the unwanted, ill-treated child. That hope has not been realised. Increasingly, abortion has become a solution to inconvenience and most terminations do not fulfil the criteria of the law. And late terminations, with the destruction of a possibly viable baby, remain an obscenity in practical as well as theoretical terms.

Not many women consulted me about the possibility of having an abortion, but there were some. I hope I was sympathetic, non-judgmental and helpful even though I felt unable to agree to their request. I always felt that few women really wanted to undergo the termination of their pregnancy, especially those who consulted me rather than more liberal doctors. We would discuss all the options and the possibility of resolving the difficulties which had triggered the request. I listened a lot. Then I would arrange a further appointment in two days with a doctor of their choice. Sometimes they would make it with one of my partners; sometimes they would refer themselves to a 'Private Clinic' but often they would return to me. There was never an easy answer. Working within a law that is contrary to one's own conscience, even though the law is permissive rather than obligatory, is never easy.

The controversy over the beginning of life shows little sign of being resolved to everyone's satisfaction. For the moment, it seems reasonable to me to assume that life begins with the fertilisation of the ovum by the sperm, for by then the genetic shape of the baby is defined and the organism begins to grow. Growth is an important sign of life.

Sometimes 'Ethics' may seem to have a negative effect of the progress of science. Yet I have always felt that ethical considerations control and restrict science as reins control and restrict a horse. The effect is positive and constructive. Without strong ethical guidance, it is tempting, when faced with a difficult problem, to simply shelve responsibility and 'get rid'. It seems easy to eliminate the incurable. But if our ethics deny the 'easy way", then we must seek another solution. "Finding another solution" is scientific. From such a start came the Hospice Movement, which, with all its limitations, has enriched our dying and our living. Science and ethics are inextricably bound together. Science gives ethics its application, ethics give science its soul.

The General Practitioner is spared many of these major medical dilemmas, though some impinge on our day to day life. For the most part, our difficulties were contained in the mundane daily grind. Certifying someone as unfit for work was by no means straightforward. It is true that there were fixed and rigid criteria for this, but they did not always cover individual cases. And sometimes there seemed to me sound moral reasons for breaking the law. Take the chap whose wife was ill or temporarily disabled and whose family was totally dependent on his income. Who was to look after the children? Neighbours are usually helpful, but not always available. Employers might allow time off, but with no pay. There was a mechanism for obtaining financial help from Social Services, but the process was slow and cumbersome. Under such circumstances, I did not shrink from the temporary expedient of a 'Sick Note'.

Prescriptions occasionally posed difficulties. By the time I retired, increasing numbers of drugs were becoming available 'over the counter'. Sometimes, like many doctors, I wondered why people continued to swell the surgery crowds when they could obtain their remedy at the pharmacist. I did not fully appreciate the impact of the cost of paracetamol or Calpol or Tagamet or many other therapies on a stretched family budget.

The whole business of money within the practice troubled me. We were officially entitled to charge for services outside the National Health Service. Now a couple of bob for a scribbled certificate did not bother me unduly, but gradually the charge crept up. All manner of forms came the way of the GP and many bits of paper were presented to us for signature. Many, I'm sure were very important to the patient, but they were always a troublesome irritant to me. Perhaps the underlying reason for the increasing charges was to reduce the demand. Certainly notes were requested for the most farcical situations. During the great drought of years ago, a lady consulted me at great length about her painful neck. Having completed the examination and arranged treatment and physiotherapy, she asked me for a note to *"..keep her water running.."* (I blinked) so she didn't have to use a standpipe. Even accepting the rising demand, I still feel uneasy that we were (and are?) the only qualified professionals to charge, for example, for passport application countersignatures. A bind, I grant you, but there were some exorbitant fees charged.

And many organisations asked for the most profound opinions and forecasts. Even Fitness Clubs sometimes requested certificates of fitness to get fit. Checking fitness for deep sea diving was a particular bane of my life, but there were so many others. How could I know, even with the most diligent examination, that someone could survive an Activity Holiday in the Andes. There were some who I felt would be lucky to leave the surgery. I have heard of a GP who kept a crystal ball on his desk. I can understand that.

I hated examining the elderly for fitness to drive a motor vehicle. For many, this was critical to their lives. I remember refusing one charming elderly man who only ever used his beloved car to take his wife to the shop a couple of times a week. I have no doubt I was justified, after all, he was virtually blind and his memory uncertain. He broke into tears and pleaded. I felt an absolute swine, especially as I had known him thirty odd years and he and his wife had been most helpful to us when we first arrived in Wakefield. But I could not sign. Both of them declined rapidly and within months had died. Balancing responsibility to the community and the care and responsibility to the patient was often a delicate matter.

In the last year or two of my practice life, drug addicts began attending the surgery. Now, of course, we had had some before, many medically created with valium and the like. There had been occasional problems when LSD was fashionable as I have already mentioned, but the new breed was different. Heroin and cocaine are nasty and demanding. Many users had already acquired criminal records. Some were plausible and my inclination was always to trust them, though this sometimes was a mistake. In fact, I never really knew how to handle them or organise their care. Eventually special care evolved in the district which was better, but the problem was already getting out of hand when I left.

Confidentiality was a straightforward responsibility when I first entered medicine. In fact, I remember being advised of the golden rule for General Practice – 'Keep your mouth shut and your patient's bowels open'. But straightforward though it was, I occasionally slipped. I was a casualty officer when several young people were admitted. They had been involved in a multiple motor bike accident. The injuries were pretty horrendous and for a couple of hours there was mayhem. Gradually, a sort of order supervened and relatives began to arrive. A tearful couple asked about their daughter. I was reassuring. I explained that she was in theatre and that her fractures should heal satisfactorily. Then I added "and I'm pleased to say the pregnancy is fine". They looked puzzled "Well," said her dad, " we knew they were going out, but we didn't know they were courting"

Retaining confidentiality became more difficult as medicine and its organisation became more complex. The private telephone was not all that common in the '60's but as more and more people acquired one so did the risk divulging private matters to third parties increase. Leaving a message was fraught with danger. I imagine the scenario at home "Why has the doctor phoned you? What's going on?" Employing staff extended lines of communication and risked leakage. Increasing numbers of agencies began to share care, social workers, liaison nurses, practice nurses. We were not always sure who we were speaking to. And of course there was the advent of the computer.

Many doctors acquired computers in the late '80's. The machines sat on our desks and displayed the patient's record. It seemed polite to have the screen visible to the patient so that information was shared. Generally this was alright, though I always felt that to see an objective history of oneself, albeit a medical one, could be a little disturbing. Some people, though, like to peruse their own records and indeed some insist it, occasionally for legal or other important reasons. There were sometimes benefits. 'Same name' patients were prone to have other's information misfiled in their own. But there were many disadvantages. Early records, before widespread litigation became a risk, occasionally included personal comments, not all of them complimentary. A letter from the enuretic clinic read "*This little lad remains dry. His mother remains wet*". An exasperated GP wrote of another patient, "*Visited this queen of hypochondriacs for the third time…*".

There were more serious concerns though. Often a doctor's notes will include 'prompts' "*Nil definite on examination, but still feel Ca a possibility*". This can be upsetting if it is about yourself. There were times when a patient would demand that their records be altered. A lady was furious when her application for insurance cover was rejected because she had attempted suicide twice in the previous year. This had been divulged with her written permission in the medical report. She insisted that these attempts had been "not serious" and demanded the record be deleted. I could not, of course, comply.

In the course of my time in the practice, much changed. In particular, the nature and the content of the consultation changed. In the early days, patients brought with them a problem they wanted resolving. If you identified that problem and provided a solution, both you and the patient were satisfied. It was said at the time that we did not have a Health Service, but an Illness Service. Gradually, the emphasis changed. We began to talk of 'Health Promotion', anticipatory care and screening for diseases before they became apparent to either the doctor or the patient. Incorporating these into a five or ten minute consultation became increasingly difficult and we needed more staff. Much of the 'lifestyle' management, such as obesity and smoking advice was gradually delegated to a new member of staff – the Practice Nurse. She took a leading role, too, in a more formalised management of chronic diseases such as diabetes, hypertension and asthma and also contributed to screening, especially screening for cervical cancer and periodic 'check-ups' of the elderly.

But it was within the consultation itself, that opportunist screening took place. In theory, this is, of course, an excellent and sensible idea, but it was not without its ethical problems. When a patient brings a specific symptom to you, there is an implied consent to the necessary investigation and treatment. However, if you suggest to a patient that you check his blood pressure and he agrees, is he giving 'informed' consent? Is he aware of the implications? A chap saw me because he had sprained his ankle. He had not had his blood pressure done for some considerable time and he agreed to have it checked. It was high. Over the next few weeks, further checks, blood and urine tests, an ECG and a chest X-Ray made him a frequent attender at the surgery. Some years later, when he came for a review, he ruefully remembered that first appointment "I came with a bit of a limp and left with a life threatening disease". I know I didn't cause the disease and I know I might well have saved him from serious disability, but I still felt sorry I had disturbed his life, especially as the treatments at that time had some drawbacks. Perhaps, though, I became over scrupulous. After all, how would I have felt if I had not checked his blood pressure and he had developed a stroke or heart disease?

Over the last few years of my professional life there were immense changes in medical education at all levels. Undergraduate education is virtually unrecognisable now to my generation. Junior hospital posts are more humane and there is an in-built system of formal continuing training. Organised systems of Vocational Training are the norm for all specialties. Care is taken to encourage 'Personal and Professional Development' for GPs and soon there will be regular assessments of competence. It is all a far cry from those 'GP lectures' of nearly half a century ago. Medicine itself has changed, patients have changed and now the government is deeply involved. The organisation of practice has been transformed. The long stints of duty which might last 72 hours or more are no longer and out of hours care is taken care of by co-operatives or call centres. For most of my career, I felt that out of hours cover was simply part of my job and sharing with partners that responsibility both eased the stress involved and maintained some continuity of care. But as I became older, the stress became greater and I am glad that I did not have the option of delegating out of hours care outside the practice. I might have been tempted – and felt guilty.

Nowadays 'Management' dominates everywhere. I am sure that professional management is a good idea, but it was not invented for many years of my time in practice. It seems to me now from the outside, that much of management exists for the sake of management itself rather than entirely for the facilitation of patient care and the efficient use of clinical resources. Is it really necessary to cover hospitals and surgeries with mission statements and notices saying their aim is to care for patients? Shouldn't that be obvious?

I am rather glad that I worked and lived when I did. Keeping up to date was fun and had a direct impact on the job. Only in the last year or two of my medical life did 'keeping up to date' begin to mean targets, filling in innumerable questionnaires and forms and all the other aspects of a growing bureaucracy. I feel my time as a doctor was a good time, not perfect, but good; I hope my patients felt so too. I could not imagine a more fulfilling life. I do hope that in thirty or forty years time, the fledgling GP of today will be able to say exactly the same thing.

Christmas

There is an emotional intensity about Christmas that is unlike any other occasion or any other time of the year. As soon as I hear the first notes of the first carol, the hairs at the back of my neck prickle. It's always been like that, ever since I was a lad. And Christmas has always been celebrated in more or less the same way. Sometimes we have tried to 'update' it, buying new fashionable baubles and even different coloured tinsel, but the family seemed to resent any fundamental change. Tradition dominates the feast and of all the traditions the most unchanging is my consistent inability to buy the right tree. I've tried to approach it in a considered manner; I've tried to drop in and buy it spontaneously; I've tried taking the family with me for advice. Yet every year it is too big, too small, too fat, too thin, too bushy or too sparse. Sometimes, I have trimmed it into shape with the hedgetrimmers. It never escapes criticism, not entirely. And every year we debate where it should go and every year, after to-ing and fro-ing, it ends up in the window.

It is probably true to say that Christmas begins with the Christmas Fayre – yes it is always spelled like that; it gives it a historical verisimilitude. How such events came to exist and what function they perform and why we persist with them is a fertile field of study for any social scientist. Worth a Doctorate at least. But for whatever reason, they are an integral part of the liturgical year for any parish worth its salt. They used to be a sort of car boot sale without the car boot and with tinsel on. It was a place and time to exchange your tatt for someone else's and at a price. How often did we empty our broken, disused or outgrown toys on to the 'Toy Tombola' only to find our kids had won them back again.

Then, some years ago and being a well-heeled parish, we decided to go upmarket, abolish the rubbish and create stalls that sold the sort of thing that presents are made of. Well, it wasn't quite like that, not to start with. I once made jewellery. Had velvet display boards and lights and things. I did alright. I put it down to my clever marketing ploy – they were dirt cheap. Many a mother spent Christmas Day with a precious stone suspended round her neck on half a yard of gold(en) chain, a present from her loving child for less than the price of a comic. It did produce an interesting selection of pathology at the surgeries the following week. Strained necks and interesting rashes were the most common. One lady, whose gemstone (several carats in weight) was suspended on a rather generous length of heavy duty chain, did require surgical release with a hacksaw when a sudden movement of her head swung her jewel over a wall light. Overall though, I reckon Julie's home made Christmas Crackers were more successful. An unexpected epidemic in the family suddenly produced a superfluity of toilet roll holders. They were dressed up and had a 'special gift' inside, some for men and some for women. Went like a bomb they did. Which was, of course, part of the trouble. We considered an accompanying note about stout leather gloves and goggles, but decided it might affect sales. I believe they caused some excitement over the dinner tables around and about. I am not at liberty to discuss her contributions to the cake stall, though I recall considerable tension about whether they were sold or not.

I took up crib making. *Every Home Needs a Crib, A Crib is Not Just for Christmas* were some of my advertising slogans. I thought the mission statements had about them a certain cachet. Which was more than you could say for the cribs. I was unfortunately lacking in even the basic carpentry skills and depended entirely on divine inspiration for their creation. I would cheerfully hum '...*his strong hands were skilled at the plane and the lathe...*' as I plied my skills, ignoring the fact that my only tools were a rusted saw, a hammer and nails. The main feature of the cribs was their crudity which gave them a limited appeal. I have continued making and selling them ever since. Generally speaking, Christians are quite nice and charitably inclined.

I say 'generally speaking' for a good reason. Most inclinations towards charity are submerged in the cut and thrust of Christmas Fayres, especially during their setting up and preparation. I have known blood spilt over the position of a stall, for to achieve successful selling, you need *location, location, location.* And a demand from an over ambitious stallholder for TWO tables produced a crisis in the ranks that verged on the mutinous. But of all the arguments integral to a successful Fayre, the most bitter is that over when to start selling. Can one sell choice items to fellow workers before the official opening time? For many the opportunist sale to other stallholders was not to be missed and they were keen to point out that Canon Law is reticent on the subject. Others, considering Moral Law to be more binding, felt that to sell choice items before the Great British Public had a chance to view, was tantamount to fraud, usury and all sorts of other sins. I learned early to keep out of it. For those who find Christmas stressful, I would recommend helping at a Christmas Fayre. After that, a simple family Christmas is a doddle.

You get a lot of religion about at Christmastime. Much is involved in your own parish of course, but a few years ago, ecumenism was gathering strength and the different strands of Christianity were beginning to weave cautiously together. Nevertheless, I was surprised and immensely complimented when I was asked to give the address at the annual carol service of the

Methodist District on the Sunday before Christmas[16]. Especially with me being a Papist.

To this day, I swear I was told that the Service began at 6.30.pm. I had spent the afternoon in the garden, taken a leisurely bath and changed into a formal suit. As I went to clean my shoes, I heard the strains of Bing Crosby singing *White Christmas.* I sat, mud stained shoes in hand, to watch the last few minutes of the film.

A little after six, the doorbell rang and there was Don Froggett - in a state. "Are you coming? We've just started the first carol". I cursed under my breath, slipped into my shoes and was taken to the chapel.

I took my place in the first pew as the second carol finished. The minister welcomed us, not from the safety of the pulpit, but informally from the dais. I looked on the gleam of his black shoes and became acutely aware of the crust of compost around my own. As his welcome finished and the next carol began, I composed myself and felt in my pocket for my reassuring notes. They were not there. *0 God Our Help in Ages Past* was not a seasonal thought, but it was appropriate.

I have often tried to erase the memory of that sermon, but I cannot quite. The theme was peace, of which I said there are three aspects. Alas, I could only remember two. I remember telling the story of Cinderella - but neglecting to explain the allegory. Ploughing on along my uncertain, lonely furrow, I exuded anything but peace.

[16] This account was first published as *Peace and Earth* in *General Practitioner Magazine* 12th February 1988

My final act was to invite everyone to shake the hand of their neighbour and wish them well. Intending to start the process, I stepped off the dais, missed the step and went reeling from the unexpected two foot drop, up the centre aisle to the fourth row where I was brought to rest by the stout arm of Albert Wilkinson.

Ecumenism did not prosper locally for a little while, but, from that day to this, I have always listened assiduously and in awe to every sermon I have heard.

The Sermon was an unusual event. Otherwise, the usually unchanging nature of Christmas makes it difficult to distinguish one Christmas from another. Some have a distinguishing characteristic. There was the 'Blue-tac' Christmas which transformed our life, it seemed, so easy was it to put up the decorations. There was the 'Penicillin Christmas' when my inadequately dried homemade, papier-mache Crib fermented in the heat of the fire and produced copious growth of the therapeutic mould. We remained very well that year. There was the last Christmas we were all together as a family in 1995. With marriages and children, the celebration has tended to become fragmented. Now we try to meet up on Boxing Day.

I do not complain about the 'sameness' of each Christmas – I even have great affection for the traditional cliches of the season. "Wont be long now…" "It's not like it used to be…" "Of course, it's for the children really…" "Too commercial…" "You don't get the carol singers these day – one verse of '*We wish you a merry Christmas*' and they're ringing the bell…" "What are you doing this Christmas? Just quiet. The family will be round/ going to the daughter's/her mother's…" "This time next Thursday, it'll be as far away as ever…"

Christmas Eve was always a tense affair. There was a great wrapping of presents and then the checking that the pile for each child was equal to the piles of the others. This was not easy. I suppose its equivalent would be adjusting the legs of a wobbly table. So far as we knew at the time, every child got what they wanted, though nowadays, when we gather, we hear of presents that were less than welcome or of presents that were expected, but never arrived. We hear tales of lying on the bed crying. The kids were very good and rarely complained, though I did once have to go to the Christmas Sales on Boxing Day to get a giant teddy bear for Dominic. In the early days we used to go out carol singing (to a very select audience) on Christmas Eve. I enjoyed that. I never thought to ask whether anyone else did.

The pattern of the Day itself was fixed. I always preferred the early Mass myself. Midnight Mass is a scrum and uncomfortable, but Julie liked it. She reckoned that the Last Day will be just like Midnight Mass only bigger. Myself and the kids would go to the earliest Mass possible when they were young. As we drove back we would see little boys riding new bikes and little girls pushing prams. Sometimes we would see fathers playing football on the Green, giving the new ball and oversize strip an airing. We returned for bacon rolls. I would bank up the fire, put on the carols and check the lights were working. Then each collected a cardboard box and we processed into the 'Carpet room' for the distribution of presents. Even now, any family members in the vicinity assemble for what's under the tree. And then to sherry, beer, G&T or whatever. One year we had proper cocktails, but they didn't half diminish the intellect. We didn't repeat it.

Everybody seemed to gather in the kitchen to prepare vegetables, though we all tried to avoid the sprouts. Some read their new books, listened to their new records or put on their Christmas sweater. I had a Christmas tie once. It played carols if you pressed the bottom. It did have a habit, though, of switching on inadvertently. Lunch was a prolonged affair with splendid wines. I don't remember a lot about the lunches when the kids were very young, perhaps I have wiped them from my memory. One could guarantee that at least one of them would be ill – even that became part of the tradition.

There always used to be a good film on in the evening, after the Comedy Special. Once the kids were in bed, we could relax with a turkey sandwich and a glass of wine. Now all you get is damned 'Soaps' – a way of enjoying Christmas by proxy for some.

Sometimes, especially as the family became older, we had a party, but as they left home and founded their own dynasties, we held the party on Boxing Day. Everyone was expected to do a 'turn'. Some were remarkably ingenious. As grandchildren arrived and grew, they joined in. The first time they performed formally was for great-grandma. The Nativity Play was quite short and took place on the landing outside her room. It was quite moving. In later years, we did a puppet show of *Cinderella*. It was alright. The trouble with these things is the casting. Kids are always prone to take their bat home and are rarely satisfied with the part they're offered. Which explains how we came to present *Snow White and the Five Dwarves*. We were down to four for the second half.

Christmas, for me though, was always dominated by the rota of duties. The organisation of the rota was always done democratically, but was rarely satisfying to anyone. Christmas Eve tended to be busy medically as well as socially, but at least you got it over with. Christmas Day was the quietest day of the lot and it was rare to get trivial calls. Boxing Day was often a nightmare. Not only were you faced with the many who had delayed their call out of consideration, but also there were those who'd had a miserable Christmas and seemed to wish to spread their misery. It was rare for anyone to have a complete Christmas off duty and many times did I dream of a job where Christmas was a holiday.

The balance between duty to the family and duty to the patients was always a delicate one. Sometimes the two combined well. We had delivered a lady of healthy boy in the early hours of Christmas Day. As I drove the kids back from Mass at about 9 o'clock, I thought I'd pop in to see her. She was well and said I could bring the family in. It was a special time, though I think some of the younger ones were a little confused about who the baby was.

Not all such 'pop-ins' were as happy and fulfilling. The 'flu was beginning to appear in late December and I had seen a youngish chap on Christmas Eve with the familiar symptoms. He felt unwell and shivery and had a dry cough, but was sitting watching television. He had a slight fever, but otherwise there was little to find amiss. Only one thing, his pulse was faster than I expected. I gave him the usual advice and asked him to ring me if he didn't improve over the next couple of days. The following morning I was off duty, but on the way back from church, I felt I ought to see him. His wife opened the door. "Oh he's much better. In fact, he's been playing silly buggers this morning", his wife said when she saw me. I went through to see him in the bedroom. He was pale and his hands were cold with a bluish tinge. He talked a lot and laughed until he coughed. His chest was moist when I listened and his pulse was rapid and weak. Whatever had been wrong yesterday, he now had an obvious fulminating bacterial infection. I admitted him forthwith, but by eleven o'clock he was dead. I went to see the family. There is little to be said at such times, but much to be thought about.

Death is always sad, but it is particularly poignant when it occurs at Christmas especially as you know that for the rest of their lives, Christmas will be blighted for the family by that memory. One Christmas, I'm not sure how it happened, but I was up for long periods on four consecutive nights. I think it was a combination of a sick partner and another who was away. In the course of that time I had four deaths. The first was quite unexpected. A man arrived home from work on Christmas Eve, took off his coat, sat in a chair and died. Another man with chronic heart failure, suddenly deteriorated and died in the early hours. On Christmas Day, two men who had terminal cancer died within an hour or two of each other. It might have been really depressing, it was certainly draining. And then I thought, suppose there had never been a Christmas Day? All this suffering would have been quite pointless. But there was and is a Christmas and somewhere in that truth is an explanation.

There was a curious sequel to that Christmas. All the people who had died were to be cremated. This meant that I had to request a second opinion as to the likely cause of death. Normally, this is a formality, but four deaths? I phoned a colleague whom I had known for years. He was obviously surprised and as he questioned me about the circumstances, I was aware of his concern. I often thought of that during the sad and terrible saga of Dr Shipman. The death rate in his practice must have been so much higher than normal. How did it pass unremarked for so long?

Not all deaths were truly tragic. That may seem an odd thing to say, but it is true. Take Jack Sampson for instance.[17] I was drifting into that curious Limbo-state that occurs in those hours on Christmas Day that lie somewhere between the extended lunch and the premature tea. A confusion of gastronomic satisfaction, emotional well being and that special sort of tiredness derived from an early morning and a smiling day.

Harry Sampson abruptly dispersed this mood with an apologetic phone call. "Ah'm sorry to bother you doctor at y'tea but dad's feeling queer like and he don't look so cracky either. Can you send somebody to have a look at him?" I couldn't remember his dad. "Aye well you won't know him. Me mam passed on in t'summer and he's been a bit low like, so we thought we'd have a bit of a family do at our house and bring him on with it being Christmas like. Our Sarah and George are here an'all from Goldthorpe" "But what actually is wrong with your dad?" I asked. "Well he's just sort of queer like. Will y'come?" There seemed no option and little else of value to obtain over the phone. "I'll be down in a few minutes."

Oddly, once I was out, I enjoyed the short drive through the deserted, frosted streets to the neat semi-detached bungalow in the neat semi-detached rows.

The sound of the Sampson family at Christmas drowned my knocking at the front door. Silly, I thought, Harry might have left the back-to-backs, but he will never be a front door man.

Sure enough, the back door was open and as I went in, I was assailed by the noise of Christmas. Walt Disney, whirring cars,

[17] This account originally appeared as *Come up Smiling* in *World Medicine*. Edited by Michael O'Donnell. 10th December 1983

205

kids shouting, laughing, crying all at once, loud grown up conversation and strident, if uncertain notes on the keyboard organ.

Edging my way around the disorganised table in the kitchen, I found Harry and his brother George pint-glassed in conversation in the small hall. "Can ah get y' one?" Harry asked. "Nay, I'll have a look at your dad first", I said.

The front room was a sea of people of all ages and activities. With difficulty, I negotiated the present-strewn floor and already sagging streamers to find Grandad. Sitting in an easy chair, Napoleonic party hat askew, mince pie clasped in his right hand, tea cooling at his left, he was obviously dead and smiling. I found my way back to Harry and George "I'm sorry", I said, "I think he's passed on'. "Ah told thee din't ah", said George.

"What's on now then," asked Harry. "I reckon it'll be a coroner's case", I said. "But it seems a pity to spoil the day", I admitted. "That's a facer! Never bother" they said, "You'll not spoil his day".

After some discussions, we thought it best to move Grandad out of the room. I knew it was not in the best interests of Forensic science, but it was Christmas. The three of us moved through the party to Grandad, moved his pie and tea and lifted him and the chair, carrying it out to the bedroom. He remained smiling.

The Police Officer standing in for the Coroner's Officer was convivial when I phoned and understood the situation. They were at the house within a few minutes. They took off their caps. I thought that was nice. After a cup of tea and informal questioning, the elder Mr Sampson was moved away in the van. His paper hat fell into the gutter

I didn't think the kids had noticed Grandad had gone, but one said "Uncle Harry, where's Grandad gone?" "Nipped up to heaven," he said. Auntie Ivy, Grandad's sister, cried a bit.

"Now then, Doctor, will you have that drink?" asked Harry. "A small sherry please", I said and then unthinkingly, "All the best, Cheers, have a good Christmas". "Ah'll drink to that", said George "but I'll tell thee what. We'll never have such a good un as Dad just did".

I have mentioned earlier that, with the exception of odd years, every Christmas tends to fuse into one. There was one year, though, which stands out. It was the year of smells. It was also the year when I was sorely troubled by the irritations of General Practice. And the biggest irritants to me were Fred and Cynthia.[18]

It all began innocently enough. In fact that particular Christmas Eve we were remarkably well ahead of schedule.

By mid-afternoon we had evened up the kids' presents. This is not, as I've mentioned, a task to be underestimated. We had even, for the first (and last) time actually prepared the vegetables ready for Christmas dinner and the turkey waited in the oven.

It was then, with some delight, that we spotted the first Christmas snow in the hitherto unrelenting rain. "Snow, snow" cried the kids and, in a flurry of coats and wellies, they rushed headlong into the wet garden.

Inevitably the bedraggled remains soon found their way back into the kitchen to change ready for the carol singing. Soggy

[18] This originally appeared as *God Rest You, Michael Balint* in *World Medicine* edited by Michael O'Donnell. 12th December 1981

coats were spread to dry, but the wellies were a problem. A child more perspicacious than the others slipped hers unnoticed onto the bottom shelf of the oven to dry. "Come on everybody - early beds, so let's go singing," cried an unusually relaxed mother and again there were flurries of activity before setting off on our round. "Won't be a minute", cried Julie. "I'll just start the turkey"

Our return had something of the Dunkirk about it. Kids full of chocolate and pop, tired and excited, wet and cold.

To our horror the house was filled with a thin, foul-smelling, rubber smoke that became denser as we approached the kitchen. Within the oven, a pair of Dali like wellies had melted over the floor of the oven. Thank God the turkey was unsullied.

The subsequent happenings were blurred and overwhelming. Consoling the crying, feeding the hungry, bathing the dirty, deodourising the odorous, calming the sleepy and all the while smiling and trying to be happy.

Then midnight. My whisky (was I ever so entitled) was nectar. Now Julie and I could glimpse the peace of Christmas and view the coming day with excited calm. And how our bed was welcoming and welcome and the dark stillness was the essence of Christmas.

Alas, it was not the Christmas bells of peace that rang at one o'clock, but Cynthia Sidebottom. "She's really bad this time doctor", panted her poor crushed, sweating husband (God why did he always sweat so) for the umpteenth time this year.

'What's up now then, Fred," I asked, fearing his reply. "Ooh, she's gone too far this time. I can't cope" (How could he even try?) "It's Christmas. It's too much for her – she's having a right breakdown. Come as quick as you can" and he hung up still panting. He hadn't told me the address. I hadn't asked. It was a time only for essentials. We all knew where Cynthia lived.

I pulled my trousers and sweater over my pyjamas and crept quietly through the darkened house, terrified of waking the light-sleeping children. "Is it Christmas now, dad?" said a voice. "Shh. Santa's about". I slipped out of the front door to the now miserable wet night.

There is something special about the night before Christmas. Many of the decorations still glowed. There was no traffic. Ghostly, hazed voices cried greetings. Late revellers sang carols of a sort.

But Cynthia was on my mind. I always found it difficult to think about Cynthia as a doctor should. That night was no exception and I arrived at the house with no clear idea of what I was to do.

Why was the house so hot? Fag in hand, knee length dressing gown revealing less than clean, black-nailed feet, Gerald panted "Oh I'm glad you've come. I can't face it". The quilted bar in the corner had seen some action, I thought, and every ash-tray was spilling its heaped contents. The socks in the hearth were not for Father Christmas. They were Fred's. By hell, were they Fred's.

Cynthia sat and lay over the pseudo-leather Chesterfield, her 'Baby-Doll' nightie barely covering her bulk. Her eyes were closed, but poured tears and her sobs stretched out across the tufted carpet. "Take a grip, lad," I thought, "Remember St Francis and Sigmund Freud"

It needed neither special communication skills, nor insight, nor empathy to open a flood of emotional enormity which threatened to drown me. "Me headache's worse and me nerves are tearing me up and Fred doesn't understand and why does his mother have to come for dinner tomorrow and we always go there and he's not brought me a present…" ("Working today", panted Fred while she drew breath) "…and the turkey's still froze and he's late again from work and …… and ……"

I made a sympathetic noise. The flood increased. Time for non-verbal communication. I leaned forward intently and deliberately to control the flow.

Deep-sunk in an easy chair, the sudden movement was too much for the button on my pyjama trousers and it popped. The resultant loss of security somewhat diminished my confidence.

I made more noises. My open statements were unheard or when they were heard, they merely increased the tide. I strove for understanding and enlightenment. The heat was overpowering and, combined with the vapours from Fred's socks, I began to lose my will to live. I abandoned my counselling mode. "Time for bed, love", I said.

I was aware that I had only minutes of standing and walking before my pyjama pants slid to straddle uncomfortably and obviously the bifurcation of my trousers. With a mighty heave I prised her off the couch - alas only as far as the floor where she remained or all fours. With persuasion, she crawled to the bedroom. Thank God it's a bungalow, I thought, but, oh Lord, there were more of Fred's socks around the bed.

She fell across the quilted bed, half kneeling, sobbing and wailing, her vast buttocks emerging from her baby doll pants. Speeded by my obviously descending pyjamas I drew up the Largactil and with admirable dexterity, I plunged in the sedative and with a final effort lifted her into bed.

"Sleep well love", I said. And then I said it and never did it seem so appropriate. "Never mind, love, this time tomorrow it'll be as far away as ever".

It might seem odd to have spent so long talking about the delights – and the vicissitudes - of Christmas, but throughout my professional life there was the continued and continual dilemma of choosing between the priorities of family, practice, patients and one's self interest. At Christmas, the dilemmas become acute. Sometimes, the choice was easy. An urgent call to a convulsing child obviously takes precedence over the ritual of distributing presents. Sometimes, the decision is more difficult. Should I leave my Christmas dinner to go (for the umpteenth time that year) to an alcoholic who is causing mayhem again? What about his wife and family?

I have to admit that when the priorities were difficult, I tended to respond to the patient on the strength of 'You never know. Even the most difficult and neurotic of patients gets ill sometimes. And all of them die eventually. Perhaps today's the day'. You can never trust the unhappy, the neurotic or the hypochondriac. A young mother from a problem family and with a problem family of her own saw us frequently with a variety of trivial matters. She seemed incapable of coping with anything. Being grossly overweight, she had referred herself to the nurse's dieting clinic at one time, but, over several weeks of trying, had lost no weight. In fact her girth was spreading. The nurse asked me to see her. She had an enormous ovarian cyst, the sort you read about in textbooks. So, you never know.

There were many disadvantages to my attitude and many of those disadvantages were borne by Julie and the family. It was not easy in those days before answer phones and bleeps and co-operatives. Families became sucked into the GP's life. And yet, at Christmas, despite the distractions and inconveniences, somehow being a GP seemed even more fulfilling. Many patients sent cards or gave presents. One patient who was acutely ill while staying in the district many years ago still sends me a card every Christmas and thanks me. The local parish church choir always called to sing at our house. Patients wished us well. I think it was all worth it.

Enthusiasms

General Practitioners mix with all sorts of people in a variety of circumstances. Moreover, in the days when I practised, it was usual for a GP to spend a lifetime in the same place. As a result, not only did you become familiar with most of your patients, you became familiar with their children and even with their children's children. This long term association and the many thousands of consultations, often in intimate circumstances, give doctors unique insights into human behaviour especially when they are under stress. The responses of people who are troubled physically or emotionally varies from the pathetic to the heroic and can fluctuate between the tragic and the farcical. This wide range of behaviour and emotion that forms and shapes the General Practitioner's day also forms and shapes the doctors themselves. It should not surprise anyone, then, that the doctor gradually develops attitudes that are a complex mixture of arrogance, cynicism, compassion, resignation, frustration and a capacity to be continually surprised. As a consequence, GPs have a tendency to philosophical meanderings and opinions about most things. And if a doctor has a literary bent, then he or she will be prone to try to express all this in writing.

For the most part, the writing is simply a personal catharsis, but since there are few more delights than seeing your name in print, some of these writings may be submitted for publication. Now exposing one's thoughts in public has its own stresses, especially if the chosen medium is the permanent one of the print. Moreover, allowing an editor to assess the value of your writing is, I think, far more fraught than exposing one's body to the eyes and hands of an enquiring doctor. I have always found rejection profoundly depressing, a bit like being told your baby is ugly. For me rejection is always personal.

Nevertheless, I enjoy writing, though I sometimes wonder if I enjoy playing at being a writer even more than writing itself.[19] I like the scenario. The concentrated pose of the figure bent over his current love. The paper and notes scattered excitingly over the table. The spot lamp drawing to higher things the languorous smoke from the half-neglected pipe. The staccato sounds of the typewriter against the background hush of inspiration.

I once tried writing in the garden. I liked it. I sat in a cane chair with a glass of coarse red wine at my right hand. The hot, still, July sun warmed over my left shoulder. Birds sang, but only softly. The pages remained empty. No matter. In their emptiness was always the potential of a great novel. This was true Bohemia. People dropped by to chat about things literary and took wine with me. (I have to admit this is something of an exaggeration, but my wife did call once, from her labours in the vegetable bed, to ask me what I was doing. "Writing," I replied. 'Oh," she said.)

I have always felt that creative typewriting should be done with, at most, three fingers. The art seems finer for being difficult and laborious. I wish, though, I could do it as fast as they do it at the 'Pictures', like Jack Lemmon in *The Front Page.*

Writing is a fine alibi when it comes to household chores and is an excuse second only to illness to avoid unwanted social contact. It also reassures your wife that your creative urges are within the confines of your own home. A problem soon loomed, though. "Dad's writing" became an increasingly common topic of conversation. We discussed at length subject and style. We anguished over the opening paragraph. We debated the relative merits of the latest "How to Write" books. We were communally

[19] A modified version of this first appeared in *The GP Writer* (No.3, 1987) and is incorporated here by permission of the editor

puzzled by the lack of appreciation of editors and publishers. The conversation was, alas, becoming all too theoretical. A large, unasked question hung in the air. "When do we get to see the printed page?"

It was not entirely my fault. I was dogged by misfortune from the time I first started. 'Dogged' is not the most appropriate word, since it was an untoward bowel movement of the cat that desecrated my first manuscript – an essay on *Anything You Can Do, I Can Do Better.* The first piece of literature that I had accepted coincided with the resignation of the whole editorial board of the journal. My second acceptance letter was followed, within a few days, by a letter expressing regret that the magazine had now ceased publication. A further manuscript was returned in an unopened envelope marked 'Gone Away'.

Well, perhaps it was all coincidence, but it made me think. It might have been my style, I suppose. I've had a lot of trouble with my style. The problem was, I had only to skim through a book, or even read a review and I fell under the influence of the author. I had firmly resisted Shakespeare because I feared literary apoplexy. I envied Somerset Maugham his long, convoluted descriptions, but tried not to emulate him for fear of constipation. Besides, he didn't give you many laughs to the page. Kipling's prose left me, I thought, unaffected, but no matter how or where I tried to write poetry, I was followed inevitably by the *Green Eye of the Little Yellow God.* Gerard Manley Hopkins seemed a better bet so far as poetry was concerned, but I never got the hang of sprung rhythm. Perhaps it would have helped had I read him aloud at the bottom of a concrete spiral staircase, as suggested in *The Times* some years ago, but I didn't have access to one. And a carpeted Victorian stair proved less than helpful. Anyway, there soon proved to be a limit to the number of objects you could describe as *'dappled'*.

A holiday in Laugharne cast me firmly under the spell of Dylan Thomas. I think I suffered from being under that influence, but then, so did he. For some time, I *"spit spewed spirit sighs on my tip tap tippety typewriter, Tipp-ex encrusted oracle of a being, breathing the life of my heron grey soul"*. I'm not sure that I have entirely recovered. If I don't watch out, I still stray, at the drop of a hat, into a winter wet outside.

I became involved in a passionate, posthumous love affair with the writings of Patrick O'Donovan. I met him once in his later years. He had about him a beautiful sadness. We were anxious as to how best to entertain such a great man, but he was thrilled with Wakefield, mainly, I think because he found a shop here that sold real brawn. His writing was like he was. I don't think I fully appreciated its delights when I read it in its original form in newspaper columns. But what great pleasure it was to see (in a book of his collected writings) those lyrical sentences spread across a proper page like rolling meadows, separated by short, sharp hedgerows of words that surprised and intrigued. The savouring of each sentence was impaired only by anticipation of the next.

I had always admired Richard Asher who was able, with apparent ease, to illuminate even staid, dust dry medical journals with the light of easy prose. I find it difficult to follow his example. I was encouraged to hear that he sometimes revised an article a score of times before he was satisfied that it was fit for publication. Now I can admire any man who is capable of writing an article twenty times, but I worry about a man who actually did it.

Our Parish Priest reckoned that writing is an escape into one's own world where no one can follow. There may be something in that. But it is certainly not the whole answer. If it were, then why publish (or in my case, why try to publish)? Perhaps it's about love. Just as one likes to share the fruits of one's love with the rest of the world, so is the desire to show to all mankind 'your' literary conception and realisation. There can be few more satisfying pleasures than that derived from an acceptance letter. Someone else appreciates, shares joy in your creation. Conversely, there is nothing more devastating than the rejection slip. With one exception. Gardening magazines seem different. Rejection by them is sometimes almost pleasurable. They seem to imply that you are far too good for their journal. That's nice. And comforting, even if it isn't true.

But I digress. That's the trouble with enjoying writing, you start off aiming for Manchester and, before you know it, you're looking at the daffodils in Farndale. What I really wanted to explain was that the rich experience of General Practice when combined with a love of writing makes it increasingly likely that you will be prone to pontificate on most things and if you find an editor sympathetic to your thoughts, you might get published. Eventually I did find such an editor and several disparate pieces were published.

Many of these reflected my interest in recording the usually unremarked hazards of a GP's life. And one of the greatest hazards I experienced in my surgery was the mucky patient. A teenager (usually) may present themselves in all the right gear with tee shirt, baseball cap, large tongued trainers and torn jeans, but it was surprisingly common to find their necks, especially, were ingrained with longstanding grime. Foot problems held special dangers. It really is true that many patients wash only the problem appendage and are horrified when you ask to see the other foot for comparison. Their horror is nothing to that of the doctor who has to view and smell the soggy nauseating extremity. But unclean bums are worse; they really do test your resolve to examine patients properly. And I never ceased to be amazed at squelchy carpets. Kneeling to examine a patient's belly risks wet knees and worse.

On the other hand, it always seemed to me, some patients were over zealous in their hygiene. I don't know how they found time to have several baths or showers every day. After I had met several of these zealots in a week, I meditated on the risks of bathing[20].

Bathing has become only recently a habit of the civilized. While it is true that the Romans did it, and with some style, it didn't catch on for centuries in the Western world. And then, for many years, the average British citizen was content with the ritual of the weekly bath. This may have had something to do with the
• lack of a defined bathroom. Certainly the delight of a hot bath in front of a roaring coal fire was hard won. Now, in our leisured, well-plumbed society, few people would care to admit to less than three or four baths a week - and some would take that many each day.

So well established is the habit, that it is no surprise to find that it has become 'medicalised'. In 1989, one medical authority stated that '*Personal hygiene is central to good health and well-being*' and implied that '*the availability or provision of help in bathing (the elderly) is an important criterion of health care.*'

---

[20] This first appeared as "*On Having a Bath*" in *Yorkshire Medicine* (Vol 4 No. 1, 1991) and is incorporated here by permission of the editor and publisher

I question the assumption that bathing is good for you - at least in a medical sense. *'Cleanliness is ... next to godliness'* is all very well, but John Wesley was addressing *'slovenly'* sinners, not members of the Royal Colleges. Are we not guilty of foisting on gullible patients our own middle-class concepts, concepts bred of the blandishments of the advertisers and the fairy tales of Hollywood? Have we any evidence in favour of bathing other than the visual and sensual images conjured up by 'a long soak in a hot tub'? Does a bath achieve any more than the removal of old sweat or visible dirt?

The best established benefit is that of assuaging the aches and pains of unaccustomed or excessive exercise. I know of no controlled assessment of this effect, but would be prepared to accept it on the basis that a little hyperaemia may ease muscle pain. And of course everybody knows it helps. So that's that then.

If we are honest, the most common motive for recommending bathing is to reduce human smells. The invention (advertisers again) of *'BO'* has produced such a complex of social guilt that to smell of honest sweat has now become the one great deadly sin left to our society. It is this guilt that we pass on to our patients, particularly the elderly.

Human smell arises mainly from the apocrine glands in groin and armpit and the hair, the feet and the excretory orifices. Old people sweat little and the smell they exude is more likely to be stale cabbage than 'Body Odour'. Unless, that is, they happen to be incontinent. If they are so afflicted, then the smell will originate from a small area of body surface and will be emitted regularly and steadily. I fail to see how total immersion, with all its attendant risks, can possibly be a justifiable remedy, especially since its benefits last, at best, only a few hours.

Jack suffered his stroke as he was getting out of the bath and slipped back in. He was unable to raise himself and lay speechless in the cooling water until his wife, missing him, broke in the door. The difficulty we had in lifting him out assumed the nature of pure farce.

If one spent a little time in planning a dangerous room, I suspect we would design a bathroom. A door, lockable and unlockable only from the inside; a tiny room with no space to fall comfortably; an exciting mixture of electricity and water; an available store of drugs and sharp instruments; and a floor which, when wet, might make the slowest turn a gamble. The temperature of the hot water is capricious and sets the stage for disaster. Who has not escaped hypothermia or widespread scalding only by speed of thought, fleetness of foot and accuracy of hand-eye co-ordination? The Home Accident Surveillance System (HASS) recorded 2,149 accidents in the bathroom in 1980.

Not that the dangers belong only to the bather. The confined space and the design and position of the bath make vulnerable those who would aid the frail and unable, especially when they are soaked and soaped. Back injuries in nurses are common enough without us inflicting on them this dangerous and hardly necessary activity. And if nurse is suddenly incapacitated, what price the patient?

There is a well established fallacy which indicates that bathing cleans the skin of infection. And yet we know that the assiduous scrubbing of the surgeon's hands makes only a transient impact on his bacterial flora. In fact, in an active skin infection such as impetigo, bathing increases the spread and persistence of the infection, allowing the comparatively immobile staphylococcus to move, effortlessly and at will, to parts otherwise inaccessible to it. As for fungi and yeasts, they thrive on moist warmth. The scabies mite is impervious to simple bathing, though removal of skin grease may make it available to more effective treatment. Lice will survive, especially if infected clothing is ignored. And nits are waterproof.

Our skin is blessed with natural protection, but in the newborn it is not developed and in the elderly it has deteriorated. The newborn infant has some temporary protection from its coating of vernix. This natural defence is however, usually washed away fairly quickly by a diligent nurse. Sometimes, this zeal exposes the infant and his companions to outbreaks of skin infections, especially with the ever threatening staphylococci. This in turn leads to widespread use of antiseptic substances in the bath water with all its possible problems. And why are little babies bathed so often anyway? Apart from their bottom ends they must be the cleanest creatures on God's earth. Perhaps the function of the daily bath is really to provide a defined period of active 'bonding' and occupational therapy for the new mother.

The elderly skin often irritates as it dries in the drought of passing years, flaking in the absence of natural oils. It is the unthinking, socially conscious and unwise carer who will further degrease this skin with frequent soapy baths. Let us hear the prayer of the elderly unwashed: *"0 Lord, let me be "topped" by a skilful hairdresser, "tailed" by a caring nurse and, 0 Lord, let me dust my bath in peace. With a long handled duster.'*

By all means, let us bathe and encourage bathing, but let us not pretend that it is 'medically advisable'. Let us rather glory in the pleasure for its own sake and in the retrospective joy of our return to the womb.

My enthusiasm for writing ebbed and flowed over the years, for it was not only the vagaries of human nature that intrigued me. The close association with people for a long period of time meant that I became involved with them on a personal level as well as being a professional adviser. As a result, I became interested in their work, their lives, their hobbies and their own enthusiasms – enthusiasms that were catching.

Which brings me naturally to my ambitions to play the violin. One of the first home visits I made was to a lady who had just given birth. Over the next few months I grew to know her and her family fairly well. Her husband was, at the time, learning to play the violin. Now, by a strange coincidence, I had a violin which had been given to me by my father-in-law and I became overwhelmed by a desire to play it. You may recall I had had an ill-fated flirtation with the instrument in my schooldays but I thought I had retained some of the rudiments of the skills of playing. I re-strung the fiddle (inscribed *Stradivarius* on the inside) and started to practise. It was a painful time. I acquired a teacher, but the pain was still slow to go away. Vic, whose enthusiasm had originally infected me, had heard of a 'Beginners' Orchestra' in Denby Dale. We joined. Within the first twenty minutes of the first rehearsal, I had moved rapidly down the pecking order from leader of the first violins to the rearmost ranks of the seconds. I suspect it was because it took me just out of earshot. My abiding memory of my time at Denby Dale was of a continual struggle with *Eine Kleine Nachtmusik*. Even now, whenever I hear it, I get palpitations of anxiety during the fast bits and consciously relax during the slow movement.

I never achieved any great skill, no matter how I tried. I think my fundamental problem was that I never listened to what I was playing, but heard only what I was supposed to be playing. Fortunately, for all sorts of reasons, the pressures of my proper job overtook me and I abandoned my orchestral ambition. I still have the violin and I sometimes look at it and wonder how good I might have been had I persisted. No, best not think about it.

I did not however entirely lose my enthusiasm for music. I had first acquired pleasure listening to music while at school and when I was studying for A levels, I had an impulse to attend the City of Birmingham "Proms" at the Victoria Hall, Hanley. I was hooked, but ignorant. A few years later I married into Music. Julie's family ate and breathed music. One morning, while I was staying at their house, I was in the bathroom, brushing my teeth and humming. As I came out, Julie's dad was waiting on the landing. Now Julie's dad sang in Opera and also taught singing. I stood there on their freezing landing while he explained the inadequacy of my techniques. He explained about the importance of my diaphragm and how my voice should travel up through my sinuses and project. Now, to be honest, I was too cold to absorb all this. Nevertheless, years later I could still recall it and the thought began to dawn that perhaps my great gift for music might lie in my God given instrument, my voice.

I had for a long time been convinced that I had an exquisitely sensitive musical ear. Though few shared my view, I remained convinced. If I drive over a certain set of cobbles in the lane, at a certain speed, I can hear the opening bars of 'The Bartered Bride' overture. I have confirmed Gilbert White's observation that tawny owls hoot in B flat (though the one in our garden was prompted to a reasonable Top C when the cat strayed inadvertently near her). Now some people might consider it a privilege, a great benefit. It is not. It lays you open to all sorts of suffering. And the greatest suffering of all is electronic music. Why are even the football results accompanied by electronic music? Who writes the stuff? If I go to Hell, I will hear nothing but electronic music played on compact discs. For ever.

I used to phone my GP colleagues occasionally and many had this bizarre invention playing while you awaited the transfer of your call. In one surgery the tune was, I swear, *'There Once Was an Indian Maid'* - a somewhat bawdy ballad last heard in the students' bar. (The Practice vow it is *'American Patrol'*, but I bet Glenn Miller would never own it). Another practice, fairly self-effacing too, played *'Thine is the Glory'*. At least it put you in the right frame of mind to talk to your GP.

I felt that I could not ignore these two priceless gifts of a distinctive voice (I always assumed that that was a compliment) and my concept of perfect pitch. This despite contrasting opinions of my qualities. I began to sing loudly in church, a most un-Catholic thing to do. At the end of Mass, the man in front of me turned round "Do you sing in a choir?" he asked. I beamed "I don't actually" "I'm not bloody surprised" he said and left. And him a Christian too. I was more influenced by two patients. One was an elderly chap who was still singing and still loved it. "Clears the tubes", he would say. And the other was a distraught lady who consulted me about the deterioration in her voice. Her pitch had deepened and she was no longer able to keep her place in the sopranos, but had been transferred to the altos. She feared worse might follow. The choir was her whole life and she dreaded losing it. I found her thyroid had slowed down and replacement therapy restored her to her rightful place. She was immensely grateful. I caught their enthusiasm and I joined the Sharlston Male Voice Choir. Of all the groups and societies I have ever joined, this was by far the most welcoming. Mind you, they hadn't heard me sing at that stage and fortunately there was no voice test.

It was a most enjoyable few years. We gave concerts, took part in competitions and enjoyed festivals. After our weekly rehearsals and our performances, we would usually go for a pint or two. Almost inevitably, we would sing and no-one seemed to mind. Unfortunately, I never quite grasped the concept of harmony and could never read music except in a vague sort of up and down way. One of the problems I had was being on call every second or third week and being unable to attend rehearsals. I grew frustrated and felt that I was letting them down. So I retired, gracefully, I hope.

At about the same time that I joined the Sharlston Choir, a group of chaps from our parish were discussing a looming crisis in the Church. St Patrick's Night was getting closer and while the disco had been planned (that is somebody was bringing a record player) there was no proper entertainment booked. And entertainment was always an integral part of such a night. Somehow, by the second pint, someone said they knew the words to *The Rose of Tralee* and someone else had a book of Irish folk songs. And there was a young chap in the parish who played a guitar. And so The Misfits were born. We decided that we were a sort of folk group. But if the concept was full of hope and joy, the birth was traumatic. Why we tried to sing *The Irish Rover* is a mystery to this day. No-one ever owned up to suggesting it. Starting in three different keys was unfortunate; trying to get our tongues round the complexity of under-rehearsed words was disastrous. We did though manage to get through *The Wild Rover* and this was sufficient to persuade us that we had something to offer the world. In retrospect it was a sort of *Folie de Cinque*.

225

We did improve slowly and we acquired more musicians until, at our peak, there were about a dozen of us. We expanded our repertoire and rehearsed every Sunday night. Our bookings increased – at times up to two or three a month. Overall, we produced quite a reasonable sound. Most audiences seemed to enjoy the evenings, but we had our share of disasters. Occasionally, we would come across an audience who didn't seem to notice we were there. This is very depressing. On one occasion we were upstaged. As we finished our first set and enjoyed the beer break, the club steward asked if we could let Martha sing one of her songs. Of course we would , we said in a condescending way and after our opening song of the second set, we announced her. There was a roar of applause which rather suggested relief and Martha eased herself slowly to the stage. She must have been nearly 90 and was blind. To make matters worse, she had a beautiful clear voice and sang one of those special Irish ballads that ooze tragedy and emotion. The audience were enraptured. She sang an encore – and then another. We fidgetted and began to feel superfluous. It was difficult getting back on and, after Martha, I don't know if anyone was really bothered.

We played together for ten fruitful and happy years in many venues throughout the North of England, usually for a variety of charitable causes. We even made a tape. But life became busier, some of the chaps moved away and we eventually disbanded. We were always proud of the fact that we had lasted as long as the Beatles. We did get together once more some years later. It was an enjoyable evening. I would like to record that we sang our greatest hits, but that was not strictly true – we were expected to occupy most of the evening after all. The concert was a sellout. This was a great comfort as we moved into retirement, pondering on what might have been.

I was slow to develop an enthusiasm for the visual arts. I don't remember noticing pictures or sculpture in my youth. Most of those I did see were the religious art in church. Unfortunately, popular Catholic art when I was young was a garish mixture of the bloody and the sentimental. How much it encouraged devotion I cannot say, but it did nothing to develop a critical sense of the aesthetic. I do however remember becoming fond of a book my elder brother gave me for my 18th birthday, *A Book of Delights*. It contained excerpts from great literature, some poetry and, above all, beautiful reproductions of paintings. I used to return to it over the years.

I did not visit art galleries in my youth; in fact the first time I did was when I went to University. It had been drummed into me that University was an opportunity to become not just trained, but educated. So I went to the theatre, went to museums and went to look at pictures. I do recall the awe I experienced at seeing original paintings, but my eye was untutored and my mind uninformed. My appreciation stopped with wonder at the skill with which fellow humans could with their minds and hands create so beautiful an image from paint and canvas or from stone and metal. I fear my critical faculty has developed little since that time. I have recently been exposed to some of the greatest examples of Western art yet that which overwhelmed me was the 'incomplete' stone sculptures of Michelangelo in the Academia in Florence. It was seeing the emergence of beauty from the unhewn stone that revealed with great clarity the wonder of the artist.

Sometimes, I bought a painting from an art student. This gave them a few bob in their pockets and satisfied me that I had become a patron of the arts and was pushing forward the boundaries of civilisation.

Yet the visual arts did not, for a long time, seem particularly relevant to everyday life. However, once we were married, it seemed natural to put something on the walls. My main criteria were, I remember, do I like it and can I live with it. We sometimes used the borrowing scheme run by the Art Gallery. It was helpful, though I think we chose them more for decoration than any aesthetic reason.

It was only after I began visiting patients in their own homes that I began to appreciate the importance of pictures. I always felt it a great privilege to be welcomed into so many homes. Apart from everything else, it seemed to me an integral part of the life of a GP. A patient on their own patch is a real person, more confident in themselves and a more equal partner in the consultation. And yet they are also more vulnerable. Their virtues and their inadequacies are exposed; their life is open. The modern GP does not seem to appreciate the immense social and clinical benefits of home visits or, if they do, consider the time taken to be better spent elsewhere.

Most of the wall decoration seemed to me of no great consequence. It was a time when various types of birds flew up and down many walls of many sitting rooms and bedrooms. Now enormous butterflies rest on the outside walls. The commonest pictures seemed to come from Boots; the child with the shining tear below its eye, the Eastern lady in brightly coloured jacket with flowers scattered about. Elephants trumpeted from some walls, but the *"Stag at Bay"* era had passed. But what some patients had on their walls was often illuminating and frequently an introduction to another, deeper layer of personality, experience or family history. "That's an interesting drawing". "Do you like it? My husband did that at Art College" "Does he still draw?" "No. His dad pulled him out to go down the pit. Never touches it now". I knew her husband well. His frustrated talent explained a lot.

I have mentioned Albert before. When I was visiting him during his last illness, we talked about all sorts of things. In his bedroom hung two oil paintings, both of woodland scenes. He said he'd had them for years and thought a friend of his dad had done them. "The wife put them up. I've never looked at them much. Not till I ended up here. Now I look at them a lot". He was not a man to talk much and it would, I felt, have been intrusive to ask him what he saw in them. Dying is a personal, private business. When he died, his wife asked me to have them. "I can't go back in there", she said, "He would like you to have the pleasure of them". They spent some time with us, then travelled to my daughter for a few years and now, with refurbished frames are with another daughter. I have learned a little of what's called 'provenance' and begin to understand that a painting is altogether greater than simply an arrangement of paint on canvas.

After Julie retired, she attended a course on Art History. The sharing of her knowledge helped me to structure how to look at a painting. I began to understand a little of symbolism in paintings; I began to understand how important it was to look at a painting in the context of its time and place. We visited art galleries and we went to some exhibitions. I began to use words like *Mannerist, Pre-Raphaelites* and the like. I tagged on to her group when they went on visits, hoping to absorb more knowledge and understanding by association. We went to Milan once, mainly to see *The Last Supper.* This must be one of the best known paintings in the world. I had seen reproductions many, many times. Nothing, though, can prepare you for the reality. 'Stunning' is an overused and devalued word, but I was stunned.

I do find it difficult to come to terms with Modern Art. I see many of the paintings only as patterns. I can see that distorted figures can emphasise or reflect an emotion, but I don't always feel it. Perhaps they are exercises in mood or a stimulus to your imagination. I do not find them easy. I see no point in presenting natural phenomena as art, not in my understanding of art. I get nothing from a dissected fish or the mould of the blood vessels of the head. Perhaps it is because I am familiar with the real thing. I remember the first time I operated on a young child. I stared in wonderment at the sheer beauty inside the abdomen, still pure and virginal, still unsullied by years of use and abuse. But then, that was created by a really Great Artist.

I have not so far talked of our family, though I hope I have at least intimated that they exist. I am uneasy at including them in "Enthusiasms". The feeling for a family is so much greater than that. Nor is it a transient experience; it is constant and so integral a part of your being that it is rarely spoken of as such and indeed hardly ever reaches conscious thought. It is bedded deeply within us, influencing and informing much of our thought, priorities and emotional lives. It does, of course also absorb much time, patience and effort. Yet the reward is enormous, the opportunity to re-live your life, albeit by proxy and often in different ways. Through our children, we were present at Dunblane on that fateful day; we experienced the tragedies of Kosovo, Bosnia and Iraq; we have taught generations of children and we have tried to be fair and just in the cut-throat world of finance and big business. And through our grandchildren we have re-discovered play and shared emerging imaginations; we have re-learned the joy of just being who we are. As they grow, we hurt again as childhood merges, sometimes painfully, into adulthood and innocence becomes tarnished.

A little while ago, I experienced one of those brief moments of absolute clarity that appears rarely, perhaps only a few times in a life. We were enjoying a somewhat advanced joint birthday when it was transformed by the appearance of all those members of the family who could travel. It was all the more relaxed because it was so spontaneous, at least so far as Julie and I were concerned. As the noise of conversations grew and children played and babies grew hungry, I drifted to the periphery of the action. I stood and watched and listened. I suddenly realised as never before that this was our family, true, but it was not simply an entity in itself. It was more than that. It was a collection of individual adult human beings related to me in blood or related to me through the love of my children. Each one was different. Each had their own concerns and the need to strive with their own demons. All of them have their own responsibilities. Petty annoyances and irritations are controlled by the good manners and mores of the group and their relationship with each other. Through these virtues, the family exists. It was easy to see what Daniel O'Leary meant when he talked in *The Tablet* of the dynamics of Love within a family, feeding each other, healing wounds, stirring growth, reinforcing goodness and the joy of life.

I remained at the periphery for a while, a little ashamed that all this had not struck me so forcibly before. Then I felt better, for I had thought of it now and was enriched. I felt able to let go of my family in a more complete, real way than ever before. I topped up my glass and re-joined the action with a new and changed enthusiasm.

Retirement

The last few months of my 33 years in the practice were the most difficult of my professional life.[21] Once the letter was sent and the resignation accepted, my whole life and thought centred on that Thursday in June. I was aware that after that my reputation would rest only in my notes and in the memories of patients and partners. And memories last only for a while.

My notes became more assiduous. I investigated everything and referred patients more easily. One of the great benefits of my time in the practice had always been that there were usually opportunities to correct errors and make good any omissions. After retirement, these second chances were no more. Inadequacy, default and frank mistakes were inherited by my partners, and, while I had faith in their loyalty, I feared embarrassment, even by proxy. My anxieties verged on the psychotic and built to a crescendo before each surgery and at the ringing of even a distant telephone. Eventually, as April became May, I realised that I could no longer cope with out of hours work and I 'bought in' a partner. While this eased some of my anxiety, it left me depressed by my own inadequacy.

Each consultation, too, was a bereavement. For many families, I had been available to three generations and more. I was there when the day was split into miners' shifts, and the sound of their boots on dawn pavements was our alarm clock. The slag heaps are now contoured into the landscape and all five pits have gone, but their painful memories remain in the minds and bodies of the patients. There are still miners' widows here and tangible

---

[21] This account of the process of retiring first appeared as *A Retiring Sort of Chap* in the *British Medical Journal* February 1997 314:612

memories of that disaster in the 1940s which killed 22 men. Old-fashioned cottages that smelled of polish and cabbage and the weekly wash are still there, but are now transformed into 'desirable residences' with pebbled gardens and patio heaters.

During the consultations, we sometimes laughed at incidents past that now seemed ridiculous, though they weren't at the time. We shared joy at the memory of confinements and sheepish teenagers were ushered in. "This is the doctor who delivered you", mother would say. We sometimes wept together at memories of more tragic times. There was much handholding, many embraces. Often, there would be a farewell gift or card. I have to admit that there were times when I would eye the plastic bag they carried and try to guess the contents to prepare my thanks. Usually it was a bottle, which further threatened my liver, but there were less common gifts - a book, plant pots, fruit bowls. Jack and I had had an uneasy relationship for many years, but he gave me his miner's lamp 'for what you've done'.

The last surgery was followed by the first of many presentations. They were all overwhelming and I never did manage to say what I had intended, though I usually did say thank you and apologise for any grief I had caused.

A few days after I had left the surgery for good, one of my partners called to ask how I was. Since I was sitting in the sun with a glass of wine, I wondered at the question. Two days later - days interrupted by many non-specific telephone calls - I called at the post office. The postmistress blanched and grasped the counter. "Are you all right?" she asked. I replied that I was. It was only later that I learnt that I had died the previous week. The rumoured manner of my going was interesting. Some said that I had collapsed in the garden, others that I had fallen asleep in my chair. Another said it had happened at church, which would have been nice, though embarrassing. A week or two later, I was invited to open the Church Garden Fete. I used a microphone. Surrounded by wires and magnified by loudspeakers, I announced how delighted I was to be 'currently appearing'. I was quite pleased with that *bon mot*, but I rather sensed that few others appreciated the wit.

Once I had left the surgery for good, my mornings were spent writing thank you letters and beginning the tidying up of a life of neglecting the day to day business of banks and insurance and the like. I grew to know my family again and visited them from time to time. We were on call for grandchildren and joined the rota for the school run.

Gradually, the process of retiring passed and I became retired. It was not the idle idyll that I had anticipated. I felt uneasy if I was unoccupied. A day without achievement of some sort would be followed by an uneasy night. I strove to avoid aimlessness. I began to dread the frequent question, "How are you enjoying retirement?" I did not know, but I could not say that. "Beats working," I would say, but I was not sure if I meant it.

My self imposed guilt fed on the casual remarks. "No more Monday mornings for you, eh?". "It's alright for some". "Must go, some of us have to work". The remarks hurt, though I'm sure they were meant kindly. But I wanted people to give me permission to relax. I wanted people to say, "You've earned it. Now do what you yourself want". But few people did.

One Thursday morning, about five or six months on, I awoke with the now familiar sweating anxiety. How was I going to accomplish all that was planned for the day? In the middle of

234

my concerns it suddenly occurred to me that I was not obliged to do anything at all. It was I who had defined and planned the day. No one else. I suppose that was the moment that I truly retired. The headaches did not go, but they eased. Now I could begin to see retirement not as a withdrawal or a stop, but as a beginning, a new life of a common man.

I no longer thought of the practice. I no longer resented seeing the local doctors on their visits. Now I could wave cheerfully. I thanked God daily that there were no more meetings. How I loathed meetings. My only regrets and self-recriminations are that I did not do more to make meetings more profitable. I used to dread the prolonged debates over trivia as each of us strove for importance. And then a partner would arrive late and we'd start all over again. I refused all offers of locums for I have never seen general practice as sessional. You were either a general practitioner or you were not.

Being a common man takes a bit of getting used to. At first, the loss of status was a shock, but I feel easier now. I have grown used to carrying means of identification, for some people ask me who I am.

My flat cap and anorak help me to blend into the landscape. And I go to night school as a new boy to learn woodwork. I have a shed. How I have managed without one for so long I do not know. I have a stool to sit on and an old green wireless that has lost its back. If you press the switch, the light comes on. My name is on the door and there is a sign saying, "Mind Your Head". It is my realm.

But becoming retired, though having its own problems, is really quite a different kettle of fish than the state of being retired. The 'holiday' feel of the first six or eight months was diluted with a sense of deprivation and ending. It was not unlike a bereavement I suppose. There was loss and there was guilt, though I never could decide what I was guilty about. Perhaps I felt I was letting the side down or wasting my expertise and experience. I don't think I felt too guilty about my medical career. I had, overall, been fulfilled and provided, for the most part, a reasonable service to my patients and to Medicine itself. It was not perfect, of course, but I gave it my best shot. But the sense of loss persisted, especially the loss of structure to my life. For a while, I continued to do part-time work at the hospital in the dermatology department. This did enable me to 'anchor' my week and I could distinguish between Fridays and Wednesdays. And it was supremely enjoyable. I attended no meetings, was comparatively unconcerned about medical politics and administration; I simply saw patients and re-discovered the special mix of compassion and joy, fulfilment and frustration provided by daily contact with people who ask for your help. But gradually, I came to need something more, a new beginning, a different challenge.

During a 'run-out' – a habit one tends to acquire in retirement – I was sipping a pint of best in the warm sunshine of the Yorkshire Dales, browsing through a magazine. I came upon an advertisement for Continuing Education. A degree course[22] appealed to me and seemed to promise so much. It would exercise my dwindling neurones and provide me with the structure I required. And, besides, I was becoming increasingly sensitive to

[22] This account of my flirtation with Continuing Education first appeared as *It Doesn't Get Any Easier* in *The Writer* (Journal of the Medical Writers' Association) Vol 1 No 1 2002. A fuller version, *A Different Journey* appeared in *Triangle* (Parish Magazine) Autumn 2001. No 29.

the boredom I was inducing in casual listeners as I ranted about the Old Days and about youth and the price of carrots.

That was several years ago. I have run the race; I have gained the prize. The part-time degree in History did everything I'd hoped, though I rather suspect that I am still boring from time to time, but about different things.

I took it for granted that I would be intellectually capable of handling the course. As a matter of fact, since I had been vaguely interested in history for some years, I rather thought it would be a piece of cake. My main preparation was buying some file paper and innumerable pens. One thing I did give a lot of thought to was how I should dress. Smart casual I went for. Tweed dogtooth jacket, a checked slim woollen tie and sensible brogues. I resurrected my briefcase. Real leather that was. 25/- it cost me. By, it had seen some action had that. I joined a group of eighteen year olds for my first tutorial and was overcome by a great sadness for them. Here they were, away from home and breathing freedom for the first time. And then they find grandad sitting with them. They were ultra polite and made the false assumption that I knew more than they did. They sat silently throughout tutorials waiting for jewels of wisdom to spring from me. They never tired of waiting.

Looking back, I realise that there were many difficulties that I didn't anticipate. Oh, I did think I might have problems with memory, but I was surprised that, when reading even the most exciting text, I had no recollection of the previous page. This amnesic tendency, combined with overwhelming sleepiness, was nearly my downfall. I should really have known. After all, I have never been able to recall dates or names, which is a bit of a handicap when studying History.

Eventually I became used to the youth of tutors and lecturers. It was, however, difficult sometimes to accept criticism, from a young woman especially. Feedback from my first essay was pretty traumatic. No one had spoken to me like that since Sister Cuthbert at St Thomas's Primary. As the tutor banged on about lack of structure, unsubstantiated statements, poor annotation and a summary that had nothing to do with what I had written, I felt my face setting into a fixed asinine grin. I was aware of the blush spreading down my chest. Humiliation is a painful experience. My arrogant belief that I was bringing fresh ideas to the dusty ethos of History was somewhat dispelled. Oh they were fresh ideas alright, it was just that they were crap, that's all.

Essays were always a problem. I had this tendency to try and make them interesting by leaving a denouement to be revealed in the last sentence. This, I soon found, cuts little ice with your average historian for, as one of them pointed out, they all know the ending anyway. There was little scope for purple prose or the odd merry quip. People didn't laugh much in the olden days apparently. No, I had to say what I was going to say, say it, then say what I'd said. So that was it then. I cottoned on only slowly.

Examinations were a nightmare. It had been over 40 years since my last. I don't remember getting in such a state then. Palpitations abounded and the Black Dog awaited me round every corner. The lack of knowledge was only one of many problems. What became a dominating concern was my ageing body. I lacked the sheer stamina to write fast for three hours at a time, especially when I had to think as well. It was inevitable that my hands should complain, those same hands that attracted holy martyrdom through their suffering in making Christmas cribs. I went to see the doctor. He smiled in a tired sort of way, but he eventually gave me the anti-rheumatics for which I craved. As I left, I saw him shaking his head sadly.

Now although the drugs helped, they needed to be taken after food, which meant a breakfast I could not eat. Nervous dyspepsia ensued. I flew to the Gaviscon. Its mildly laxative effect could have capricious effects, especially when the adrenaline is running high. I found I needed a modicum of conscious sphincter control. Simple enough normally, but deep involvement in Tudor inflation did create a certain insecurity. The prostate was another organ that had remained quiescent in my youth, but grew in size and importance with advancing age. Three hours is a long time these days. Fluid intake therefore required careful planning if I was to steer that middle way between dehydration and embarrassing discomfort. With such problems as these, the nuances of the development of the Tudor and Stuart town seemed mere bagatelles.

Eventual Graduation posed new problems. The suit I last wore nearly three years ago had mysteriously shrunk. Diet alone was insufficient to reduce my bulk. At my age, buying a new suit is a major decision. I mean, I would like to get some wear out of it. And I didn't know what to do about my gammy knee. Should I use a stick and aim for sympathetic applause? Or should I simply limp, hoping people will notice and admire my self-effacing courage? Do I need to ask for assistance up the steps?

These were heady concerns, though. For a while, I relaxed in my new intellectual achievement. It was a comfortable state.

In fact, graduation was a delight. I did buy a new suit and a fancy shirt. I had my hair cut two weeks beforehand - to 'let it settle down'. I slept badly the night before and awoke at about 4.00am. The breaking dawn found me barefoot on the lawn in my pyjamas. I showered, using a trendy body wash that promised invigoration. I arrived very early. I became quite emotional

239

when I was gowned. I think it was genuine, though the fact that the gown was made to fit someone 42 inches high may have contributed. Some of the family came. And my long suffering wife. (Say *Pilgrimage of Grace* to my wife and you risk all.) It was a splendid day that mellowed into a heady, euphoric night.

The photograph posed its own problem. Generally, only graduation and wedding photographs appear in our best room. While I qualified on the first count, the fact remains that the photograph gallery was full. An option of a 3ftx2ft portrait over the mantlepiece was not greeted enthusiastically. My elegantly framed image remains on the move. It has left its temporary resting place on the fridge, bypassed the downstairs toilet and is currently reared up against the wall. In the best room admittedly, but only just.

After graduation, I admit I felt somewhat bereft, but the thought of hitting the books again did not immediately appeal. My wife was a little concerned that I was not looking for a job. I rather thought I might lie on the settee for a while, like all the other graduates have done in our house. But, on the other hand, the grass grew and the paint peeled. I got up.

Once again, I felt a sense of loss, but day to day living took over. I found that there is a general assumption that retired people have nothing to do and are therefore immediately available for a variety of tasks and duties. To my displeasure, there was a plethora of committees awaiting me. As I have already implied, I am not much good at committees for I never seem to grasp things like 'implications' and the 'overall view'. Thinking on my feet has never been my forte.

It also became obvious that as a retired person, and particularly as a grandparent, one becomes part of real, but subtle, social chain and process. The expanded life choices open to women over the last twenty odd years have led to most mothers combining their maternal duties with a career outside the home. As a result it has become increasingly common for both parents of a family to be working. In the normal course of events, providing they are well organised and the relationship is both strong and just, this works and the children are both cared for and have a fair slice of the family cake. But life is rarely smooth for long and easily available back-up becomes essential. Which is where grandparents come in. Not that I mind, you understand. Our family are fair and pretty undemanding and sharing the delights of growing children has its own pleasures; I am assured that it 'keeps you young', but it doesn't half make you feel old. I have always felt that visiting grandchildren is a bit like visiting the zoo; it's nice to see them playing and feeding and chattering, but there's no need to get into the cage with them. I must say, I cannot understand those families – and especially the grandparents – where the routine care of the children is in the hands of Grandma and Grandad. But even without these extreme examples, it is now an established pattern that grandparents fill an increasingly important role as childminders. Which enables the young parents to work in order to pay the taxes which help to maintain the grandparents' lifestyle in the manner to which they have become accustomed.

One becomes prone to drifting into philosophical meanderings when one has the opportunity for thought that retirement provides. The snag is that ideas and attitudes – which you may well have held for years – become increasingly crystallised and sharply defined and tend to develop inexorably into bigotry and prejudice. Becoming such an opinionated old man, provided it is diluted

241

with a little humour and personal awareness, may be endearing – at least that was my impression – but I have been disabused of that of late. It has been pointed out to me in no uncertain terms that not only is it not endearing, it is fairly tedious. Well, perhaps so, but it seems to me that some things cannot be said too often. I cannot understand why England has adopted the baseball cap, for instance. What image do people wish to project? It's alright for a good looking young woman to look a bit cooky, but anyone else? Dear me. And people never take them off. They even wear them indoors. I once visited a rather large middle aged chap because he had a temperature. He was wearing his baseball cap in bed. When he sat up, he turned it back to front and when he lay down, he turned it the right way. I am sure there is a surgical manoevre available to remove them.

The English summer is a nightmare for anyone with a modicum of the aesthetic. Why do people dress as if for a track and field competition when they are all too obviously not athletic? Why do men think it acceptable to wander streets and supermarkets bare chested or, worse still, wearing a black vest? And who persuaded young women that showing your belly button was attractive? Or those big tackety boots? In fact, our whole culture seems to me to have become a culture of ugliness and indignity.

You will not be surprised to know that things were infinitely better in my day. I remember as a medical student in Dublin for a few weeks in the '50's my immense pleasure in sitting in the sun on St Stephen's Green, watching the office girls come out for lunch. They were smiling and laughing. Their long hair danced and glistened in the sun, their floral, full-skirted dresses fluttered and billowed and they walked proudly and lightly in elegant shoes. Now young women seem to dress either as a

242

dark-suited business man, slop about in clothes more fitted to a building site or wear clothes deliberately too big for them, which makes them look terribly depressed and slovenly. For reasons beyond my comprehension, leaving laces undone is fashionable. And, of course, everybody carries a bottle of water from which they drink at frequent intervals. Where did this come from? Who spread the threat of impending dehydration? When was the last occasion that someone died of thirst on the streets of Wakefield?

When I get too angry – and anger is increasingly common when you have the time - I seek solace in my garden. Increasingly in recent years, I have a tendency to rush back from wherever I am and sit in the garden[23]. I have often wondered why, especially when no task was pressing. Only recently have I realised that I have grown to love my garden and want to be with it. I had never thought of it before, not consciously. It had simply been there. When I opened the door or looked through the window, it was there, sometimes demanding, sometimes peaceful in the warmth of the sun, sometimes turbulent in wind and rain. Sometimes it had a great sadness and at other times it was exuberant. In my working life, it maintained my sanity; in retirement it maintains my creaking body and softens my emotions. It is my companion. We have grown together, me and my garden.

I don't know if it's a 'nice' garden. It is simply my garden. I cannot see it as others do. We are too close. Most of it I have planted myself and I know each plant individually. The gentle

---

[23] This account of my relationship with my garden was a runner-up in the Gardening Essay Competition 2003 organised by *The Times* and *Hortus*. Permission to publish has been granted by *The Intellectual Property Licensing Authority* and by David Wheeler, Editor and Publisher of *Hortus*.

majesty of the Silver Birch marked our Silver Wedding; the enormous ceanothus was once a cutting from a bereaved wife.

That primula transports me to Scone Palace; the Lady's Mantle to South Wales and the poetry of Dylan Thomas. And Frank gave me that Taxus on one of his better days. The *lithospermum* was from Gladys' garden, a postage stamp of happiness in her tragic life. The arch came from a crowded, expensive Chelsea. It has style, though now it functions mainly as Gothic goalposts. A major life change is marked by the shrubbery which, in one cathartic week, replaced the herbaceous border. Various beds mark the weddings of my daughters. It may be an exaggeration to say that my garden is a horticultural autobiography, but it's not far from the truth.

My garden is not perfect. Not by any means. But one of the great gifts of any gardener is the ability to live with error, perhaps even smile a little, though wryly. If I become complacent, I simply recall the courgette in the hanging basket or wonder at the 'dwarf' conifer now 20 feet high and climbing. Oh yes, I am familiar with imperfection and can cope. But I can't adjust to the vagaries of the Creator with whom I share my plot. I know He provides the basic ingredients for procreation and growth, but I do find His timing and proportions a little unsatisfactory.

The resultant uncertainty has led to the evolution of empirical but inviolable laws and rules. Onion seeds should be sown, in heat, on New Years Day. Dahlias should be planted out no earlier than the 22nd of May. Roses should be pruned on Good Friday and on that same day, plant potatoes. Beds should be dug and fertilised before St Nicholas Day. Saws and sayings abound and in them I find comfort and security. But, like all gardeners, I am defensive and paranoid. Faced with a visitor's compliment, I automatically respond "You should have seen it last week" or, conversely "It'll be a picture next week when theflocks/lilies/roses/dahlias are out". Today is never the right time.

Gardeners develop their own language. For some it is a living form of Latin, with a hint of Greek , a soupcon of French and, more recently, snippets of Japanese. The opacity of such a hybrid vocabulary lends itself easily to misunderstanding. (A passing remark, that I had noticed thrips on my polyanthus, caused my wife some anxiety for a while). There is, too, the vernacular. When we talk of a 'picking' or a 'boiling' we immediately define ourselves as of the soil, separating ourselves from those whose leeks are ever clean and encased in plastic. The vernacular implies our traditional role as providers.

Which raises embarrassing questions. Each Spring, my heart fills with hope. Time to prepare for the next Winter. I have a fixed assumption that, without my produce, we may not make it next time. I envisage myself struggling through autumn rains and gales, knife in hand, to claim the bounty that will sustain my family through the long nights. It is rarely like that. In fact, I often have to plead to be allowed to bring in a soil encrusted cabbage, delicately laced by voracious caterpillars. Mutterings of 'added protein' cut little ice. My cucumbers are OK, but I regret the banning (by our European Masters) of the *Burpless Green Wonder* - always a boon in company. But my beetroots are always 'baby beets'. My tomatoes cost me about £2.50 per pound. My onions, ravaged by the dreaded fly, are stunted. My calabrese are overtly important ingredients of some food chain. My lettuces sustain a vast slug population. My parsnips bear little resemblance to the picture on the packet. The *Super Prizewinner* beans proved ill named.

Yet, if I despair of my repeated failures, I am consoled by the joy I bring to the many other inhabitants of my garden. So many birds. A sparrowhawk visits occasionally and we see woodpeckers. The tawny owls are no longer seen, though we hear their call at night. I take delight in sustaining the sparrows. We don't often see small mammals, except as a present from the cat. The hedgehog visits the bird feeding area each night for the leftovers. Their innocent, self-assured charm appeals to me. Squirrels are another matter. My initial delight changed to frustrated fury when they became invasive. I don't talk about them any more. Their very presence disabuses me of my Franciscan self image

It is impossible to work in a garden without being conscious of the wonder of creation. I have already mentioned the joy of walking barefoot in the garden as dawn breaks; but I still think of it. The grass was springy and cold moist beneath my feet. There was a rustling in the undergrowth. The black cat stretched himself under his favourite tree and opened an eye. A wren began to sing. A gloriously clear sound that pierced my very being. The moon faded and the sun rose, dappling the lawn. Another resurrection morning. I felt I walked with God.

My delight in caring for my own garden soon made me wonder why other people didn't share my enthusiasm. Few people seemed to see gardening as a pleasure and a privilege. Some people 'tidy' their garden, some 'do' their garden; for many its seems an intolerable chore. They 'had better cut the grass' in the same way as they 'had better hoover the best room'. I began to be concerned that others were missing out on the delights of their plot. I began to fume when I saw an untended garden and wondered how people could tolerate an overgrown lawn or a weed ridden bed. Within me grew the seeds of a crusade to convert the world to gardening. Inevitably, I began with my own family. After all, they must have some genetic predisposition to love their land. Well sort of. But, it seemed to me, the big problem was how to start, what do you do first. I started to volunteer my services.

There is a particular pleasure in gardening for someone else, especially when you are faced with the horticultural equivalent of a blank canvas. For a start, you can, with luck, avoid the errors inherent in your own garden. You can explore new plants and exciting designs. It's not quite the same as 'trying it on the dog', but I have to admit there's a bit of that about it. When you have finished there is the joy of having improved the planet and continued the work of Creation. And then there is the special delight of seeing your baby grow and develop.

Needless to say, there are disadvantages. It is essential that you remember it is not your garden. This is easier said than done and I need to be continually reminded that it is not 'ours', but 'theirs'. I try to think what it would be like if someone 'did' my garden. I cannot watch these 'garden makeover' programmes for that reason. Can you imagine what it must be like to return after a weekend away and find your garden transformed? How do you regain some ownership, that fundamental necessity of enjoyable gardening? I am also aware of the influence of my creative activities on my childrens' marriages. "I see your father's been round again. Can't you tell him I do not like rhododendrons?" "He means well and it keeps him happy" "Tell him to be happy in his own place, then". Gardeners must, above all, be sensitive to the human condition.

There are times, admittedly, when gardening is not pleasurable. Heavy rain, bitter frost and chill winds freeze my joints and diminish my enthusiasm. Under such circumstances, my greenhouse[24] provides refuge and its own delights. Sometimes I potter as one is supposed to do, but sometimes I don't. Sometimes I just wonder and wondering, as often as not, leads to contemplation. And contemplation in a greenhouse drifts easily into allegory, allegory of biblical proportions.

My greenhouse is very small, but you can't miss it – it's just round the back of the house. It is my retreat, my recuperation, my own monastery and of silent order. Like all monasteries, though, this quiet, apparently negative retreat, is a hubbub of life. All the world is within its fragile glass. In there, the violence of the spirit is tempered with the peace of well ordered tranquillity. Man's petty scientific knowledge vies with the Natural Law. Life and death walk hand in hand and arrogance and humility succeed each other in turn, constant only in their inconstancy. Contented warmth is spiced with the ever present danger of obliteration.

It is the womb from which my garden springs. In good times, the moist warmth pervades one's being with the heady scent of growth and health. At those times, it is an explosion of Nature's bounty. But in the bad times, it has about it the dank reek of dying things. A dying greenhouse is the essence of decay. The dumb helplessness of a sickly plant evokes guilt and impotence in the most casual observer.

In the greenhouse, I catch a glimpse of what God must feel like. I built it myself - not exactly out of nothing, though there wasn't a lot there when I started, just a mess of rubble and a highly complex kit with instructions written in Swedish. I bet God was glad He didn't have Swedish instructions. It would have been

[24] Originally appeared as *The Man in the Greenhouse* in *Triangle*. No 3. April 1987. Reproduced with permission from the editor, Rosie Shaw.

'ir ferni alt verld'. Trust Him to have no trouble with his umlauts. My lips were pursed for days afterwards.

You won't be surprised to hear that it took me about six days to build it. After all the hassle with aluminium and glass and concrete and all, I rested on the Sunday, sitting at my ease in my new domain. The March frost cut no ice with me. Immune was I to the vagaries of the English Spring. I sipped a rather elegant Chablis and looked around. And, as I looked, I saw that it was good.

It was not enough, though, for very long. I needed living things to share my existence. I can't remember now how I filled my greenhouse; whether I just put plants in it, or whether I set seeds and encouraged their growing. The exact origins of my creation are now irrelevant. I do remember my first cutting, though, taken from my favourite geranium during its dormant period. There was joy in its growth, but, inexplicably, it was a little different from its parent. Once plants were established, it was in their growth and reproduction that I found most fulfilment. Usually, cuttings were easy, but growing from seed was a capricious exercise. A poor compost would result in ineffective germination. Too much water and the seedlings flourished only briefly before they faded. On occasion, rogue seeds distorted the symmetry of my trays. Sometimes I tried to grow inappropriate plants. Seduced by the bright images on the seed packets, I would spend all my pocket money on the dream they promised. I never actually melted down my gold and silver, though, mainly because I didn't have any.

Getting plants to fruit is a delicate procedure. I'm a bit shy about it really. Tomatoes and peppers are alright. They just need an occasional passing bee, but melons and bisexual cucumbers are different. It's a bit rude, all this feather duster business. When I do it, I'm always looking over my shoulder. That might explain my lack of success. I could do with blinds really.

Alas, all is not joy in my greenhouse. Show me a gardener who has never suffered disaster and I'll show you a man who has never lived. And of all the people I've ever known, none can have suffered so much or so often as I. I reckon I have had at least seven major catastrophes, some, I'll admit have been self induced.

There was the time of the great damp. In my early days, I was obsessed with watering and the more I watered, the unhappier my plants became. I gave them still more. They lost their roots and the stems rotted to a gelatinous mass. Conversely, one holiday I overlooked their care. They shrank, waterless, and failed. My tears of regret were insufficient to irrigate the desert of their destruction.

There was the night of the great wind. An airborne dustbin lid smashed the glass and the primitive paraffin heater was extinguished. The temperature dropped below zero and the plants expired. All of them. Together.

The plague of greenfly started quietly enough - just a few to start with. I'm sure I've read somewhere that if a single greenfly is not interrupted in its reproduction, within six months England would be three foot deep in a moving green mass. I can believe it. You should have seen my little patch after only a week. They've no morals, you know. Perhaps there's no need when you're bisexual, it wouldn't be fair. At any rate, in the wake of their sticky presence came more pestilence in the shape of the creeping grey soft death known as botrytis, feeding on the weak in the still cold damp of early spring

Looking back, I think the white fly were the worst. A delicate, pretty creature at first sight, it was voracious in its appetite for life and within days, a white haze filled the house. They flew and dived from all angles to wreak havoc and destruction. In silence. The weight of their presence bowed my plants. They were immune to chemical and biological assault. There seemed no answer.

Paradoxically, it was another disaster that eradicated the white fly. A substandard batch of paraffin produced clouds of thick black smoke throughout one night. The following morning, everything was covered in half an inch of thick, tenacious, tarry soot. Days of patient washing revealed little permanent damage to the plants. But the white fly were no longer white and they were grounded. This particular black cloud had stilled their flying.

Then, one Christmas time came a great gift to my special world. By the courtesy of my wife, I have a cable linking it with the mother house. This brings a great power and gentle warmth to my world and makes all living things flourish. Even in the ice cold days of dark midwinter. So lush is the growth, in fact, that I need a compass with me, lest I lose my way in the profusion.

I am usually to be found in my greenhouse, potting on, pricking out, gently watering - or just being. I can see out in all directions, but it is difficult to see me from outside. People know I am there though, or, at least they know somebody's doing something there - they can see the plants through the glass dimly. I realise I have great power over my plants, but I wouldn't want to harm them, they are an extension of my being.

You can understand how I feel when I am in my domain. I am happy and content in this world of my creation. I would like it to go on forever. Perhaps it might. So long as Julie doesn't turn the switch off in the house.

It is self-evident that one cannot spend all one's waking life in the garden and greenhouse. The vagaries of the English climate do impose some limits. In fact, one of the most striking things about retirement is how much one's day is influenced by the weather. When I worked, the weather was almost irrelevant. Rain or sun often went by unnoticed in those now far off days. Now a passing cloud or sprightly breeze can transform my mood and determine what I do. But even in the most inclement weather, I am able to resist painting and decorating. There is always a more attractive alternative. And there are few better alternatives than to repair to the shed.

Exactly what I do in my shed is often ill-defined, but on a frosty Saturday afternoon, with snow threatening, there are few more contented places to be than in a shed with the heater on and Radio 5 on the wireless. Of course, I timp about, but it all gets more serious and creative as Christmas approaches, for, with Christmas comes the Crib Season. I have long been obsessed with the Christmas Crib – or 'Nativity scene' as it's called these days. Their creation occupies me most of the autumn and early winter and has done for nearly 30 years. I sell them at sundry Christmas fairs. Some people buy them, which is nice. As our family has grown up, married and moved away, they have provided me with an expanding market. I enjoy the 'Crib Parties' they have organised – a bit like Tupperware parties, but religious.

Recently my interest has expanded. For some years, Libby Purvis has exhibited a collection of Cribs from different parts of the world. We went to see it at Norwich. I found it fascinating and determined to follow her example. Since I am not a man to travel far, I encourage anyone who does travel to bring me back a sample. I write to people working abroad and to missionaries. The Fair Trade organisation has provided some. I reckon I've about sixty or seventy now. How the Nativity story is represented in different cultures intrigues me. For instance, in many, the shepherds are not represented at all; in the Nigerian one the 'shepherds' are fishermen, carrying fish. The further east you go, the more likely it seems for the poverty aspect of the story to be played down —the Chinese cribs I have show the Holy Family in very grand circumstances indeed. The allegory of the Polish *Skopje* is a lesson in Christianity. The Crib is tiny and simple and sometimes difficult to spot against the background of the vast (sometimes several feet high) cathedral-like structure, sparkling, lit and with moving scenes and ringing bells. You may find the Family huddled insignificantly near one of the entrances, as though sleeping rough. Yet you have to pass through them or near them to enter the church. Makes you think. I would love to make a *Skopje*, but it is beyond my skills. The humble stable, crude and ill-formed is more appropriate to my style of woodwork.

Not that I haven't tried to improve. I think I have mentioned my woodworking class. I loved every minute. People who work in wood must be the most blessed of all. The smell and feel of wood is intoxicating. Alas, I never got much beyond the periphery of the art. I think I was born with a genetic incapability of measuring anything accurately. It's all very well for the tutor to go on about 'measuring twice, cut once' and I really did try,

253

but I was always a thou out. But people were very tolerant and encouraged me. I was allowed to use machines that amazed me. I learned to sandpaper assiduously. I learned the power of glue. But by far the greatest pleasure I had was bringing home something I had made. This is a pleasure denied by a life in Medicine. Of course there was the pleasure and satisfaction of seeing someone who was ill, become whole. But this is different. This was sharing in creation itself. I would bring my work home and arrange it sacredly in the kitchen. I would look at it and my eyes would moisten. I would call Julie and the family in and we would stand and look at it in wonderment. Julie always said the right thing, though I have to admit she rarely became poetic. The family would shuffle a bit, say 'very nice' or some such and return to their telly or homework. Then I would sit alone, sipping a glass of wine and look at what I had made. And I found it was good.

In fact, it seems to me that complete fulfilment of the retired life is to be found in the full development of life at home and within one's self. I appreciate that I have many priceless advantages. I have a splendid house and a large garden. I am fairly well and I have a wife who not only tolerates my idiosyncrasies, but always seems pleased to see me. My family are well and still talk to me. We are agreeable companions. Why then should I ever want to leave here? Yet whenever I meet someone who is about to retire and I ask them what they want to do, almost inevitably they will say that they are planning to travel. And many of my retired acquaintances never seem to be at home. Now I know that it is sometimes necessary to travel to visit friends or family, but travelling for pleasure, especially abroad, is, to me an oxymoron. "We go abroad for the sun", they'll say, or "It's really exciting" or "It's wonderful meeting the people, seeing the Taj Mahal, Eiffel Tower, Statue of Liberty in moonlight/at night/ arising from the early mist…" and all that. Well perhaps. It does not do for me. I think my time in General Practice did for me so far as travel was concerned. You get a different view of other people's holidays when you're a GP[25].

There was a time when the holiday season was limited to a few weeks in the summer. No longer. Holidays are big business and therefore at the mercy of the advertisers. Their systematic promotion of the Great Escape has convinced the Great British Public that if it does not have regular getaways, the chances of survival are very poor indeed. And year after year, the greatest confidence trick of modern civilisation creates stress and chaos where there was little before. Year after year the population throws itself into the strange and tempting arms of fates known only through the gloss of The Brochure. Year after year the Great British Public are lured to expensive disappointment by the sirens that sing between the pages of every newspaper and seduce from every television channel.

There is an overiding assumption that holidays do you good. Perhaps I am biased, but it never seemed that way to me. How my heart used to sink when another lovely couple, happy for years to paddle in the North Sea at Bridlington, came to ask me what injections they needed for their month's holiday in South East Asia. "We've saved for years for this, Doctor. It's the Holiday of a Lifetime." Oh Lord why didn't they spend it on a picture or central beating or something more tangible than a dream.

From May to September, Friday evening surgeries bulged with 'emergencies' created and exaggerated by the impending trip to wonderland - tomorrow. Antibiotics are ladled out 'in case' the snuffle becomes double pneumonia in the temperature of

[25]Originally appeared in a modified form in *Pulse Magazine* 3rd October 1987.

Torremolinos. Asthmatics wanted nebulisers lest they became breathless in Benidorm. The calm reassurance of the Airline advertisements were no longer sufficient to still the beating hearts of our holidaymakers and airports must been filled with the chemically tranquillised.

Expectations and demands went beyond reason and common sense. "Can I have something for their skin. You know how they get sunburned". Of course I knew. Debbie was hospitalised in Estartit and both she and Emma suffered mightily in Majorca. "Where are you going this year?" I would ask. "We thought we'd try Paxos". Oh God. What chance is there for education and self learning in the face of the blandishments of the purveyors of dreams.

And Monday mornings were like the aftermath of Dunkirk as the survivors struggled back to collapse into the arms of the Health Service. Many were still wearing the tattered remains of their uniforms. Their trainers and sandals were blood-stained and scuffed from their last fandango. Their short sleeved shirts and shorts were no longer white, but discoloured with red wine wounds sustained in the final battle of the Bodega. Their deep tans were fading already in the pale Yorkshire sun to a crinkled yellow green and they remained prone to mutter foreign words like peseta and lira.

They told tales of heroism and drama that defied the imagination. They would produce communiques in foreign tongues and assumed I understood - "With you being medical". They often had more X-rays than they had holiday snaps. They tipped up their plastic bags on my desk and cascades of strange drugs spread around. Ointments and sprays and pills and suppositories, most of them containing steroids and antibiotics and other dramatic remedies that bedazzled me. The amounts and selection made me feel like a therapeutic nihilist.

Katrina got a virus in Vladivostock and she is still wammy. Jennifer had a brief affair with an Italian, but not brief enough. Her memories did not fade over the next few months. That was one souvenir she hadn't bargained for. Albert was mugged in Miami and Richard vomited his way down the Loire Valley - and back. Jeremy and Catherine found their motor tour of Switzerland somewhat curtailed by the failure of their big end in Basle. Philip went off it in Bulgaria – his paranoia may have been justified, but the police would not allow it. Mrs. Rowbottom got mennorrhagia in Bled and collapsed.

Everybody complained about the cost of medical treatment 'over there' but they didn't seem to appreciate the dear old N.H.S. any the more. No one ever kissed my feet.

Oh I know I'm biased, even jaundiced, but I am sure that the whole holiday business is a gigantic confidence trick. I'm sure we only go because if we don't the advertisers will make us feel guilty and deprived. You work twice as hard before you go and the same again on your return. And when you get there, you spend most of your time doing with great difficulty the things you do in comfort at home; simple things like eating, sleeping and going to the lavatory. Another thing, I find endless sun rather tedious after a while. As for all these wondrous sights and experiences, well I've seen the pictures and watch them on the Telly.

Mind you, Britain is different. You know where you are in Britain. No passports, no injections, no language problems (generally speaking) and you have the everlasting excitement of not knowing what weather it will be tomorrow – or this afternoon for that matter. A full tank of petrol and the world's your oyster.

257

Which brings me naturally to Robin Hood's Bay. On retirement from the Health Service you are granted not only a pension, but also a Lump Sum. Perhaps a private pension scheme becomes mature too. At retirement, therefore, there is more money about than ever there was before. The mortgage was paid, most of the family married and fairly independent. School expenses and University fees were a thing of the past. The question is what do you do with it. Of course, it has to last you out and that is a difficult equation to resolve, what with the variables involved. There is no shortage of advice, most of which falls into the two categories of provision for oneself and provision for one's family. This involves lots of financial faffing about and while I'm sure it was all very sensible, I felt tarnished by the whole business. Not for the first time, Julie resolved the problem. We have a large family, most of whom are married and with a young family of their own. Why not invest in a 'Holiday Home' which would give us a bolt hole, provide welcome and cheap breaks for the family and at the same time, hopefully, protect and employ our money. And so it was that we bought 'Friends' House'. At the time, I had some reservations. I was aware of the impact of 'Second Homes' on local communities and particularly on the young people of those communities. On the other hand, might not we contribute to the locality, providing we tried to depend on local services? It has, I think worked well.

The red roofed houses and cottages of Robin Hood's Bay tumble in profusion down a great cleft in the East Yorkshire coast on the edge of the Moors. The hinterland is both beautiful and majestic and dotted with attractive villages. It demands exploration. Whitby is to the north and Scarborough to the south. The area is steeped in the history of religion and industry, shipping and smuggling Many of the cottages are recently restored, but there is sufficient dilapidation to give a feel of authenticity. Over the years, we have begun to feel at home there.

Those early days of the house were days of hard work, frustration, excitement and great joy. We gradually transformed the rather stark and run down building into a simple but comfortable dwelling. Various members of the family would spend time doing various jobs there. On a couple of weekends, the men of the family spent a weekend, knocking it down and building it up. It was a formative time in so many ways. But I remember most the times Julie and I spent in the winter and early spring of '97-'98, painting, papering and cleaning. There were frustrations and errors and misfortunes of course, but there was an immense satisfying, joyful delight in seeing the 'new' house emerge. You can't beat creation. I even created a garden and terrace. The garden is best described as bijoux. I can 'do' this garden in less than a couple of hours, but I usually take my time. If you sit on the terrace, you can hear everything that goes on in the street below. It is excellent entertainment. We used to be able to watch everything, too, but the plants have flourished too well and we can't easily put sights to sounds now.

The house is well used by the family and their friends and ours. Of course, we enjoy it too, but increasingly we take greater pleasure in other people's enjoyment. Julie tells me I am too nosey and grill people after they have been, wanting to know what they did and where they went. Well, I don't care, I just love it, that's all.

Despite, or as well as, my delights in the pleasures and beauty of the British Isles, I feel I must come clean and admit to a sneaking delight in being in Italy. Not the travel to and from, you must understand, but the being there. There is something special about it. As soon as you leave the airport you are a walk-on part in a gigantic Grand Opera.

We stayed at the English College once.[26] One morning, we left very early to walk to Mass at St Peter's. The streets were still and even the Tiber was barely moving, its level low after weeks of the Italian summer. The Castello San Angelo materialised through the dispersing mist as we crossed the Ponte Vittorio Emmanuel.

We turned into the deep shadows of the Borgio S. Spirito and walked alongside the forbidding hospital walls. I was moved again by the human tragedies associated with the curious trapdoor in those walls; the rotating opening through which despairing mothers had, for centuries, passed their unwanted babies anonymously to the nuns within.

At the end of the street a figure and a handcart were silhouetted against the now bright sun shining down the Via della Conciliazioni. The street cleaner was brushing the gutters with slow, methodical sweeps of a large rustic broom and emptying the shovel into the cart with a noise that reverberated down the street. We drew closer to the bent back of the cleaner, who turned as we passed. "Buongiorno", she called, flashing eyes and smile beneath the waves of her black hair. As she spoke, her earrings moved. They were large, pendulous, jade coloured triangles that complemented her colouring and matched the tone of her overalls. I was taken aback by the vision. "Buongiorno, signora", I replied. This was Rome. Even I have to admit you won't find that in Wakefield.

As I have meditated on a life of retirement, I realise how fortunate I have been. I begin to realise that I have changed and grown. I am more happily married than I have ever been and I am conscious of the beauty of the world and goodness of so many people in it. I am aware that I live in a special environment and that my world is a quite different world from that of many others and that portrayed by

[26] Originally appeared in *Yorkshire Medicine* Vol 3 No 2 Spring 1991

the media.   I think, though, I would be dishonest if I gave the impression that my retirement has been non-stop joy and contentment. That is not my nature, nor, so far as I can judge, the nature of any other human being.

I get angry and frustrated at watching others make the same mistakes as I made or following a path I feel to be wrong. I become anxious about the most trivial matter. The Council has recently issued our household with a special 'Green Waste Bin'. If I have not filled it and collection day approaches, I worry at a possible lost opportunity and rush about the garden collecting bits.

I feel the need to be fully occupied. This is not entirely altruistic. My ambition for the higher things would, I suspect, not satisfy St Paul. No, the need to be busy stems from the need for distraction. There is no doubt that being retired means being old and being old means that you are creeping nearer to the ultimate denouement. No matter how strong a faith you have, there are times when you ponder.

And between finishing one job and starting another, the gap is all too prone to be filled by despondency. Melancholy awaits behind every door and all too readily prompts temptation to pointlessness. Fortunately, distraction is rarely far away. But if depression does set in, I find Mahler, or Wagner or Foure or even Puccini have the ability to transform the ugly, paralysing depression into a gentler shape which is altogether more creative and hopeful.   Overall, though, I am pretty happy with my current state. As a matter of fact, I begin to doubt whether I'm a proper Christian, for I would happily settle for this for eternity. I occasionally mention this to God, but I continue to get older and the creaking louder. I suppose He knows best.